Israel's New Future, Revisited

Manfred Gerstenfeld

ISRAEL'S NEW FUTURE
REVISITED

Mordechai Abir · Moshe Arens · David Bar-Illan · Miriam Ben-Porat ·
Yehezkel Dror · Abba Eban · Daniel Elazar · Menachem Friedman · Yaakov
Gadish · Israel Katz · Uri Marinov · Peter Medding · Sergio Minerbi ·
Moshe Sanbar · Dan Segre · Abraham B. Yehoshua

RVP Press
New York

RVP Publishers Inc.
95 Morton Street, Ground Floor
New York, NY 10014

RVP Press, New York

Israel's New Future: Interviews, the original edition, was published in 1994 by Robin Mass Ltd. and Jerusalem Center for Public Affairs.

Photo cover: Reporters/AP/Ron Edmonds

This book was published in collaboration with the Canadian Institute for Jewish Research.

The publication of this book was supported by International Center for Western Values, Amsterdam.

Library of Congress Control Number: 2013947650

ISBN 978 1 61861 337 0

www.rvppress.com

To my sons Dan and Alon
who are part of Israel's future

Table of Contents

Acknowledgments

First and foremost, I would like to thank all of the people who agreed to be interviewed and to be a part of this book.

I am grateful to Moshe Alon and Ze'ev Sher for their kind help.

I would like to thank especially Carl Schrag, who edited the manuscript. Without him the book would not have reached publication.

Lastly, it bears noting that interviews with several of the individuals who appear in these pages appeared in shorter forms in *The Jerusalem Post*, *Israel Scene* and *Jerusalem Letter/Viewpoints*. All material published here has been expanded and updated extensively.

For the 2013 edition, I am grateful to Jamie Berk for her diligent research of sources for the new introduction. I also want to thank Leah Horton for her frequent re-typing of the introduction and for reviewing the text.

Twenty Years After Oslo

I N 1994, this author's book *Israel's New Future: Interviews* was
published.[1] It recorded the expectations of 16 prominent Israelis
about future developments after the official signing of the Oslo
Accords on September 13, 1993.

In the interview with former Israeli Foreign Minister Abba Eban,
he noted that, "Israel is engaged in direct negotiations with Syria,
Jordan and Lebanon," and what he termed, "the mainstream Palestinian movement." He added, "We are desired guests in Morocco and
in Tunisia," as well as, "there are contacts with Saudi Arabia and the
Gulf States. Moreover, the Arab boycott is now in the first stage of
disintegration."

Eban remarked that these developments pointed to a total change
in the Arab approach. "Never have Israelis and Arabs been meeting
in so many ways in Washington, Tokyo, Moscow, Ottawa, Rome
and our region. Militarily, the Arabs have been very unsuccessful
against Israel. Now they want to be free of the traumas of defeat.
Before the collapse of communism and the Gulf War, the two main

developments of the last few years, nobody foresaw that this would happen."[2]

Political dynamics in the Middle East move quickly and in several directions. Today's political situation in the Middle East is far from the one Eban perceived a few months after the Oslo Accords were signed. Many major developments have taken place since in Israel's immediate environment. Israel was directly affected in some, as in the Second Intifada which started in 2000.

In others, it was involved as the initiator, e.g., the unilateral withdrawal from Gaza in 2005. Many other important events took place with no, or relatively minor, Israeli involvement, such as revolutions in what came to be falsely known as the "Arab Spring" or—at least until now—the Syrian Civil War.

Not only have circumstances changed. Perspectives on many statements by the interviewees in this author's book 20 years ago have varied according to the point in time in which one analyzed them.[3] Had this essay been written a year ago, several parts of it would have read differently, for instance those about Egypt and Syria. Rewriting this text say, a year from now, will almost certainly have to relay a different emphasis due to new developments.

Israel's New Future: Interviews dealt with both external and internal Israeli perspectives. However much the internal situation has changed, the reality in the outside world is even more different from what it was 20 years ago. Thus, attention must first and foremost be given to the global political situation and the one in the Middle East.

Prospects for the Western World

Before discussing Israel's prospects in a changing world and an unstable Middle East, several issues concerning the overall outlook for the Western world must be assessed. An assortment of global structural developments has become increasingly apparent in recent years. One of them concerns the many possibilities created by rapidly advancing technologies, concurrent with their multiple resultant problems. Cyberwar is only one among many. To defend oneself against it has become increasingly difficult.

As technology advances and permeates society further, more and more people find difficulty in functioning efficiently with it. Such a rapidly changing and increasingly complex environment also leads to more individual and communal feelings of fear and insecurity.

Governments can barely cope with the many challenges that have gradually emerged over the past decades. Their tasks will get even more difficult in the future. National authorities are likely to become increasingly powerless unless the rules of democracy are modified. The nature and *modus operandi* of democratic states at the end of the 21st century are likely to be substantially different from those of today. Value systems will undergo major changes; one can only speculate in what directions. The same will be true for the world's economy.

Demographic changes are likely to have major influences. The Organisation for Economic Co-operation and Development (OECD) forecast for Europe is that it is expected to shrink both economically and in terms of population. As Europe's public ages and families remain small, the younger generation will bear the burden of supporting long term care systems, and the reality of living in stagnating economies with higher unemployment rates.[4]

Power relationships between various nations will shift. No one is able to quantify how they may develop. For years, much has been written about the fast economic growth of the BRIC countries, Brazil, Russia, India and China.[5] Recently however, problems have emerged in each one of them. The fall of communism and the disappearance of the Soviet Union have been very beneficial for Israel. Developments in China and India are also of great importance to Israel, as both have become important trade partners.

Tensions between nation states and trans-national entities are likely to increase further. This is already clear as far as relations between the European Union and some of its member states are concerned. In May 2013 in the United Kingdom, high-ranking members of Prime Minister David Cameron's cabinet stated that they would vote to leave the European Union if a referendum were called.[6] In July 2013, the European Parliament criticized Hungary for making undemocratic constitutional changes. However, the Parliament only has the power to investigate these breaches, not to put a stop to constitutional changes prior to them being passed.[7]

Downgrading the Welfare State

One hardly takes risks in predicting that many characteristics of the open democratic welfare state will be downgraded in coming decades. This includes disparate issues such as social entitlements, relative employment security, government guarantees for bank accounts and freedom of expression. Individuals will have to shoulder more responsibilities and face greater risks.

In Europe—for the first time since the Second World War—new generations are growing up that will, on the average, be economically worse off than their parents were. A far bigger problem is increased unemployment, in particular within the young adult population. German Chancellor Angela Merkel has gone on record saying that this is currently Europe's most pressing problem.[8]

Is it daring to forecast that many legally enshrined freedoms that Westerners presently enjoy, combined with individualism, may make democracies increasingly unmanageable and therefore must be limited? Privacy is one of them. This has already occurred in practice. In summer 2013 it was disclosed that the National Security Agency in the United States was carrying out a widespread surveillance program of its citizens and those of many other nations.[9] There are indications of similar situations in some other Western countries. Yet individual freedoms are the hallmarks of contemporary democracies—however flawed. This contradiction will be difficult to resolve and may also lead to further conflicts within Western societies.

Post-Modernity

A number of features from the post-modern period will become more dominant. Globalization in multiple fields is one of them. Some of its main characteristics are mass communication and an overload of frequently distorted information. Another feature of post-modernity is the fragmentation of many issues. This includes for instance, the slow disintegration of a variety of societal structures, the further dissipation of authority, as well as an increase in vulnerability of complex systems. All this favors asymmetric warfare by enemies of the existing social order.

The September 11 attacks in the United States perpetrated by mainly Saudi Muslims, and Wikileaks, are two disparate examples of how a few individuals—far from the seats of power—can cause major damage to society at large. A recent example concerns leaks about the United States spying on some of its "allies." A single person may be at the origin of disclosures about this.

Similarly, one terrorist, Richard Reed the "Shoe Bomber," made a significant negative impact on society.[10] Since his failed aircraft bombing in 2001, millions of people in many countries have had to remove their shoes during security checks at airports and elsewhere.

The Crumbling of Norms and Values

Post-modernity has also brought with it the deterioration of tradi-tional norms and values. This has led to increased individualism, pluralism, relativism and subjectivism. Political correctness is an effort to establish often distorted norms for conduct in post-modern democracies. Analysts can only wonder where the borders of cur-rently acceptable behavior are.

In such a complex and opaque situation, many people doubt their own identities. At the same time, the number of those who flee post-modernity into fundamentalism becomes significant. These forms of counter-culture expressions give their adherents feelings of belonging and authenticity.

The current Western system is neither stable nor sustainable. Judging from current events, a clash of cultures between signifi-cant parts of the West and extensive segments of the Islamic world seems inevitable. This will further accelerate some of the changes mentioned before. In such a situation, attempting to ask the right questions often has more merit than making forecasts. This is not only necessary in order to follow future developments, but also to attempt to assess that which can be reasonably predicted.

Twenty Years after Oslo

Today, asking the correct key questions about Israel's future is similarly difficult. The American government is once again attempting to initi-ate peace negotiations between Israel and the Palestinian Authority. These efforts take place in a much different political climate from that of 1993. Expectations of the people on both sides have also changed.

Israeli optimists who believed in the Oslo Accords with near-Messianic enthusiasm were radically wrong. The Palestinians have not turned themselves into reformed democrats. The political concept of "land for peace" can also be considered a failure after Israel's unilateral withdrawal from Gaza in 2005 and its takeover by Hamas in 2007. A fashionable new expression is "one makes peace with one's enemy," to which one answer could be, "but not with those who consider a peace agreement as a step on the road toward Israel's extermination." Regarding the pessimists who saw the Oslo Accords as "the beginning of the end of Israel," the jury is still out.

The threat of fundamentalist Iran acquiring nuclear weapons and possibly using them could materialize in a not-too-distant future. Israel occupies a central place in the genocidal hate-mongering by Iran's leaders. Muslim and other countries are also among those potentially menaced. This existential threat to the Jewish state lessens the importance of peace negotiations with the Palestinians on Israel's agenda.

Iran's criminal attitude is mainly publicized in one field—its nuclear threats against Israel. Yet, former Canadian Justice Minister Irwin Cotler stated that its criminality prevails in many other areas: "Iran is in standing violation of international legal prohibitions with respect to its nuclear weaponization. Iran supports Syria's Bashar al-Assad killing his own people. It is also the world's leading state sponsor of terrorism, killing innocents from Argentina to Lebanon, Afghanistan to Syria. Furthermore, it has the highest per capita rate of 'executions of minors worldwide.'"[11]

The 2013 Iranian presidential elections handed victory to whom many call a "moderate" Prime Minister Hassan Rowhani. In many circles, hopes run high that he will change Iran's attitude toward the West. However, shortly after his election, Rowhani already stated that the uranium enrichment in his country will continue as planned.[12] Yet the real power in the country continues to rest with Supreme Leader Ayatollah Khamenei. Only candidates vetted by him were allowed to participate in the elections.[13]

More International Issues

Many major international issues concerning Israel come to mind besides the Iranian threat and possible peace negotiations with the Palestinians. The United States' position as leader of the free world has been eroded under the George W. Bush and Barack Obama administrations. The departure of the last American troops in late 2011 from Iraq marked the end of the war for the Allies.[14] The lethal violence in the country has continued. That is one of many negative issues which have impacted on America's image.

The same is true for the inability of the American-led Allied Forces to rein in the Taliban in Afghanistan. The United States, unable to defeat this terror group, has indicated that it considers conducting "peace negotiations" with them. David Miliband, who was British Foreign Secretary from 2007 to 2010 in the Labor government, said in July 2013 that the "overall reckoning" concerning Iraq was "strongly negative." He added that Afghanistan would most likely face many years of civil war after the Western troops leave.[15]

One sees the erosion of American power in various continents. Another example is the strengthening of the anti-American ALBA bloc of Latin American countries under the leadership of Venezuela. The late Venezuelan President Hugo Chávez developed close relations with former Iranian President Mahmoud Ahmadinejad. They were based on their common rejection of U.S. ambitions in both the Middle East and Latin America. Chávez also facilitated the development of Iran's relations with the other ALBA bloc members Nicaragua, Cuba, Ecuador and Bolivia.[16]

The weakening of the United States is a major aspect of the waning power of the Western world. Another issue is the European Union's financial woes. Problems surrounding the Euro currency were close to causing worldwide financial chaos, and this may still happen. Massive destruction of international wealth should not be excluded either.

The Arab World in Turmoil

Large parts of the Arab world and the Middle East are in turmoil. The "Arab Spring" movements have been hailed by some Western politicians and "experts" as the beginning of a more democratic Middle East. In September 2011, then-French Minister of Foreign Affairs Alain Juppé said: "The Arab Spring holds out tremendous hope—hope for democracy and the rule of law, hope for peace and stability, hope for a better future in which every person can pursue goals commensurate with his or her needs, talents and ambitions."[17]

In July 2012, *New York Times* columnist Thomas Friedman wrote about the election of President Mohammad Morsi and the Muslim Brotherhood in Egypt that it could be "the beginning of real peace between the Israeli and Egyptian peoples, instead of what we've had: a cold, formal peace between Israel and a single Egyptian pharaoh. But, for that to be the case, both sides will have to change some deeply ingrained behaviors, and fast."[18]

Old established dictatorial regimes in Tunisia, Egypt, Libya and Yemen have disappeared to different degrees. One wonders however, how democratic those currently in power are and how long they can maintain their positions. In Egypt, after mass protests, the military deposed elected President Morsi in summer 2013.

Tunisia is presently considered the greatest "Arab Spring" success in terms of peaceful democratic transition. Yet there is a basic lack of agreement between its dominant Islamist party and other factions in Parliament. Nearly two and a half years after the revolution, the new government has still been unable to hold a successful plenary debate to draft a new Tunisian constitution.[19] If passed, the new constitution is likely to contain a widely supported clause condemning Zionism and the normalization of relations with Israel, the first section of its kind anywhere in a constitution throughout the world.[20]

The "Arab Spring," with all of its initial hopes, has rapidly turned into the beginning of a nightmare outside of the Arab world also. This is not necessarily for Israel alone, but potentially as well for the Western world. Where will weapons from these countries—including chemical ones—end up? Stable dictatorships, however ugly, have made way for unstable regimes. One wonders what type of rulers Egypt, Libya, Tunisia and Yemen will have 10 years from now? And further away from the Middle Eastern scene: what is the future of Pakistan? This is the more important, as it is a nuclear power that possesses many atom bombs. The nearby end of the regime of the Ayatollahs in Iran has also been forecast incorrectly by many pundits for several years now.

The war in Iraq and the continuing terror attacks after American troops left the country, have enhanced a long-existing Sunni-Shiite conflict. Will Iraq still be a single state ten years from now? Will violent Sunni-Shiite confrontations increase further and become a major element of developments in the Muslim world?

The temporary increase in power of the Muslim Brotherhood in Egypt was not an indicator of more democracy or of greater economic wellbeing. The rule of fundamentalist Islam in Iran could have taught the world that already. So far, Arab monarchies and emirates have weathered the revolutionary storms, but one wonders whether they can continue to do so.

Syria

For many months, the Syrian civil war drew much of the world's attention concerning the Middle East. Information from The United Nations in summer 2013 shows that it has caused the world's worst refugee crisis since the Rwandan genocide about twenty years ago. There were at that time 1.8 million Syrian refugees, of whom two-thirds have fled the country since the beginning of 2013, at an average rate of 6,000 per day.[21] Currently, approximately 5,000 people are killed per month and many more wounded.

However, much of Western interest in Syria faded away after Egypt's military deposed President Morsi. In 2012, "experts" and senior members of the Obama Administration stated that the fall of President Bashir Assad's regime in Syria was a matter of weeks or months.[22] This has not happened, which once again illustrates the many uncertainties involved in forecasting events in the Middle East.

By the end of July 2013, UN Secretary General Ban Ki Moon stated that 100,000 Syrians had been killed in the war.[23] Violent conflicts have taken place among Assad's opponents.[24] The participation of foreign combatants in the war has gradually increased. Lebanese Shiite militias of the Hezbollah terror group are fighting alongside President Assad's forces. Syrian rebels have been joined by many who ideologically support Muslim terrorist movements. This war also illustrates a number of aspects of the Sunni-Shiite conflict.

Further internationalization of this conflict is possible. If Assad's regime deteriorates, will Iran send troops to help its ally? Western intervention is another possibility. The United States and Russia hold opposing political positions. The U.S claims that the Syrian government has used chemical weapons against its civilians.[25] The Russians attribute the use of the nerve gas sarin to Syrian rebels.[26]

In July 2013, the British Parliament's Intelligence and Security Committee's annual report stated that there is a risk that Al-Qaeda could gain access to Syria's stockpiles of chemical weapons with "catastrophic" consequences. Intelligence chiefs considered this "the most worrying emerging terrorist threat" for the UK.[27]

For Israel, the Syrian civil war has so far led to a number of incidents on the Golan Heights. There are reports that Israel bombed a Syrian weapon depot.[28] Israeli government officials have indicated that Israel may have to intervene in the Syrian war, whether it wants to or not.[29] There are also reports of Israel making preparations to counter additional problems emerging from the Syrian border.[30] Israel may have to increase strikes on Syria to ensure that no weapons end up in the hands of Hezbollah and other groups whose primary mission is the destruction of the Jewish state.[31]

Had Israel reached a peace treaty with Assad's Syria years ago and returned the Golan, its military position on the Syrian border would have been much worse. This leads to a hypothetical question—if Syrian opposition forces come to power, would they respect a peace treaty with Israel after the Golan was transferred to Syrian control?

Erosion of Israel's Position in the Middle East

Israel's current position in the Middle East is more complex than it has been for a long time. In past decades, three major powers dominated the area, Turkey, Iran and Egypt. Israel lost Iran as an ally after Ayatollah Khomeini came to power in 1979. Israel's relations with Egypt improved after their peace treaty was signed the same year.

After the Egyptian people overthrew President Husni Mubarak in 2011, Egypt's relations with Israel deteriorated. Terrorists have stopped Egyptian gas deliveries to Israel by frequently blowing up the gas pipeline.[32] Under the Mubarak regime, Israel got about one third of its gas deliveries from Egypt.[33]

During his regime, President Morsi as well as Muhammad Badie, General Guide of the Muslim Brotherhood, made constant mention of re-examining the successful 1978 Camp David Accords. Morsi said that they were unjust in their current state, because they were a bilateral agreement. He added that it was necessary they become multilateral to include provisions for Palestinians, a sentiment never expressed as forcefully by prior Egyptian leaders.[34] After the overthrow of Morsi's regime by the Egyptian Army in July 2013, the situation in the country is puzzling.

Erdogan's Provocations

Israel has had good relations with many past Turkish governments. Yet Prime Minister Recep Tayyip Erdogan has aimed at weakening Turkish-Israeli relations for many years. Already in 2004, he falsely accused Israel of state terrorism.[35] To mend the fences between the two countries, he came on a state visit to Israel in 2005.[36] In hindsight, we can understand this as an early sign of his policy of duplicity.

In May 2010, the Turkish ship Mavi Marmara tried to break the Israeli blockade of Gaza as part of a flotilla. Its crew refused to obey the orders of the Israeli Navy. Israeli commandos landed on the ship, where passengers who had boarded in Turkey attacked them with home-made weapons. Nine passengers were killed in the ensuing battle. Erdogan used this incident for a major anti-Israel campaign and downgraded diplomatic relations between the two countries.

Steven Merley, who specializes in the study of political extremism, uncovered facts which showed that the Turkish government was heavily involved in many aspects of the flotilla's provocation. He exposed Turkish government support for the flotilla that was channeled through the Turkish Muslim Brotherhood network. This included the attendance of officials from Turkey's ruling AKP party at many important Muslim Brotherhood network events in support of the flotilla, as well as a meeting attended by Erdogan himself, with a delegation of the Global Muslim Brotherhood and flotilla movement leaders from Britain and France. This meeting took place shortly before the ships left port for Gaza.[37] Without Turkish governmental support, the Mavi Marmara would probably never have approached Israel's waters.

Erdogan may be able to maintain his ambiguous and provocative attitude for a long time. Israel is just one of his targets. Fundamentally, however, Turkey remains a regional power in an economically weak environment. Yet it cannot project itself as being far above its league forever. This becomes even clearer when one learns that its Gross Domestic Product per capita is about half that of Israel's.[38, 39]

Peace with the Palestinians?

Many ethnic groups in the world strive for an independent state of their own. The Palestinians already have one such state—on territory of the former British Mandate of Palestine. Jordan has a majority of citizens of Palestinian origin. On various occasions, Palestinians have turned down opportunities to establish a second state on the West Bank and in Gaza. They refused the United Nations offer in 1947.[40]

In 1967 after the Six Day War, they did not distance themselves from the Khartoum Declaration which stated "The Three Nos"—no peace with Israel, no recognition of Israel, no negotiations with Israel.[41] The Oslo Agreements in 1993 gave the Palestinians a further opportunity to work toward their own state.

In 2000, Israeli Prime Minister Ehud Barak made a far-reaching offer of peace which was rejected by Palestinian President Yasser Arafat.[42] During the following second Intifada, Arafat personally authorized suicide attacks against Israel.[43] The Palestinian Authority refused to negotiate on the transfer of Gaza under Prime Minister Ariel Sharon. Israel therefore withdrew unilaterally.[44]

The Gaza strip came under Hamas control after violent attacks on Fatah supporters in 2007.[45] Since then, the area has been the main ongoing source of rocket attacks against Israel. Israel has also paid for its unilateral withdrawal from Gaza by having to undertake two military campaigns against Hamas. This has led to massive international criticism of Israel for defending its own citizens.

Ehud Olmert made another unsuccessful peace offer to President Abbas when he was Prime Minister.[46] A large number of Israelis doubt whether Palestinian leaders want peace, or they consider any such agreement an intermediary stage in plans for Israel's annihilation. The latter opinion is further fed by the huge ongoing incitement against Israel by Palestinian sources. A few years after *Israel's New Future* was published, it became clear that none of the interviewees had mentioned how the way the Palestinian Authority educates children is a key indicator of its true intentions. The inability of prominent Israelis interviewed to foresee this should be cause for deep concern regarding the accuracy of forecasts on important issues.

Palestinian and Arab Incitement

During his service as an Israeli government minister, Natan Sharansky coined the notion of the 3 D's concerning anti-Semitism—Demonization, Double Standards and Delegitimization.[47] Arab incitement has played a central role in the international demonization of Israel. The Palestinians have often been the major actors. The Oslo Accords have enabled the Palestinian leadership to obtain a territorial base to organize both their Muslim and Western supporters in massive campaigns of presenting Israel as a demonic state. While the PLO and Arafat were in exile, they could not promote hate against Israel on such a massive scale as both the Palestinian Authority and Hamas have done since. The Palestinians have gained many allies from this incitement.

Attempts to delegitimize Israel can be illustrated in many ways. One instance is how some Palestinian Christian leaders demonize Israel. The Kairos document is a prime example of this. Dutch theologian Hans Jansen summarizes: "The central argument of the Kairos document is that only Israel is responsible for the problems in the region. The document called for considering the Israeli occupation policy as 'a sin.' The main aim of the document is to achieve an international economic boycott against Israel."[48] At the same time, these and many other Palestinian Christian leaders hide the major discrimination and harassment of Christians suffering under Palestinian rule.[49]

Palestinian Media Watch (PMW) provides many examples of Palestinian anti-Israel and anti-Semitic incitement. The PMW website divides them into categories such as "animalization," "Jews and Israelis are evil," "Jews and Israelis are cancer and other diseases," "Jews/Israelis endanger all humanity" and so on.[50]

One among many examples of extreme incitement was in 2013 on Palestinian Authority TV, where two young girls recited a poem which included the following lines: "You who murdered Allah's pious prophets [i.e., Jews in Islamic tradition], Oh, you who were brought up on spilling blood, You have been condemned to humiliation and hardship, Oh Sons of Zion, oh most evil among creations, Oh barbaric monkeys, wretched pigs.'"[51]

The MEMRI website provides translations from contemporary Arab sources. One finds there many examples of extreme anti-Israel hate-mongering by Arab and Muslim leaders as well as in the media.[52] Many other grassroots organizations fight incitement in specific areas. Some examples: CAMERA[53] and Honest Reporting[54] mainly address bias in the English-speaking press. NGO Monitor deals with anti-Israel hate-mongering from non-governmental organizations.[55] Scholars for Peace in the Middle East exposes anti-Israelism and anti-Semitism on college campuses.[56] Major long-established American organizations like the Anti-Defamation League, the Simon Wiesenthal Center and the American Jewish Committee deal with a variety of matters. Hundreds of other organizations can be added; however, there is only sparse coordination between them.

The aim of the incitement is to achieve the Arabs' political goals which they have failed to reach through military means. This incitement has been successful to a substantial extent. It has, for instance, led Israel to a situation where it appreciates when Western leaders affirm its right to defend itself, which should be self-evident.[57] Israel has received some benefits from the Oslo Accords such as diplomatic relations with more countries. In the long run, the damage of Arab incitement may by far exceed whatever benefits Israel has gained from the Agreements.

American Attitudes toward Israel

The American public remains favorably disposed toward Israel. Several polls indicate this. Since 1967, Americans have consistently polled around 50% in favor of Israel over Arab nations. A February 2013 Gallup poll showed support for Israel at 64%; this was the highest figure since the First Gulf War in 1991.[58]

During its first term, the Obama administration was supportive of Israel after an initially hesitant period. This manifested itself in the supply of military equipment, assistance in fighting the cyber war as well as broad strategic collaboration. The United States has also consistently supported Israel at the United Nations. Furthermore, President Obama personally intervened in the life-threatening situation for Israel's embassy personnel in Cairo during the Egyptian mob attack in September 2011.[59]

Two major issues can explain why most Israelis did not have a positive opinion of the U.S. President. Firstly his image as an internationally weak president is bad for Israel, as the United States is Israel's main supporter. Furthermore, his appeasement policy largely ignored the massive violence coming out of parts of the Muslim world. This was clear from his 2009 speech in Cairo.[60]

During Obama's first term, many highly problematic extremist

Islamists were hosted at the White House. In addition, the American betrayal of the United States's long-time political ally Egyptian President Hosni Mubarak was a worrying event. It raised the question—to what extent can Israel count on the U.S. President in crisis situations?

Obama's re-election increased fears in Israel. Many thought that he no longer had to take into account reactions from pro-Israel Jewish-American organizations and their allies. Yet these fears have largely been unfounded. Obama visited Israel in March 2013. He—and his speech writer—made a major effort to please the Israelis. This was in part successful because expectations before his visit were low. Obama's popularity rating in Israel increased considerably due to this visit.[61]

During his stay in Israel, Obama gave a lecture to Israeli students. He said that he genuinely believed that Israel has true partners in Palestinian President Abbas and Prime Minister Fayyad.[62] Within a short time, these statements turned into a lesson of how weak Israel's Palestinian negotiating partners are. Fayyad resigned a few weeks later. His successor Rami Hamdallah stayed in office for less than a month.[63] Abbas' own legitimacy is non-existent: his mandate as elected President ended in 2009. All this casts further doubt on Obama's advice to make peace with such leaders.

It may well be that the Obama administration realizes that in a Middle East of such great turmoil, the Israeli democracy is the only reliable ally the United States can count on. This doesn't necessarily mean that the United States agrees with all elements of Israel's foreign policy. Yet at present, there seems to be no good reason to stress such differences.

Erosion of Israel's Position in Europe

A major issue requiring attention is that Israel's standing in European public opinion has greatly eroded in the new century. Concessions made to the Palestinians by Israel in the Oslo Accords, as well as the unilateral withdrawal from Gaza in 2005, are long forgotten.

After the Oslo Accords, Europeans continued their bias against Israel. Dore Gold, former Israeli Ambassador to the United Nations said, "Many people have been under the illusion that Israel's relations with the United Nations—and therefore also European voting patterns therein—actually improved in the 1990's during the period when the Oslo Agreements were implemented. One of the first things I did when I arrived in New York in 1997 was to take out the thick books of voting patterns to see how various UN members voted on critical issues relating to Israel.

"My findings were completely contrary to this myth of a wonderful Israeli romance with the UN during the 1990's. The first Oslo Agreement was signed on September 13, 1993. Within three months and one day from the signing, on December 14, 1993, the UN General Assembly began to adopt its usual series of anti-Israel resolutions."[64]

150 Million European Anti-Semites

Many Europeans hold a demonic view of Israel. A 2011 study in seven E.U. countries by the University of Bielefeld on behalf of the German Friedrich Ebert Foundation, illustrates this.[65] Researchers polled 1,000 people of 16 years and older in each of them.[66] They were inter alia asked whether they were in agreement with the assertion that Israel is carrying out a war of extermination against the Palestinians.

The lowest percentages of those who agreed with this statement were in Italy and the Netherlands, with 38% and 39% respectively. Percentages for Hungary were 41%, United Kingdom 42%, Germany 48% and Portugal 49%. In Poland the figure was 63%. These seven countries combined account for well over half of the E.U.'s population.

The E.U. counts over 500 million inhabitants. Of these, about 80%, or 400 million people are 16 years or older.[67] One may assume—in view of the University of Bielefeld study—that in the entire E.U., the average percentage of those holding demonic beliefs about Israel is at least 40%. One thus obtains a figure of over 150 million E.U. citizens who consider Israel a genocidal nation. This current widespread demonic view of Israel is a new mutation of the diabolical beliefs about Jews which many Europeans held in the Middle Ages.

Those who agreed with the statement expressed deeply anti-Semitic views. Genocide or behaving like Nazis is the "absolute evil" of our time. The European working definition of anti-Semitism includes drawing comparisons between contemporary Israeli policy and that of the Nazis.[68]

Additional Reports

Several additional reports support the aforementioned findings. In the first years of this century, a study was undertaken by the University of Bielefeld, relating only to Germany. More than 2,500 people were asked whether they agreed with the statement, "What the State of Israel does today against the Palestinians is in principle nothing different from what the Nazis in the Third Reich did to the Jews." Fifty-one percent of those interviewed answered in the affirmative.[69]

Reports in two European countries outside of the European Union show similar data. A study published in Switzerland by gfs.bern found that 50% of the Swiss population view Israel as "'the Goliath' in the extermination war against the Palestinians."[70]

The first comprehensive study of Norwegians' attitudes toward minorities was published in 2012 by the Center for Studies of the Holocaust and Religious Minorities. It was carried out at the request of the Norwegian government. It found that 38% of Norwegians agree with the statement that Israel behaves toward the Palestinians in the same way that the Nazis acted toward the Jews.[71]

These views are not rational. The number of deaths in the past fifty years in the Palestinian-Israeli conflict is a small fraction of the most lethal conflicts during that period.[72] The Palestinian population has grown greatly. Israeli hospitals save Palestinian babies and children every day. Yet, over 150 million adults in so-called "civilized" Europe do not seem to have an interest in facts, in particular whenever Israel is involved. That was also the case concerning Jews in Medieval and nationalist eras in Europe.

A number of other studies confirm the negative viewpoint many Europeans have regarding Israel.[73] They have not been given much publicity, either in Europe or in Israel, nor have obvious conclusions been drawn from them. The fact that so many in Europe hold a demonic view of Israel is a major problem for Israel. What lives in the minds of a huge number of citizens will, over time, influence politicians. One can only wonder why the Israeli government has not launched a major study into what extent European public opinion can be recaptured.

Anecdotal Information

There is much anecdotal material available on the widespread negative views of Israel held by Europeans. A number of interviews in this author's book, *Demonizing Israel and the Jews*, illustrate this concerning a variety of European countries. These interviews provide answers to: who promotes hateful anti-Israel views, with what messages and how are they transmitted to the public at large.

There are many such promoters of anti-Israel incitement in

Europe. They also include governments, of which Norway's current Labor party-dominated government is among the most extreme. Other anti-Israel hate-mongers can be found in many circles. They include extreme leftists, other parties including several Green and Social Democrat ones, trade unions, NGOs, academics, church leaders, parts of local Muslim communities and many others.

Senior European hate-mongers do not necessarily believe that Israel exterminates the Palestinians, or behaves like Nazis. Their biased statements have, however, contributed to this image. On an individual basis, none of these attacks has caused the dramatic data the studies show. However, together they have created the climate which makes this anti-Israel atmosphere possible.

A Different Method of Demonization

The current demonic view of Israel has been created in a different way from that of the Jews in past centuries. Jews were repeatedly and explicitly portrayed as "absolute evil" by Catholic and various other Christian churches. This image resulted from the false and devilish accusation that they were responsible for their ancestors' killing of Jesus. The latter was a false allegation in itself. This accusation of deicide was the worst possible against any grouping in European societies at the time.

The perception of what "absolute evil" was changed with the advancement of the Enlightenment. In nationalistic societies, Jews were increasingly presented as "foreign elements." The Nazis turned them into "subhuman," "bacteria," "vermin," etc. This rhetoric contributed to making the Holocaust possible.

In today's society, the major notion of "absolute evil" is committing genocide, or behaving like Nazis. Yet, the demonization process of Israel is far more complex than that of the Jews. The demonization process is mainly carried out through what can be called the "method of the million cuts." Its rhetoric is far more indirect than that of anti-Jewish inciters of past centuries.

This rhetoric frequently includes condemnations and attacks on Israel by leading E.U. officials, politicians of European countries, media, human rights organizations, trade unions, Protestant church leaders and so on. Very few of them accuse Israel of committing genocide or behaving like Nazis. Yet, the accumulation of all these statements has created a picture of Israel as "absolute evil" among huge parts of Europe's population.

The Methodology of Demonization

The current methodology of demonization is complex. It has many components. One of its pillars is frequently reporting negative news about Israel. The exaggeration of negative issues concerning Israel, as well as putting forward lies and false accusations is another.

A different category of anti-Israel hate-mongering is false arguments. Prominent among them is the use of double standards and moral equivalence. Another important fallacy is scapegoating, which means that Israel must always take the blame, instead of the real culprit. All of these are part of the method of the million cuts.

One key example of the double standards applied by some European politicians is that they accuse Israel of transgressing international law. This is done while European states have not lived up to their legal commitments under the UN Genocide Convention to bring planners of genocide, such as Iran and Hamas, before an international court. Material on the ongoing declarations of intent of the Iranian leadership to destroy Israel is easily obtainable.[74]

A further element which enhances the demonization of Israel in the Western world is the muted attention given to the huge criminality and hate-mongering in many Arabic and Muslim states. If mass murders, terror attacks and other major crimes were highlighted proportionally to the size of the population and misconduct in those countries, news about Israel would be comparatively negligible.

Yet another element that contributed to the delegitimization of Israel is the downplaying of horrific events in European countries' own pasts. In this way, a far too rosy picture of their society's history is painted, which is then compared with the greatly falsified picture of Israel.

Hiding Europe's Moral Decay

Europe's political and opinion leaders are not interested in having it become widely known that over 150 million Europeans hold demonic anti-Semitic views about Israel. If this were to become a substantial topic of debate in Europe, the possible consequences for the continent's image could be major. European countries present themselves as "models of democracy and promoters of human dignity." From the large number of citizens with demonic views of Israel and the huge anecdotal pool of anti-Semitic incidents, the E.U. also emerges as an ugly conglomeration of many people with criminal opinions of others, i.e., Israel.

If this reality became widely known, it could raise many other extremely unwelcome questions about Europe. Who will investigate how this repulsive mass of extreme Israel-haters came into existence? Other unwelcome questions would be asked. To what extent has hateful rhetoric by European Union and member countries' politicians contributed to this widespread demonic picture of Israel? What is the role played by the European media in hate-mongering? Are schools involved at all? What have so-called "humanitarian" NGOs added by their bias? And so on.

The main candidates to be investigated however are the E.U.'s leadership and national governments. This could lead to explosive results. One will have to name senior people in the E.U., member states' governments and civil societies who have contributed to this demonization. It could even have dire political consequences. Furthermore, the outcome of any reliable study would be a massive assault on the "humanitarian image" of the European Union and of many of its components.

A detailed analysis of the incitement process against Israel should lead to demands that the E.U. and individual governments act accordingly. This would mean as a first step, silencing the frequent incitement against Israel emanating from their midst.

This is a giant task. Yet an even more damaging question would become part of public discourse. The widespread criminal world view regarding Jews in Europe was the precursor to mass atrocities committed there in the 1940s. The peak of these was the Holocaust. In view of this, one should now ask: Will these present widespread criminal opinions lead to major crimes once again, this time against Israel? Or alternatively, will Europeans become criminal "bystanders" while many in Muslim countries may try to commit extreme crimes against Israel?

One might sum this all up by concluding that for Europe's leadership, this Pandora's Box is just too big to open.

Laboratory for the West

In *Israel's New Future: Interviews*, it was mentioned that many of Israel's political, military, cultural and economic experiences were precursors to what would later take place in the Western world. In other words, to a certain extent Israel was functioning as a laboratory for the West.[75]

This role that Israel plays has evolved further. By the 1990s, Israel's military experience had already provided lessons for the West for many decades. In the new century in Afghanistan and Iraq, Western forces were confronted with terrorism. Palestinians and other Muslims have contributed to the development of innovative terrorism.[76] One way in which this expressed itself was how the war experiences of allied armies in Afghanistan and Iraq were often similar to Israel's.

One specific case became extremely instructive for how double standards are employed against Israel. Israel had decided to make use of targeted killing of terrorists. The execution which received the most publicity was that of Hamas leader and founder Sheikh Ahmed Yassin in 2004, which was widely condemned by the UN and leaders in the West.[77] However, during the Afghanistan war, allied forces frequently executed such killings without due process. They also did this in the lawless areas of Pakistan.[78]

The Obama administration's expansion of targeted drone strikes against terrorists in Afghanistan and Iraq has gained some acclaim for lessening "boots on the ground" in these dangerous environments. In other cases, the Obama administration brought both U.S. troops and mercenaries to kill terrorists, often without due process.[79] The most publicized targeted killing of a terrorist by the United States was that of Osama bin Laden, founder and leader of the Muslim terrorist group Al-Qaeda, in 2011.

This targeted killing was seen as a cornerstone of the Obama administration's success in combating terror worldwide. Other democratic countries have implemented similar successful targeted killing policies since 2000, largely inspired by the Israeli model created in the 1950s.[80] Yet, only Israel faces significant criticism by Human Rights Watch and Amnesty International when investigations of their targeted killings are compared to similar investigations of these other Western nations.[81]

In addition to facing formidable opponents from state militaries, Israel has also been fighting asymmetric wars with terrorists since its independence. Although some groups like the Palestinian Authority no longer commit terror acts even though they may condone them, new major threats emerged such as terror organizations Hamas and Hezbollah.[82]

Richard Kemp, former Commander of British forces in Afghanistan, credits the Israel Defense Forces (IDF) for helping him develop a policy to counter suicide bombings that was subsequently adopted by all British forces, thus saving many lives.[83]

Amos Guiora, presently a Law Professor at the University of Utah, wrote that interactive software developed by the IDF to prepare for ethical dilemmas, "has been called the best and most advanced of its kind by senior officers from many foreign armies. The IDF has received numerous requests for the video from other armies." He based this conclusion inter alia on conversations with senior American, Canadian and British officers. Guiora added that, "As more and more nations encounter the new form of armed conflict, they too will have to develop models relevant to their particular needs, rules of engagement, and standard operating procedures. Meanwhile, this author's research clearly indicates that the IDF has 'defined the field.'"[84]

Terrorist Attacks in Western Countries

Terrorism against Western targets has evolved swiftly. Initially, major terror attacks by Muslim "militants" against the United States were outside of its borders. They include the Al-Qaeda-coordinated twin attacks on U.S. embassies in Tanzania and Kenya in 1998 killing 224; the suicide bombing on the USS Cole in 2000 killing 17 U.S. sailors and countless terror attacks against members of the armed forces and civilians during U.S.-led operations in Afghanistan and Iraq from 2001 until the present.[85]

The September 11 mass murders however, took place within U.S.

borders. Like later attacks in Madrid, London and Bali, they were no longer aimed at military personnel or even officials of the state, but randomly at civilians.

Many terrorist attacks have been launched by Al-Qaeda at civilian populations in Muslim countries through its international proxy networks.[86] Many of these attacks by terror networks, especially in Iraq and Afghanistan, mimic attacks Israeli civilians have faced since Israel's independence. Like terrorists who attack Israelis, these international Muslim terrorist networks strive to attack civilians, either to weaken their governments, or to coerce them into complying with their demands.[87]

After terrorist attacks aimed at an Israeli airport, airlines and air travelers, Israel developed advanced security measures in these fields. For decades, they have served as examples for many other nations. Yet there remains much for many in the West to learn from the Israeli approach of profiling suspects.[88]

In the United States, both a 1997 commission headed by Vice President Al Gore and the 9/11 Commission recommended various airport security measures—from luggage screening to background checks. It was clarified that no person should be suspected of terror based solely upon "national origin, racial, ethnic, religious or gender characteristics."[89]

In 2009, there was a failed attempt by terrorist Umar Farouk Abdulmuttalab to detonate an explosive device on a flight from Amsterdam to Detroit.[90] The Obama administration subsequently reevaluated the security provisions, allowing for screening based largely on nationality. This addition to the protocol was mainly inspired by Israel's advanced system of profiling terror suspects on El Al flights and at Ben Gurion International Airport.[91]

Israel as a Sensor for the Western World

In recent decades, a new role for Israel has emerged. It has increasingly become an indicator of the state of mind of the Western world, as well as its widespread dubious morality. The issues concerning Israel and its interactions with the West are so numerous, one can learn "where the West is at" from them in many fields. A similar role was played in previous centuries by the Jews. That continues until today.

The aforementioned figures regarding the huge number of Europeans who hold a demonic view of Israel illustrate a variety of aspects in contemporary European society. One is how successful inciters of hate can be there. In this case, the hate-mongering concerns Israel. Yet it seems logical that it can be used against other targets too.

These figures also show how absurd and extreme views can be instilled in large parts of the European population. The accusation that Israel is exterminating the Palestinians is criminal slander. During the two years from the end of 1941 until the end of 1943 in the extermination camps of Treblinka, Belzec and Sobibor alone, 2 million Jews were murdered by the Germans. Technology has greatly "advanced" since then. If this genocidal accusation against Israel were true, the last of the Palestinian adults and children would have been murdered long ago.

To the contrary, the number of Palestinians has continued to *increase* greatly in the last decades. The belief that Israel behaves like the Nazis toward the Palestinians, while Palestinians are being treated and cured in Israeli hospitals, is just one example of how easily large numbers of Europeans can be duped into believing the absurd.

It has already been mentioned that while today many see Israel as "absolute evil," similar views about Jews were held in Medieval

Europe. These views returned massively in the years leading up to the Second World War. They were a clear indicator of Europe's moral decline. This issue of Israel being a sensor for European development has many other aspects. It is a subject for a major essay and only a few disparate examples can be given here.

From Overall to Particular Degradation

The overall moral decay of Europe as expressed by the widespread diabolical views about Israel has more particular aspects as well. One concerns the extensive moral decomposition of many socialist parties. There were social-democratic politicians such as French President Francois Mitterrand,[92] Swedish Prime Minister Olof Palme and Greek Prime Minister Andreas Papandreou, who compared Israel's actions to those of the Nazis.[93] However, politicians who accuse Israel of being "absolute evil" by comparing it to Nazi Germany are the exceptions. Less extreme socialist anti-Israel hate-mongers are more common.

Former Swedish Liberal Deputy Prime Minister Per Ahlmark observed about Palme: "To compare the bombs over the capital of North Vietnam with the gas chambers in Treblinka was thus a false parallel. . . It contributed to the trivialization of the Holocaust. If all killing is the same as Hitler's, one conceals what is unique about the Nazi genocide. We should also note that Olof Palme during his time as party chairman twice made statements where he equated countries with Nazi Germany. One of those states was built by the people who were Hitler's primary victims. The other was the nation that came to decide the victory for the free countries over Nazism in World War II. And both—Israel and the United States—were and are democracies."[94]

The extreme negative attitudes toward Israel also show that

Scandinavian socialist parties are erroneously considered "progressive." One example concerning the Norwegian government is that it co-financed a hate-promoting anti-Israel exhibition in Damascus before Syria's murderous civil war broke out. The same exhibition was also shown in Beirut, Lebanon and Amman, Jordan.[95]

During Israel's Cast Lead campaign in 2009, there were large anti-Israel demonstrations in Sweden. Thanks mainly to Swedish bloggers, it is known that prominent members of the Social Democrats, the country's largest party, took part in hate demonstrations against Israel. Mona Sahlin, then-party leader, participated in a rally in Stockholm[96] where Hezbollah and Hamas flags were flown and an Israeli flag was burned.[97] Jan Eliasson, former Foreign Minister,[98] and Wanja Lundby Wedin, Chair of the Swedish Trade Union Confederation,[99] also took part in that event. In Norrköping, another senior Social Democrat, Lars Stjernkvist, spoke at a demonstration with a Hezbollah flag as well as swastikas in the background.[100] In Malmö, a Social Democrat parliamentarian, Luciano Astudillo, spoke as someone next to him held up a picture of Hezbollah leader Hassan Nasrallah.[101]

Israel, A Sensor Elsewhere Too

Israel is not only a sensor for the moral degradation of Europe, but for many other countries. A few examples will indicate this. Most Western countries are signatories of the UN Genocide Convention. As previously mentioned, none of them have moved to bring Iran before an international court.

Israel is also a sensor for the moral degradation of the UN and many of its subsidiary bodies. One example concerns the double standards it applies. United Nations' declarations illustrate this well. After the United States executed Osama bin Laden in 2011,

UN Secretary General Ban Ki-moon told reporters that, "The death of Osama Bin Laden, announced by President [Barack] Obama last night, is a watershed moment in our common global fight against terrorism."[102]

After Israel killed Sheikh Yassin in 2004, then-UN Secretary General Kofi Annan said, "I do condemn the targeted assassination of Sheikh Yassin and the others who died with him. Such actions are not only contrary to international law, but they do not do anything to help the search for a peaceful solution."[103] The now-defunct UN Commission on Human Rights condemned "the tragic death of Sheikh Ahmed Yassin in contravention of the Hague Convention IV of 1907."[104] In the Security Council, the U.S. had to use its veto power to prevent condemnation of Israel.

One of the most morally perverse bodies of the United Nations is the UN Human Rights Council. This has been exposed by organizations such as UN Watch[105] and Eye on the UN.[106] Anne Bayefsky of the latter wrote about a 2013 session: "From the start on Monday, May 27, the UN Human Rights Chief Navi Pillay issued an opening statement highlighting her major human rights concerns the world over. Her preposterous series of countries having "crises" worthy of specific criticism were Syria, Myanmar, Iraq, the Central African Republic, Israel and the United States. On the other hand, in Pillay's view, Egypt, Libya and Yemen were "progressing in different ways and at different speeds."' She did not mention major human rights offenders such as China, Russia or Saudi Arabia.[107]

Israel's Progress

Israel has developed greatly in the past 20 years. Its internal changes merit a detailed analysis like those of its external environment. Yet the latter have been more profound.

One major area of internal change has been the political one. Perhaps Israel's most tragic event here was the murder of Prime Minister Yitzhak Rabin in 1995.[108] Its impact on the spirit of the nation was major. It is difficult to assess to what extent it had a lasting political influence.

The second Intifada in 2000 was a major challenge to Israel's democracy. In October 2000, former Supreme Court President Moshe Landau stated in an oft-quoted article that he feared for the State's survival. He added that the internal dangers were even greater, mentioning the general feeling of bewilderment and social disintegration in the country. He also wrote: "And the weakness of the national will, the lack of readiness to fight for our lives. The illusion that peace will obviate our need to fight and defend ourselves. These things give me no rest. They really keep me awake and are affecting my physical health."[109] Yet, Israel rose to this challenge relatively well.

A major change in Israeli politics between 1993 and 2013 has been the muted political role the Labor Party plays nowadays. One has also seen new political parties come and go. The main one was Kadima, founded by former Prime Minister Ariel Sharon in 2005. In the 2013 elections, it dropped to two seats. The center-left Shinui party lost all of its seats in the 2006 election.[110] A pensioner's party entered the Knesset in 2006 and was a one-time occurrence.

In the 2013 elections, a new center-left party Yesh Atid (There is a Future) under the leadership of media personality Yair Lapid, obtained 19 seats out of 120 in the Knesset. It became the second largest party in the current government, led by Binyamin Netanyahu of the Likud. The percentage of floating voters was high. One can thus assume that in future elections there will also be major changes in the Israeli political scene.

Additionally, there have been significant developments in demographics. At the end of 1993, the Israeli population stood at 5.3 million.[111] Presently, it is around 8 million.[112] Economically, Israel has advanced well. Its GDP in 2011 was 242.9 billion dollars.[113] Israel's unemployment figures are lower than those of many member states in the E.U.

There has been sizable social unrest in recent years. Yet partly due to the Israeli population's common and difficult past, added to external pressures, solidarity, coherence and commonality of purpose seem stronger than in many European countries.

There has also been outstanding technological progress. Israel's high-tech sector has been greatly successful. The number of Israeli companies on the NASDAQ exchange in New York is exceeded only by the United States and China.[114] Several Israeli or Israeli-owned companies have been sold to foreign investors in the new century for amounts exceeding one billion dollars. In 2012 alone, Israeli start-ups were sold for a combined 5.5 billion dollars.[115]

Israel won six Nobel prizes in Chemistry and Economics in the new century, including the first Nobel Prize awarded to an Israeli female scientist. There were also four prizes for Literature and Peace awarded to Israel earlier.

Conclusion

After the Oslo Accords, perspectives on Israel's future changed in a major way. This was expressed in the title of this author's book, *Israel's New Future: Interviews*. Many forecasts of several interviewees were correct, a multitude of others were mistaken. Yet looking back, the Oslo Accords indeed represented a turn in a different direction for the State of Israel.

Unrest in the Middle East today exceeds that during the time of the Oslo Accords by far. Events that cause possible curves and bends in Israel's future now take place with much greater frequency than at the end of the previous century. A major one was the "Arab Spring," another was the beginning of the Syrian civil war and a third was the deposition of Egyptian President Morsi by the Egyptian army. All of these took place over a period of a few years.

Since the signing of the Oslo Accords, one has seen the Second Intifada, the attempts to break Israel's spirit by a large number of Palestinian terrorist attacks—partly suicidal—mainly against Israeli civilians. There was the powerful political rise of the Hamas terrorist organization in 2007 after Israel unilaterally withdrew from all of Gaza in 2005. This led to murderous rocket attacks on Israel, aimed randomly, and thus primarily harming civilians.

There have also been a series of major Israeli military campaigns into terrorist-held territories, since the signing of the Oslo Accords. In the years immediately following, there was a barrage of Hezbollah rocket attacks on Israel followed by airstrikes on Lebanon and operations conducted to free Israeli soldiers held captive by Hezbollah.[116]

In the 1996 "Operation Grapes of Wrath" campaign, the Israeli Air Force was deployed into Southern Lebanon to stop rocket fire into Israel by Hezbollah terrorists.[117] After the start of the Second Intifada by the Palestinians in 2000, a series of ground operations were deployed, including "Operation Defense Shield" and "Operation Days of Penitence," to stop terror groups and suicide bombers.[118, 119]

In 2006, the Second Lebanon War began. After rocket attacks and ambushing of Israeli soldiers patrolling the Lebanese border, the IDF launched a series of aerial attacks on Hezbollah targets and also carried out ground operations.[120]

The Israeli military was forced to launch two major campaigns in Gaza to stop rocket fire from there. In 2008-2009 and 2012, Israel engaged in operations Cast Lead and Pillar of Defense against Hamas to prevent rocket fire targeted at civilian populations in Israel.[121, 122]

In such a volatile and rapidly changing reality, can one predict Israel's future correctly? What comes to mind first is that Israel's domestic situation must be kept under control. Key economic requirements should be studied carefully and internal social discord should be contained within reasonable limits.

One major phenomenon in the last 20 years has been the increasing demonization of Israel worldwide. Methods used differ from those employed against the Jews by Christians in the Middle Ages, or by the Nazis in the first half of the previous century. The ultimate aim of many present demonizers has major similarities with those of the latter.

The diabolical view of Israel held by many in Europe is a great potential danger to Israel. The demonization of Israel in Europe has so far only marginally affected economic, cultural, technological, research and sports ties. In view of the favorable balance for the E.U. in its trade with Israel, its economic interests can be easily explained. The same is true for technological relations, as Israel has been so successful in this field. Israel's enemies have increasingly attempted to damage European-Israeli relations primarily since the World Conference against Racism held in Durban, South Africa in 2001. The question remains—to what extent will this damage increase in the future?

The unilateral withdrawal of Israel from Gaza enabled Hamas to take over the area and attack Israel, mainly with rockets. Israelis may ask themselves what would have happened if Arafat had accepted Prime Minister Barak's peace proposal in 2000 and Hamas had later taken over the Palestinian Authority.

There seems to be another important indication for the future. Making far-reaching concessions for a doubtful peace in a quickly changing environment and an unstable and largely unpredictable world would be irresponsible. Yet, Israel may be pressured to make such concessions by many worldwide.

Introduction

I SRAEL IS a complex, contradictory country that is often misunderstood. Sometimes I ask European or American acquaintances, "How would you feel if some of your neighbors told you for decades that they intended to wipe you off the map? How would you behave toward them?" The more intelligent ones realize soon that they cannot place themselves in such a different mindset.

For this reason and others, Israel's day-to-day experience and strategic position differ radically from those of countries in the West. So do its geographic environment, the origin of its population and many other characteristics.

When travelling abroad, I am often asked, "What's new in Israel?" My usual answer: "I don't know, I've been away more than a day." It's not a joke. Israel's reality and pace are different from those of the rest of the world. In this country, a day can make all the difference.

The history of the Jewish people in its own country was interrupted for almost 2,000 years. When watching Israel, one often senses that what was lost, in terms of common history, over many centuries must be made up in one or two generations. In quite a few fields, Israeli developments are indeed very fast.

The motif of rapid change repeats itself in a multitude of stories and anecdotes. A pungent one is that of the Israeli politician who desperately wanted to read some books. The only way he could find the time, he decided, was to give up newspapers for a week. After a day or two, so the story goes, he put away his book and returned to the dailies. He had no choice; without the newspapers, he no longer understood what people around him were talking about.

A New, More Complex Dimension

The peace negotiations and ongoing developments have added a new, more complex dimension to the Israeli-Arab reality. Forecasting shortly after a trendline has been broken is even riskier than when the present seems to be an extrapolation of the past.

When a fast-moving process is underway, developing systematic thoughts about the future becomes more important than ever. Israelis have long been accustomed to government procrastination in many fields, and to a hostile stalemate in the relationship with most of their Arab neighbors.

Now, suddenly, they see their government taking far-reaching decisions—on which no national consensus exists—concerning their future at great speed. Quite naturally, this makes every thinking Israeli question where the country is going, and whether our leaders know where they are taking it. These are only two of many major national perplexities.

How does one assess government decisions, and how can one assess what the future will bring? Nothing useful comes out of evaluating new events in a vacuum. To gain insight, radically new inputs must be plugged into an existing frame of reference. At the same time, one must reassess whether the set of coordinates against which these new developments are gauged is still valid.

All of this adds up to a complex thought process which requires great discipline. Few people bother to develop such forecasting skills systematically over decades and hone them on an ongoing basis. Those who do apply this methodology understand that they often will be wrong, but that this is the only way to achieve any results—comprehending events ahead of, and slightly better than others.

Vision and Fantasy

The alternatives are confusion in the best case; euphoria and deep pessimism in the worst. Paranoia and self-defeating humanism are strange twins which immigrated from the diaspora and have played a major part in the building of Israel's national identity. Some people viewed the September 1993 Israel-PLO agreement with messianic hope. Others saw it as the beginning of the end.

Some Israelis believe that from the moment the peace process started going their way, the Palestinians will behave like old, established democrats. Others say the Israeli government has laid the groundwork for the destruction of the Jewish state with its own hands, like the Hasmonean rulers did two millennia ago.

Such statements usually are accompanied by a mixed bag of prejudices, judgments, risks and fears. The next step is to promote fantasy at the expense of vision.

When Yitzhak Rabin and Shimon Peres shook hands with Yasser Arafat on the White House lawn on September 13, 1993, the old framework of thought no longer sufficed. Events caught the population by surprise and the opposition off guard. The latter was totally unprepared for the agreement with the PLO, and did not know how to react.

This is natural, as the negotiations were conducted in secrecy, and the approach proposed was highly unexpected. Nobody could say that a strategist should have expected the unexpected. Had the opposition been kept abreast of the negotiations, its leaders could have developed a frame of reference in which to evaluate the dynamic processes.

The radical change in the peace negotiations is only one example, albeit a major one, of the importance of developing a systematic, ongoing approach to assessing what the future may bring. Regardless of what happens, Israel will be faced with major changes and the search for new equilibria in the coming years. This makes it one of the countries where the establishment of a methodology to judge events during transitionary periods is crucial.

A Conceptual Mistake

In the course of Israel's short history, some Israelis have hoped that it would become a country like all others. They saw this as the essence of the Zionist dream, but their vision was based on a fundamental conceptual mistake. With peace negotiations underway, these ideas re-emerge. Many Israelis admire the hedonism of those who do reasonably well in the West, and wish they could live that way.

Israel's origins are radically different from those of other nations. The Jewish people's long history in the diaspora, and the short one in its modern state, have developed differently from those of other people. As Israel lives in a unique context, its present cannot be like that of other countries. The same goes for its immediate future. Neither the peace process nor anything else will make Israel a nation like all others.

In the meantime, elsewhere in the world, other equilibria have been disturbed. In several important ways, the world's reality starts to resemble the environment of uncertainty which long has been a key characteristic of Israel's situation. With the fall of communism, worldwide risks have fragmented and multiplied.

While new opportunities always are welcome, new threats merit much more attention. For instance, what are the dangers to the West if extreme nationalists, or semi-fascists, rule Russia at some point in the future? This is only one of many questions in a new, uncertain world.

Few Westerners seem to care about such threats to their own future. Is it because these are not significant, or is it because they have never grown accustomed to caring? It is difficult to assess to what extent risks exceed fears.

Forecasting in a Dynamic Reality

How does one assess the future in such a dynamic reality? This has always been a valid question for Israel. Now, in a perturbed world order, it is becoming increasingly relevant for many other players as well.

The more uncertain the future, the greater the need for forecasting and planning. Developing potential scenarios and speculating about their impact is becoming more common in many societal situations around the world. It is also increasingly rewarding, as society has become so much more confused in recent years. People with strategic minds who can assess the future better than others can—and do—reap the rewards on a daily basis.

Israel must continue to assess its future, despite all of the old and new uncertainties. What has changed is that it is no longer alone. Today, many other modern societies must learn fast how to plan better for the future, despite their unstable starting positions.

Germany after unification, and Italy with its supermarket of political scandals, are two among many countries which come to mind.

The Rationale for This Book

Why didn't I write a book on Israel's future by myself? In a complex, highly dynamic situation, the risk of injecting too much of an individual's own bias into forecasting developments in a wide array of fields is unavoidable. Besides that, taking on such a project alone would have been far too ambitious a challenge.

These considerations led me to base this book on interviews with leading Israelis of varying experiences, cultures and political views. They share a common search, among the infinite number of inputs, for those most relevant to the country's future.

In these pages, some of Israel's most knowledgeable citizens assess where this unclassifiable country is headed. The interviewees are all leaders in their fields. Their backgrounds are highly varied. Some are native Israelis; others came to the country as children or when they were already adults. By distilling their knowledge and insights, I seek to give the reader a multi-faceted view of Israel's present and future. Only time will tell how the effort fared.

The Subjects Chosen

This book deals with likely changes and those considered critical to the country's future. It develops new perspectives on geopolitics, the economy, the impact of immigration, the changing social and health scene as well as major political, cultural and religious aspects of Israel's future. At a time of uncertainty, this book attempts to open as wide a horizon as possible.

The chosen approach has another advantage. To make this book more useful to readers, it should involve them interactively in forecasting. The variety of opinions offers more than just a glance at matters from different viewpoints as they exist at the moment the book was compiled or read.

Readers will draw full benefit from what the interviewees have to say if they integrate the thoughts expressed in each chapter into their own views of the country's future, and test them as major events unfold. This is not an easy task, but it is worthwhile, as we live in times where major history is being made.

Why have certain themes been included in this book and others left out? All Israelis who saw the proposed table of contents had ideas about additional issues which could or should be investigated.

Many of their considerations were valid. Nonetheless, I preferred to stick to a select group of interviewees and a mix of themes which I thought would enable the reader to confront, analyze and understand new events as they develop.

The Optimists

How does one use all of these inputs to chart a course for the future? How might Israel change? How should it change? How will it change? How can it cope with its enemies, who perhaps are becoming partners in peace? How will the peace process and internal developments in the United States influence Israel's special relationship with the US?

What can one forecast with some certainty? Can Israel really have moderately peaceful neighbors in a Middle East that will remain turbulent even if Arab-Israeli peace is achieved? Few doubt that the Islamic world will remain in continuous ferment for decades.

One should not gloss over the peace issue, however opaque it is.

People look desperately for clues from the past as to what the future in this totally new situation may bring. Some consider that because the Palestinians, who could have had an independent state with no strings attached in 1948, have made such major mistakes in the past, they will be very careful not to throw away what they can gain now.

"They have suffered enough, and controlling their own destiny will make them reasonable, like most other nations," commented one of the people interviewed for this book. "The promised funds from donor countries should provide an additional incentive to minimize violence."

Those who are of this opinion say that the Palestinians' ongoing contact with the Israelis, however unpleasant, has given them more of a taste of democracy than they could have had under Arab rule. Important roles in the administration of several Arab states have prepared many of them to fulfill government functions in self-rule.

The Pessimists

The other school says that the internecine killings of the intifada were just a prelude to inevitable civil war among Palestinians. There is no way that neo-fundamentalists who want an Islamic state and those who look for a semi-secular society can coexist peacefully in a near-democratic society.

In this school's view, the economic incentives offered by donor countries are meaningless in view of such a major ideological struggle. Those committed to an extreme ideal will not compromise it for material considerations. Another important charge lodged by Islamic neo-fundamentalists against the PLO concerns its corruption.

What may be worse, from an Israeli point of view, is that the Palestinians, however diverse their aims and ideological approaches, may find common ground for just long enough to ensure that transition to self-rule over most of the administered territories takes place. The explosion of violence, and its inherent threat to Israel, would come at a point when the process of self-rule can no longer be halted.

Minimum Requirements for Peace

Nobody has certain answers to these profound uncertainties. In order to discern orderly indicators of whether their country's situation is improving or worsening, Israelis must define their minimum expectations from the peace process. Opinions vary, but the following three considerations could be considered mainstream attitudes as to what would make a peace accord worthwhile.

First, events should be judged as to whether they lead to the end of the killing of Israelis by Arabs. In the coming years, the peace process will require Israel to make sacrifices despite the opposition of a significant part of the population. Ongoing terror attacks on Israelis will only hamper the process.

Second, the peace process is only worthwhile for Israel if it does not cause unbridgeable tensions between those in power and the country's mainstream opposition. This is not only a function of external events and what the government decides; to a large extent, it will be determined by how the government treats its internal opponents.

This nation has exercised incredible self-discipline, under great pressure, both before and after independence. As events such as the Hebron massacre of February 1994 prove, however, it is wrong to assume that all extremist individuals or groups will maintain this restraint in the future.

Last but not least, as Israel's adversaries are not democrats, one should assess whether Israel runs increased risks if the governments of its partners in the peace process, are overthrown and replaced by crazy rulers. As all Arab states today are dictatorships—their nature ranges from somewhat enlightened monarchies to sinister perpetrators of genocide—the threat is not imaginary.

Economic Development

Despite major constraints, Israel's economy has developed remarkably over the decades. Its ability to export a wide range of products worldwide is one of its strengths. Even without the peace process, its prospects were promising, so it would be strategically wrong to take security risks in order to enhance economic prospects.

If the peace process holds, the business experience gained in a tough environment indicates that Israel will do economically much better under easier trading conditions. New markets will open, and investors will look differently upon the country's potential. Peace and tranquility are not classic resources to which economists give value, but there is no doubt that they will further contribute to Israel's economic development.

Some new problems will emerge as well. For instance, many of Israel's agricultural activities are likely to become uncompetitive due to the lower costs of farming in the Palestinian entity.

The Alternating Challenges

While the question of peace is important, it addresses only one segment of the country's future. Many other variables must be considered when trying to predict Israel's development. An issue like environmental policy, which has been neglected so far, must get more attention. Transnational issues such as water availability can be viewed differently when regional relations change.

Beyond the sweeping changes that have affected the entire world, Israel faces many challenges not found elsewhere. But even if forecasts can be only partly valid, the process and methodology of how to develop them have become more important than before.

Within Israel, some communities are undergoing major change. They must redefine their identity regardless of what happens with Israel's relations with its neighbors. Two examples: neither the kibbutzim nor the ultra-Orthodox community can remain as they have been. Both must ask themselves what the future holds for them.

Any systematic approach to understanding Israel's present and forecasting what might and should happen must rank challenges according to order of priority. Israel's main preoccupations in the past have alternated continuously between external and internal ones. Priorities have been imposed, rather than chosen. A country threatened by enemies that want to exterminate it cannot afford the luxury of defining its own agenda at any given time.

This book is divided in two distinct sections. The first looks at the country's outside, or external, relations, while the other focuses on inside, or internal, developments. This division reflects the seesaw of priorities that has characterized Israel's history.

At moments of temporary external quiet, the internal challenges come forcefully to the fore. A key question: how can one determine common long-term priorities in a heterogeneous country with a large population of immigrants who come from very different backgrounds?

This influences the country's character profoundly in many areas. One aspect: the very fact that a basically normative approach to government has been achieved in Israel should be seen as something of a surprise. Another: questions concerning national identity will become much more forceful if the peace process holds.

One More Major Variable: Immigration

As if all of this was not complex enough, other major uncontrollable events must be taken into account. Israel's future can be changed dramatically not only by a reasonably successful peace accord or its failure, but also by massive immigration.

In all likelihood, such major migration flows will be imposed by external forces. One can imagine, for instance, a multitude of political or economic scenarios under which many more Jews will leave the former Soviet Union for Israel.

It would be too simplistic to base forecasts about immigrants' integration into Israeli society on examples from the past. Israel has coped, more or less, with the streams of immigrants in recent years, but that is no guarantee that it will do so again in the future.

If another half-million or million immigrants come from the Soviet Union within a few years, they may well perturb many internal equilibria in an unforseeable way, even if only because enough work cannot be created for them quickly.

The notion of such a large part of the Israeli population coming from one country of origin raises the clear possibility of emerging cultural tensions. These could cause greater concern if such an influx comes at a moment when the peace process may sharpen the debate on Israel's identity.

Taking in massive numbers of immigrants must also create future political tensions, as their representatives will have to find their way into society's decision making bodies. Expanded immigration, and the many resulting problems, will by necessity influence Israel's welfare policy as well.

The Unique Experience

There are other immigrant states, such as the United States, Canada and Australia. None of them give immigrants citizenship as fast as Israel does. The boat is full, said a leading European socialist politician referring to immigrants, who are rather unwelcome in the EEC member countries.

Israel starts from assumptions which differ from those in other nations. No immigrant state has gathered such a large percentage of its citizens from all corners of the earth in as short a time as Israel did. It is a state that wants to be a national home for the Jews, a people with diluted common experience, tradition and religion, and without a common language.

The ancestors of the Israelis left common ground almost 2,000 years ago. Israel takes people who have lived in totally different conditions and tries to fashion a new nation from them in a few decades.

Whether one stands inside or outside, one can only watch in amazement at how the country absorbs immigrants at a time when immigration has become a pain in the neck in the Western world. Some come with no Jewish background and no affinity for the country.

Others arrive in Israel straight from the Stone Age. Many immigrants will remain a lifelong burden to the state. As one observer reflected on the 1991 airlift of the Ethiopian Jews to Israel: "No other country on earth (with the possible exception of the United States) would have admitted, let alone sought out for rescue, people suffering from intestinal parasites, infants and aged people without means of support, a population that had not been introduced to cutlery and indoor plumbing, much less computer technology. If the nations of the world were capable of recognizing political truths, they might have seen that for the first time in history African blacks were being brought westward for purposes other than slavery."[1]

Israel takes the burdensome together with the promising ones, and gives them citizenship immediately if they want it. One wonders whether such a generous citizenship policy is wise. What comes fast, without effort or merit, is not appreciated. How easy should access to Israeli citizenship be for those Jews who remain abroad for much of their lives, immigrating when it suits them, without regard for Israeli society's interests?

This factor will play a crucial role in the changing relationship between Israel and the Jewish diaspora. Israel's identity must change, as its weight in the Jewish world will continue to increase.

How to Judge

This book is meant for both a foreign and Israeli public. Quite naturally, many of the concepts expressed have a different meaning to locals than to foreigners. Sometimes, Israelis who go abroad despair when they try to make themselves understood to those who live a totally different life, devoid of existential threats. How does one cater to two totally different realities?

How can an Israeli convey what it means to have children in the army, where they risk their lives for their country, to Westerners for whom the army was at most an obligation that passed relatively quickly, and who are not called up for reserve duty? Israelis abroad, in societies with a totally different reality and value system, are forced to examine their own country from a different perspective.

Foreign observers often say that they want to understand, not to judge. Human nature being what it is, these people frequently do pass judgment, even if they lack knowledge. In order to judge fairly and competently, one must first define the main criteria the Jewish state, with its unique constraints, should meet.

My claim, in endless debates and discussions abroad over many years, has been that the first criterion for comparing Israel's behavior with that of other nations is how it has dealt with its enemies. "If members of an ethnic minority under your government's rule had attacked your citizens in the way Israelis have been attacked over the years," I often ask, "how much restraint would your country's most extremist citizens have shown toward that minority?"

If that question does not convince them of Israel's reality, I ask them to explain why foreigners who do not belong to nations which have threatened them are assaulted and sometimes killed only because they are foreigners in several Western European countries. Unfortunately, in view of the rising violent xenophobia in Europe, the question becomes more and more convincing.

A second major yardstick to measure Israel's behavior is to analyze how Israeli democracy has held up under the existential threat. I am not the only one who considers Israel's adherence to democracy in spite of all the pressures nothing short of a miracle. At the same time, progress in the quality of governance remains a necessity, and peace may provide a useful stimulus.

A European Country?

People around the world are woefully misinformed about Israel. Overestimating the size of its Jewish population or thinking that most Israelis are of Western European origin are among the most common errors. Then there are the stereotypes about Jews, which have been around for centuries and refuse to die. They have been transposed to Israel in recent decades. Anti-Zionism is a new form of anti-Semitism.

While the Catholic Church, from which the oldest anti-Semitic stereotypes originate, has changed its attitude toward Judaism in the post-Holocaust period, the process remains incomplete and problematic. In a world where equilibria have been distorted, additional clarification is necessary on this issue. The slow, cumbersome and tortuous development of Vatican-Israel relations is a symptom of how the present continues to reflect a burdensome past.

Many people abroad consider Israel a European country, but that does not make it part of the West. Its development is usually out of synch with mainstream developments there.

Foreign interest in what happens in Israel is out of proportion to the size of its population, its GNP or any other standard indicator of a nation's relevance in the world. What lies at the heart of this exaggerated media interest, and what does it do to Israel's image?

In the last few years, it has become fashionable for foreign presidents, prime ministers and other high political dignitaries to visit Israel. On many days of the year, foreign flags wave at the entrance to Jerusalem and near the residence of the Israeli president, indicating such a visit.

Israel's Ministry of Foreign Affairs can barely cope with the great number of visitors. Why do they all have to visit such a small country at this time? A decade ago, when the Arabs tried to isolate Israel politically, it could have used more high-level foreign visits, but then most of the visitors were absent. It is a safe assumption that the current mode will pass eventually.

Unique countries cannot have a simple life. Even if the world has been growing more tolerant toward cultural differences among nations in recent years, it remains difficult to understand somebody else's experiences. Westerners want to relate to Israel in the context of their own reality, but this approach is doomed to fail. Moreover, the pendulum may be swinging the other way. Basic tolerance for other people may be on the decline in democratic society.

Out of Synch

When talking to Westerners, I often feel that Israel's main problem is that it is out of synch with the Western world. For years, I foresaw that many of the problems Israel was facing would sooner or later come to haunt the West.

While many of Israel's experiences are truly unique, others prove indeed to be precursors of what the future holds for the West. The West has often refused to see events in this light. Often, years pass before the world realizes that Israel again has played the role of its guinea pig.

The most obvious example concerns terrorism. When Israeli planes, travellers or other targets were attacked abroad after the Six Day War, most Westerners thought that a Middle Eastern conflict was being fought on their territory. Only later did it become clear that this was a precursor of a much larger battle in which outsiders were testing the vulnerability of modern society. Due to Western neglect of the problem, terrorism has become universal.

This long-held conviction that Israel functions in many fields as a laboratory of the future for the West is proving itself as time passes. Many of Israel's experiences are being repeated, in slightly modified forms, by others.

To predict this a few years ago to a Westerner was meaningless. In the best case, it drew a blank stare. How could one prove such a thesis based on events which had not yet occurred, events which no discussion partner could imagine would take place?

A Laboratory for the West

Few biblical texts have been more abused than that of Isaiah, which says, "I shall guard you, make you the people of my covenant and you shall be a light to the nations." It clearly indicates the importance of Israel's religious message. One of the text's multiple misinterpretations is that Israel must, in essence, be a masochistic state, subjecting itself to a higher standard than its enemies or, for that matter, anyone else. This interpretation stems from humanistic considerations which have more than a small element of perversity, but little to do with Judaism.

Israel's political, military, cultural and economic experience also is relevant to the world. Today, when an Israeli observer sees the Western world in disarray, he cannot help but think that his experience in many fields could go a long way toward understanding the West's problems and seeing them in the right perspective.

He may even try to suggest solutions. There is nothing pretentious in this. After all, for decades, Western politicians—many of them incompetent—have been trying to suggest how Israel should behave and how it could solve its problems.

A few examples that identify the similarities and differences between the Israeli and Western experiences go a long way toward understanding the potential contribution of the Israeli experience. In 1991, part of the Western world, under a thinly veiled United Nations cover, went to war against Iraq, which had invaded Kuwait. The return of the local regime was considered a matter of crucial importance for the West, which constantly fears oil shortages.

Despite the precision of modern weapon systems, it was inevitable that many Iraqi civilians would be killed. Western media stationed in Iraq showed the destruction and civilian victims. In the general turmoil, a variety of Western nations executed under an internationalist flag de facto what they had often reproached Israel for doing in Lebanon, a country which had been a base for terrorists for many years.

This was only a prelude to the cruelties of the Yugoslav war. After years of paying lip service to the European idea, the EEC was totally unable to cope with that war. Some of its initial actions even fanned it. Now, hundreds of thousands of dead, mutilated, raped and ethnically cleansed later, the European leaders' main goal is to distance themselves mentally from what is happening.

Are the various nations which made up Yugoslavia not Europeans, or have they been stripped of that attribute? What in the history of the past decades justified such cruelty in their battles? Why didn't the Israelis apply such methods against the Arab enemies which had tried to exterminate them? It sounds like a logical comparison, but European leaders dislike this kind of argument.

The Relevance of Israel's Experience to the World

Europe's bankruptcy in Yugoslavia offers telling indicators about the future relationship between Israel and Europe. For years, those same European nations have been ready to tell Israel how to behave. Suddenly, years of Israeli protests about double political standards take on new significance.

It does not seem bold to predict that there will be more analogies in the future. After all, the UN intervened in Somalia for humanitarian reasons.

Their troups could not protect themselves against attacks by Somalians. After their first dead, some UN troops killed scores of civilians, claiming there were armed men among them. The UN has a long record of condemnations of Israel for more restrained behavior. Now the whole world watched as the UN behaved more cruelly than Israel did in situations which were infinitely more important to it than Somalia is to those nations which have troops there.

It is all a question of timing, and what comes first. Had Israelis followed the United Nations approach when the intifada started, years of fighting and terror could have been avoided. Similar riots in Jordan in late 1987 were immediately suppressed. The Jordanian approach, not the Israeli one, served as the United Nations' model in Somalia.

When forecasting the future of Israel, these comparisons are of major importance. With the advantage of hindsight, one must ask whether any other nation would have had similar self-restraint if it had lived through Israel's experiences.

Learning in Dissimilar Situations

All of this is only a partial list of reasons that the Israeli experience and its prospects merit a closer investigation by readers around the world at a time of increasing turbulence in many areas. As time passes, additional reasons will develop.

It would be mistaken, however, to assume that Israel's laboratory role for the West is limited mainly to lessons in dealing with violence. In the West, issues such as the lack of solidarity and the need for more clearly defined responsibilities are becoming focal points of the discussion on modern society's values.

Here also, Israel's experience—especially that of certain subgroups, such as the kibbutzim—can be meaningful to the West. This is an unexplored area, which, as Western discussions get more focused, may open up valuable new perspectives.

Even if Israel's immediate future is very different from that of other nations, it is not the only democracy to face huge challenges. How can a society in major transition learn from situations abroad which are not similar?

In an uncertain world, where many new risks have arisen in the past few years and more are likely to emerge soon, finding new methods to answer this question is of utmost importance. It is my hope that the interviews in this book will be helpful in this process.

Section One
Outside

ABBA EBAN

Challenges in the Aftermath of Peace

ABBA EBAN was born in Cape Town in 1915, and grew up in England. He made his worldwide reputation as a diplomat, statesman, scholar and writer. He studied Oriental languages and classics at Cambridge, and later became a lecturer in the Arabic language.

In 1946, he was appointed political information officer of the Jewish Agency in London. After Israel gained independence in 1948, he became its first representative at the UN. His brilliant performance and oratory there drew world attention. From 1950 through 1959, he served simultaneously as Israel's ambassador in the United States and chief delegate to the United Nations.

In 1959, Eban was elected to the Knesset on behalf of Mapai. He became Minister of Education and Culture, a post he held until 1963, when he became Deputy Prime Minister. In 1966, he assumed the post of Foreign Minister until the Labor Party lost power in the 1977 elections.

Eban is a prolific author. His books include *The Voice of Israel,*

My People, My Country, and The New Diplomacy. He has also hosted a number of television series, including *Heritage*, which was broadcast on the U.S. Public Broadcasting Service and worldwide.

Eban considers it extremely difficult to assess how Israel's global situation will change as a result of new peace agreements, beyond the strategic implications that such treaties would bring. The same goes for the structural changes that would occur in Israeli society. Until the framework of any peace agreement has been formalized, he says, predicting what will follow it is a very difficult game.

Nevertheless, he outlines certain general lines along which he expects Israel to develop in a post-peace treaty era, and forecasts what awaits the country—and the world—once regional peace is reality.

"The changes that would result from a peace settlement are so revolutionary that it is hard to describe them," Eban says. "We must remember that the attainment of peace has always been a central objective of Zionism."

He stresses that Israel has never sought to destroy its Arab neighbors, adding that it couldn't even if it wanted to. "The aim was to change their minds," he says, but this was no easy task. "We developed an ambivalent strategy based on strong military resistance together with keeping the door open for negotiations.

"This in the hope that our strength, international relations and stability would convince the Arab world that they have no choice but coexistence. This was our policy for nearly all the decades of our existence."

Today, Israel faces a new dilemma: what happens if the country gets what it has always wanted? While many Israelis and supporters abroad display total solidarity when Israel is preparing for war, Eban says that when the preparation is for peace, many supporters find themselves facing a new, unfamiliar paradox.

"When they see that we are exploring peace, they are gripped by a hysterical frenzy," Eban says in a cool, analytical tone. "In some parts of the Jewish world, the fear of peace seems to be stronger than the fear of war. Or, better said, the fear of concessions without which this peace would not be feasible."

Eban notes that Israel's persistence and tenacity over the years were motivated by a will to survive and the hope of changing the enemy's mindset. "If our strategy was not ridiculous," he says, "there was always the chance that one day this change of mind was liable to happen. Now we are in one of the great revolutionary periods of the Jewish people and of Israel's relations in its region and in the world.

"Nothing that has happened in the 1990s has ever happened in our history," he continues. "I would not have expected such a succession of events. Even those who support the peace process tend to underestimate its significance."

To gain perspective, Eban points to the situation as recently as 1990, when he says the notion of the Arab states abandoning their taboo against contact and discourse with Israel was unfathomable. In those days, he says, their refusal to recognize Israel was a cornerstone of Arab policy.

Today, all that has changed. Eban notes that Israel is engaged in direct negotiations with Syria, Jordan and Lebanon, as well as what he terms the mainstream Palestinian movement. "We are desired guests in Morocco and in Tunisia," he says, "and there are contacts with Saudia Arabia and the Gulf States. Moreover the Arab boycott is now in the first stage of disintegration."

Eban says these developments point to a total change in the Arabs' approach. "Never have Israelis and Arabs been meeting in so many ways in Washington, Tokyo, Moscow, Ottawa, Rome and our region. Militarily, the Arabs have been very unsuccessful against Israel. Now they want to be free of the traumas of defeat. Before the collapse of communism and the Gulf War, the two main developments of the last few years, nobody foresaw that this would happen."

Eban says the change in Syria's approach has been especially surprising. Who imagined that Syria would join the U.S.-led coalition against Iraq, or come to Washington to discuss full peace with Israel in return for a full withdrawal?

"This proposal is not only based on the abolition of belligerence," Eban stresses. "It is based on full peace with the exchange of ambassadors. The Syrians are very late in proposing this. They are now suggesting an agreement identical to what the Israeli government of Eshkol, Begin and Dayan proposed on June 19, 1967."

The reasons for these changes are clear to Eban: first, he says, Syria lost its alliance with Egypt, and then the Soviet Union collapsed. He notes that Syria never considered attacking Israel unless two conditions were met: first, Egypt had to be attacking simultaneously, and second, the Soviet Union had to provide a safety net, guaranteeing to stop the Israelis in the event that they approached Damascus. "Let us be quite frank," he says. "Only the Soviets prevented Israel from going to Damascus."

Eban says that he never really expected what he terms the "mainstream Palestinian movement" to discuss "the very same proposals which they threw in the wastebasket seven, eight years ago when they were originally proposed by Israel; namely self-government, which is short of statehood, without, of course, their closing the door to the dream of statehood."

This approach lies at the heart of the Camp David accords. While the Palestinians are prepared to accept it now, he says the Israelis are more cautious.

"Another change I would not have expected is that the United States, with Israel's welcome, does not simply provide meeting rooms, paper and pencils, but has become a full partner in the negotiations. It is carrying out a very active mediatory role, at the request of Israel and all the Arab sides.

"One more thing I would not have imagined is that Russia has not only given up the role of the great spoiler, but has become one of the architects of the peace process. We have to understand that the existential threat to Israel was always essentially a Soviet one. It was never so much an Arab threat, especially after 1967.

"There are still more unexpected things," he continues. "Because of the peace process and the image that Israel projects, Third World isolation of Israel has collapsed, in particular that of the giants, China and India. Israel now has diplomatic relations with 120 nations, making those who do not recognize Israel the isolated ones. This is an irreversible change."

Eban's analysis cannot ignore the fact that in 1992 Israel's government returned to the hands of his own Labor Party. Noting that the government's positions have changed, he stresses, "Israel is now proposing what it has not done for more than ten years: territories for peace, in accordance with UN Resolution 242."

All of these new developments combine to create a totally new environment, Eban says, one which fosters the possibility of a broad peace agreement that seemed impossible just a few years ago.

"Once we have a Sadat-type process going on, peace will not be inevitable, but it will be much more realistic than it ever was," he says. "I would say that the absence of peace is an unrealistic expectation. I expect that soon we will be discussing in great detail the complex, painful but pragmatic problems of 'what is peace worth?', the ideological and structural changes necessary and of course the territorial aspects. Territories for peace has been tried only once, and with success. The issues at stake are thus more or less exemplified by the Egyptian treaty relationship."

The treaty with Egypt reinforced Israel's logistic superiority, Eban says. It made Israel a safer place, both for the individual and as a nation. He stresses that Israelis do not die on the southern border anymore.

"Surprise attack is impossible," he says. "The possibility of war with Egypt is so remote that both sides are probably not even making contingency plans for it."

Had there been no peace treaty with Egypt, Eban says, Israel would have had to station 100,000 soldiers in the Sinai today, along with thousands of tanks and massive amounts of other equipment. He recalls that during the period when he chaired the Knesset Foreign Affairs and Defense Committee in the mid-1980s, then-Defense Minister Yitzhak Rabin said that if Israel had not reached a peace agreement with Egypt, it would have no choice but to beg the United States to defend it.

"The current developments are things which have never happened before," he says. "They are so swift that they have not yet been fully absorbed. We need pragmatic diplomatic thinking about the whole idea. What was frankly a fantasy is now a diplomatic possibility and reality, which is much more likely to happen than not."

Despite this optimistic prognosis, Eban has a stem warning: Israel faces grave risks if peace does not evolve. "If it does not happen, we are not back in the status quo," he says. "Our position will be much worse than before. The idea of peace will be so discredited that nobody will think about it for ten years."

Indeed, Eban doubts that Israel will ever enjoy such an optimal convergence of circumstances again. After all, he says, Israel did not cause the fall of communism, nor did it bring about the Gulf War, but these two events create a window of opportunity that will not last forever.

"The psychological change after peace will parallel the one with Egypt," he says. "We will have to rearrange our relation ships. The neighboring world will be cautiously open. More remote countries such as Pakistan also will open up. We are thus dealing with a far-reaching change of horizon, not with another simple disengagement treaty."

Asked what other changes will result from a peace treaty, Eban turns to the economic front.

"We are basically a small trading nation," he says. "The first President of Israel, Chaim Weizmann, spoke of the country in terms of Switzerland, the Netherlands and Denmark. These are countries which, though small in territory, can have high economic and cultural standards.

"Our trading pattern will be different. Toynbee said, 'History means response to challenge,' and it was one of the few occasions he was right. Somebody who writes 20 volumes cannot be wrong all the time. Response to challenge explains why we became an important military power. From a military point of view, we are probably the fourth or fifth power in the world.

"Israel is undoubtedly the most powerful small community that exists," he says. "There has never been a small country with such defensive and deterrent power. Deterrence requires four conditions: power, willingness to use it, clear drawing of red lines, and the consciousness of these things in the mind of your adversary. If he does not believe that you have that power, it is as if you do not have it."

"When peace comes," he says, "Israel's military structure will change. The present Chief of Staff is working to make the Israel Defense Forces a leaner army with fewer soldiers in the reserves. Deterrence will be based on technology as well as the topographical arrangement of forces."

In describing the future treaty he envisions, Eban continually returns to the Egyptian example. The areas to be evacuated will have to be demilitarized, as is much of the Sinai. "Militarily, we did not give back the whole of Sinai," he says. "One-third of it is totally without Egyptian forces, another third has limited forces, and only in one-third can they do what they like."

Eban stresses that the world has changed, and that these changes affect Israel.

"We seem to live in an era of great power passivity and non-intervention," he says. In the past, the communist threat had a certain energizing effect. The Americans were willing to go in with military might if they saw a nation which might go to the other side.

"Nowadays, passivity seems the policy rule. Previous American regimes were basically interventionist. Not only the Nixon one. Carter was willing to risk sending some military people to Iran, which was a fiasco. In the past, there was a general feeling that small countries had to be careful. One never knew what the United States might do."

Today, he says, the United States has changed its approach. Without a Soviet superpower, and with no other power filling the void, America is allowing itself to turn inward, at least somewhat.

"In such a situation of passivity, Israel has to be much more rigorous about a security set-up. Before, there was always the feeling that America would come in.

"Today, there are far-reaching contingency plans if Israel is existentially threatened," Eban says. "It would not be necessary to have another Nixon-Kissinger airlift. That was a very precarious way to live.

"The Clinton administration does not seem to care very much about foreign relations," he says. "One does not really know what America will do if Israel gets into serious trouble." In light of the current world political situation and the probability of peace, Eban says, "On the military side, there will be an enormous release of energy. We do not have to apologize that for many years military equipment has been a major Israeli export item.

"In the future, we will face a problem the U.S. already faces, namely, how can we put military technologies to work on the consumer side? Since the fall of communism, we have lost many customers for our military goods, so peace is in the first place a dislocation."

Eban is unsure whether Israel's international trade patterns will change much as a result of peace. Israel has developed what he terms "a marvelous, eccentric international commercial structure," because the Arabs did not open their markets to it, "so it had to go across the world to look for export markets.

"Some people think that this has done Israel a lot of good," Eban says. "By exporting cheap plastic toys or oranges to Egypt and buying their cotton, we would have had a Third World economy. The development of high technology and high-priced exports came about as a result of the Arab boycott. "Some people believe that it is helpful for a country to be under siege," he adds. "We had to make the best of it. This has created bonds of solidarity and a certain background of international and Jewish concern. Now, some of these people are worried that we will become a little lax.

"A large part of Jewish solidarity derives from a feeling of vulnerability. This vulnerability is a key of Jewish history. For Israel to be vulnerable means two things. It is not attractive, but it does mean that people care more about Israel. They express this caring through a much greater solidarity than any other group abroad. American Italians or American Irish have nothing to compare with the solidarity of U.S. Jews with Israel.

"Here, I see a cloud on the horizon, and we will have to work very hard to chase it away," Eban says. "Jews in the United States are assimilating fast through intermarriage. American Jews merge easily into the general community. There is much less rejectionism on the part of the gentile population than in the past. Thus, we must fight very hard to keep the sense of the particularity of the Jews in the world.

"They will support us as long as they are Jews, but what will happen if they stop being Jews? Again we come up against a paradox. We want the countries in which Jews live to be liberal. The more liberal they are, the less incentives there are for Jews to preserve their identity.

"There is something rather specific about the American Israeli relationship," he adds. "The American political leadership wants domestic tranquillity. This cannot be had if the Jewish community is very nervous. I think we made a mistake in stressing the strategic importance of Israel to the United States too much, and stressing the value system too little. We go back to the same Judeo-Christian values."

Eban stresses that one should not belittle these common values. "If you don't have these Judeo-Christian values, you tend to be excessive in your utilitarianism. This becomes clear if one considers that with the Japanese, for instance, we do not have a common spiritual-cultural background."

What is peace going to do to anti-Semitism? Eban is not optimistic. He terms anti-Semitism "an endemic disease of the gentiles. There seems to be something in human personality which rejects difference.

"There may be more resistance in the world now specifically against anti-Semitism," he notes. "In general, however, distrust of somebody who is foreign and intolerance towards him has not changed. We see this everywhere in the world."

On the other hand, many people overestimate Israel's capabilities. "I do not understand why many Chinese believe that we can solve their problems, but why should I tell them or others that they are exaggerating our power?"

He pauses a moment, and then corrects himself. Recalling the years before black Africa broke diplomatic ties with Israel, Eban says that on his visits to countries such as Ethiopia and Nigeria, he met hundreds of Israelis who were working on projects related to agriculture, water problems, health and many other local issues. Israel may be a small country, but even though it faces so many external threats, it has always found the wherewithal to help less fortunate countries. After peace, he says, the possibilities could be even greater.

"Much of the help we gave to the Third World survived the breaking of diplomatic relations," Eban says. "It is amazing how much you can do without having ambassadors. We had no official relations with Iran, yet we did many things together. We have a certain vitality. The question is: if there is peace, how can we be more selective in putting it to use?"

Eban recalls his one and only meeting with Pandit Nehru, in the 1950s. "He said to me, 'Israel is very fortunate to be so small.' I asked him why, and he said, 'because in my country no man can live long enough to see the results of his work. In Israel, within a decade you can see results.'"

The advent of peace will not change this, Eban stresses. If anything, it will expand the horizons on which an individual can create change.

Eban sees one other important area of change. "We will have to give attention to maintaining our culture," he says. "There are streets in Tel Aviv where on the signs and billboards you hardly find a Hebrew word. We may have even less resistance against that after peace. Nobody shares our language, faith or historic experience.

"Our generation has had the traumatic experience of World War Two and the Holocaust, and the ecstatic experience of the creation of Israel," he says, intentionally referring to high and low points. "The uniqueness of our experience is difficult to transfer to the generation of our grandchildren."

After peace, Eban says that Israel will have to rethink its approach to education. "Israel has given the world fundamental concepts such as peace, justice and conscience. In the Babylonian civilization, one will not find much about the need to choose good over evil. If you killed somebody, punishment depended on who you were. Somebody from the upper class paid compensation, those who belonged to the lower classes had their heads cut off. The Romans and Greeks valued war more than peace."

Eban is preoccupied about the future of Israeli society. "There is too much hedonism and permissiveness about our society," he says. "Educationally, Israel will be challenged very much by peace. When meeting young people in schools, I used to quote our founding fathers, who had rather utopian views. Chaim Weizmann and Ben-Gurion spoke about am segula, a chosen people. The youngsters say, 'what the hell, we want to be like everybody else.'

"It might have been very pretentious to have this burden of being a light unto the nations," he concludes, "but it will be quite a problem to search for a new identity."

YEHEZKEL DROR

Israel's Long-Range Prospects
A State at Its Best Ever

Y EHEZKEL DROR is one of the most original long-term thinkers in Israel. In *Crazy States*, he predicted the advent of irrational rulers. The book was published in 1971, long before state-sponsored terrorism, Khaddafi and Khomeini emerged. At the time, his ideas were considered science fiction; today, we know better. One of the many plans Dror has is to update the book, changing its title to *Fanatic States*.

Dror is professor of political science and Wolfson Professor of Public Administration at the Hebrew University of Jerusalem. Currently, he is completing a corpus of six policy-oriented books on Israel, co-sponsored by leading Israeli policy research institutes. Three volumes have been published. The fourth is due in 1994, along with the first volume of the English translation.

He is also engrossed in a major assignment for the Club of Rome, a prestigious group that sponsors studies on long-term problems facing humanity. Entitled *On the Capacity to Govern*, Dror's study will be published as a report to the Club of Rome and distributed globally. Its major thesis is that many core elements of governance have remained relatively stable for centuries, making present patterns of governance increasingly obsolete.

Accordingly, he recommends a number of ways to redesign governance, such as learning opportunities and incentives for elected politicians, counter-measures against elections being dominated by television theatrics and intense efforts to enlighten the public on complex issues.

Dror was born in Vienna in 1928 and came to Israel a decade later. He studied law, political science and sociology at the Hebrew University of Jerusalem, and received his doctorate from Harvard. From 1968-1970, he was a senior staff member at the Rand Corporation in California. From 1975-1977, he was senior planning and policy advisor of the Israel Ministry of Defense, and from 1985-1988, he directed the Center for Security Studies at the Hebrew University's Leonard Davis Institute for International Relations.

Besides being a prolific writer, he has advised major international organizations such as the United Nations and the OECD, held several distinguished professoral and guest appointments, and edited leading academic journals.

The first question one often asks a policy planner is: "How can one make very long term forecasts in a situation which is in great flux?"

In his answer, Dror underlines the limitations of the process. "One cannot forecast," he stresses. "All exploration of the future is subject to significant uncertainties. One can only reconnaissance how future possibilities can evolve while realizing that radical unforeseeable jumps can happen.

"One obvious example of the latter is the sudden apocalyptic breakdown of Soviet-style communism. This was not and could not have been predicted. This unforeseeable impact changed the trajectory for Israel in a revolutionary way."

Despite this unpredictablility, Dror says, "Some important matters are relatively stable. Israel's location within the Middle East is a basic historic, geo-strategic and geo-cultural fact. The demographic developments in the Arab countries have a very high probability unless there are apocalyptic catastrophes. Therefore, parts of problems can be analyzed with high probability, while others are in the domain of fortune."

Against this background, Dror sets out on his voyage in the future, describing changes Israel may or will encounter and how to prepare for them.

In 1988, Dror termed Israel one of history's greatest success stories, but he said the country was on a temporary downswing. When he returned in 1991 from a two-year stint at the European Institute of Public Administration in Maastricht, Holland, he changed his view. "Looking at it from abroad, Israel today is in one of its best situations ever," he says since then.

He attributes the change to the massive wave of immigration that began late in 1989. "Aliya changes the Israeli situation radically," he states. "This immigration is the single most important event that could happen. It goes against all that had been predicted in earlier decades."

Dror places the size and education level of Israel's Jewish population at the top of his list of factors influencing the country's future prosperity and success. He predicts that immigration levels will remain high enough to push Israel to even greater heights.

If such praise of immigration seems exaggerated, Dror hastens to point out that the educational level of the newcomers in recent years has catapulted Israel into the position of being the most schooled nation in the world.

"Israel benefitted from a mutation in history, due to the fall of communism," he says. "More than ten percent of its Jewish population are already Russian olim. This immigration agitates and disturbs society, which stimulates cultural creativity and will improve the country's cultural level. This aliya is the biggest opportunity Israel has today." Dror terms the government's ineffectiveness in dealing with it "a historical crime."

Dror analyzes the uncertain future with razor-sharp logic. "The peace process is a gamble," he says. "Therefore, it is so important to follow those possible trajectories which are sure to give positive results. Strengthening the demographic basis of the Jewish inhabitants of Israel, quantitatively and qualitatively, is positive in all imaginable future scenarios for Israel."

When referring to the societal turbulence massive immigration inevitably must cause, he observes in a detached tone, "So what if we have ten years of major problems absorbing them? If history had let us choose the rate of immigration, I would have considered that preferable. But I do not have that privilege. My choice is to try to bring the maximum number of olim now, or risk that they will not come at all. In this case, I prefer ten hard years for the country to the danger of not getting them."

While very few criticize the influx of immigrants, some experts have warned that the collapse of the Soviet Union did more than open the floodgates of immigration. It also spells serious problems for Israel. After all, the argument goes, much of Israel's special relationship with the United States was based on its importance as a strategic asset, which led to major economic and military aid.

Dror admits that Israel's strategic importance has lessened, but says, "If I could make a bargain with history, trading Israel's strategic value against aliya, I would consider it an excellent deal."

Where does that leave Israel's relations with the United States? Dror: "We are undoubtedly going to get into trouble with the United States in the long term, independent of the personal inclinations of who is president of the United States. Because of America's economic situation, major aid to Israel will raise problems domestically."

What catches a president's attention depends in part on external pressures and in part on his personal tastes, Dror maintains, adding that if Eastern Europe's major upheavals and the United States's domestic problems are considered, it seems clear that Israel will get less attention.

"This is both an advantage and a disadvantage," he says. "Israel will be subjected to less pressure during the peace process. It will also get less economic and political help. This may increase Israel's leeway for some time."

After setting the tone of the discussion, Dror turns his focus to the global turbulence that shows little sign of subsiding. Does it ultimately spell opportunity for Israel, or merely problems?

"The dynamic world presents Israel with great opportunities which can be Pandora's boxes if they are mishandled," Dror says. "The more the world changes, the more success depends on our ability to change."

In his analysis, he focuses on four major fields: science and technology, geo-economics, geo-strategy and the Middle East.

In the realm of science, he says, the country's excellent situation keeps improving. "Israel has potential advantages as a knowledge economy," he explains. "As time passes, the inherent birth defects of Israel—lack of raw materials and the distance from large markets—become less important.

"Israel is a small country," he continues. "Small niches in the world economy are important for us. Many countries are interested in receiving technology, and that opens up a great many new niches. The demand is very good for those things Israel has a specific advantage in and which have a high added value."

He points again to the Russian aliya as a positive factor. "It opens a possible bridge for the transfer of technology to the Eastern bloc," he says. "We have both good knowledge and access. Israel is good in the transfer of hands-on technology. Israeli patterns of behavior fit societies that are not yet highly industrialized. Assuming that those countries will be able to pay or provide goods in barter, we can expect expanding Israeli trade with the Eastern bloc."

The question of changing technology in the defense sphere raises more subtle issues. Dror points to Israel's technological advantage and says that new technologies can improve the country's situation on the battlefield. On the other hand, he says, the Gulf War demonstrated that even total air superiority won't stop primitive missiles. The wildly expensive Patriot anti-missile defense systems proved, in the end, to be woefully inadequate.

Israel's technological edge will be hard-pressed to combat another changing trend. Dror points to NATO literature, which says battlefields are becoming deeper. "The classic battlefield was ten miles deep," he says. "This may become 100 or 150 miles in the future." For a tiny country like Israel, the policy implications are obvious.

"As future wars may be very costly, one implication is the urgent necessity to try and reduce their probability by a commitment to the peace process.

"Another is that, following the shock of the Bosnia war and other events, there will be more innovative efforts to redesign some form of international regime. As the security of Israel depends on global situations, Dror says this will be in its interest. Israel should play as important a role as possible in pushing for a new international order.

If, however, this fails, and Bosnia becomes the benchmark of the future, Israel will have to stand on its own. This is underscored by the fact that the Middle East can suffer destabilization despite Israel's peace efforts, due to factors in the Arab world. Furthermore, he says, Israel must be prepared in case peace does not last.

In other words, unless we see that the world changes, Israel must be able to back peace with a strong defense. Israel should not tempt an attack by being too weak or looking vulnerable, Dror warns. This requires an Israeli image of total deterrence, together with high tech defense and preemptive strike capability against the background of a Middle East doomsday threat. All arguments thus point in the direction of the continued development of advanced technological capability.

"The next conclusion is that wherever peace leads, we will have to continue to invest heavily in defense for the next 20 or 30 years," Dror says. "What Israel can get from the United States or others is, of course, preferable, as you do not have to develop it yourself.

"Much also depends on what the Arabs do. If the peace process leads to a reduction in the arms race, this is in Israel's best interest."

As far as geo-economics are concerned, the world is being influenced heavily by the emerging power of South East Asian countries, and Dror notes that, "The Bible is for them as strange as Confucian writings are for most of us. From their perspective, the classic legitimation of Israel and Zionism based on the Bible, Western guilt and the Holocaust—is not valid. We have to face them on our present merits, and we must deal with the fact that in the background, they are thinking about *The Protocols of the Elders of Zion.*"

Turning his view to Europe, where the EC is bringing about major changes in the concept of sovereignty, Dror says, "The shifting division of labor between the United States and Europe will make Europe much more important for us. Most of our politicians do not like this change," he says.

"Another issue is that Western nations may not stick to free trade policies. Clearly, free trade got major support from countries which benefitted from it. If these same countries, those who are in power now, will not benefit from it in the future, no ideological hypothetical position will stand up for long.

"Regulated trade may gradually become the norm. Restrictions in free trade may pose some problems to Israeli exports, even if being small immunizes the local economy from world trade policies to some extent.

"The detachment from part of the Palestinian labor force may be very helpful in reducing the activities based on cheap labor in the Israeli economy. Also, Arab markets may open up a bit.

"Israel will probably not be a major producer," Dror says. "It is more likely to be a major designer, or a specific component producer. There is historic irony here. Classic Zionism wanted to normalize the Jewish state as far as the type and mix of labor is concerned. That holds no great promise today.

"Rather, our economy will be based on a modern version of the so-called *Luftmensch*. Israel is well tied-in globally, and it will become more active in the 'manipulating of symbols,' i.e., it will provide global services, if we are wise, in selected aspects of research and development, such as software, biotechnology, and perhaps also consulting as well as banking and insurance, which Israel cannot engage in as long as there is a state of war."

On geo-strategy, Dror remarks that the world today still reflects the after-effects of the demise of the Soviet Union, even if the focus is shifting. "The world today is a global system. The question is: will the world move into a global regime stopping local wars, or will it be unable to control them?"

The situation is complicated by nuclear weapons, Dror notes. "There can be a nuclear war and 30, 40, or 50 million people could get killed," he says matter-of-factly. "After that, humanity will learn to control nuclear and biological weapons.

"It's unpleasant, but I have to ask whether—in historical terms—this is an optimistic or a pessimistic scenario. It can be a realistic one."

What does it mean for Israel? Dror says the implications would be good if the United States, Europe and Japan were to impose global peace. "Outbursts in the Middle East will be reduced, global guarantees will have meaning and there will be some arms control. This increases the probability of a lasting peace in the Middle East." But he warns against building on this scenario, saying that past shock waves have not had the effect that might have seemed likely.

"If the global system is not yet ready for control, then additional explosions are necessary for human learning," Dror says. "The geostrategic situation remains open, maybe even less controlled than before. The probability of superpower nuclear confrontation has been nearly eliminated, which makes things much better from an overall human perspective."

But, he hastens to add, all signs are not positive. Local wars may become harder to control, as in the case of the devastation of the former Yugoslavia. Summing up, he says that either the world will impose order to control local wars, or it will face an increasing number of them.

This brings Dror to the more specific issues of the Middle East, which must be viewed against the background of the overall potential conflict between the West and the Islamic world as well as on their own.

Dror sees Bosnia as a test case, and he believes the world will pay a high price for failure there. Bosnia, he says, represents a major failure for Europe as it strives to build a significant European community. It is also a failure for the United Nations, the United States and the rest of the Christian Western world. Their lack of effort to help European Moslems in trouble reinforces the image that the Christian world is not terribly concerned if Moslem blood flows.

"This necessarily puts the Islamic world in a more aggressive posture towards the West," Dror says. "It pushes in the direction of the development of an Islamic bomb, as it tells them they cannot rely on a world that does not care about Moslems. Bosnia is thus more than a major failure; it is one of the historic mistakes of the century."

Dror sees a major problem in the lack of Western understanding of the Islamic world. He notes that the West has been surprised to learn that there is not necessarily a contradiction between fundamentalism and technology. "Modern technology is flowing into the Middle East," he says. This has good and bad aspects. "More universities are being opened, and Iran is moving faster than we thought toward becoming a nuclear power."

In addition to the role of technology, the influence of Islam's growing role must be considered. Dror calls it "a very successful religion, as far as society-building goes. It has been repressed by Christian colonialism, but now Arab Islam is looking to stand up again. Regretfully, the notion of transforming the Middle East rapidly into some kind of European liberal democracy is absurd. It is worse than a mirage.

"The Western policy of supporting democracy in inappropriate conditions, such as in Algeria, derives from ignorance. Those who think that Western-style democratization will cause Islamic fundamentalism to disappear are crazy and blind.

"The present cultural, political, social situation of the Arab Islamic countries will lead them to an evolutionary path which will be different from the democratic system of Europe and the United States," Dror predicts. "Various types of Islamic democracy may emerge, but this will take a generation. I do not know what they will be. I wonder whether anybody knows.

"The Western misunderstanding of Islam sharpens the issue of Israel's external image and self-image. There are three possibilities here. The first is that Israel is a bridgehead of the West in the Middle East. If Israel is perceived as a land-based Western aircraft carrier, that is very dangerous."

The second possibility is that Israel will make a major, concerted effort to integrate in the Middle East, without reducing its quality. The third is a kind of bridging role. Dror says Israel should strive to play between the second and third options.

Israel, he says, has both an important role and a long-term problem in the region. "If West and Middle East blend nicely, then Israel can be a bridge between them. If they have a conflict, then Israel looks like an implant of the West in the homeland of Arab Islam.

"Israel can reach accommodation in the Middle East and with a better understanding of long-term problems, concrete action would be easier to choose," he adds. At the present juncture, he suggests that Israeli political and spiritual leaders should express a more respectful attitude toward Islam as a first step on a long, necessary road.

"Israel should have a pro-Islamic public stance, and demonstrate it wherever possible," he says. "In the United Nations, Israel should have been a major backer of protecting the Moslems in Bosnia. Another example: the government should not have allowed a Hebrew version of Salman Rushdie's book, *The Satanic Verses*, to be published in Israel. It could have explained publicly that the ban was enacted out of respect to Moslem feelings.

"The prime minister of Israel should have said in parliament, 'While we favor freedom of opinion, out of our special sensitivity to the feelings of our Moslem cousins we will prohibit the publication of the book in Israel. At the same time, we abhor blind hatred and murder, and totally oppose the threat of death to anyone because of his opinions.'

"We should also have recommended to the West that while allowing freedom of expression, it should take into account Islamic sensitivities," he says. This could have been achieved by accompanying publication of the book with suitable declarations by government and spiritual leaders of respect towards Islam. At the same time, the West should not tolerate threats by an Islamic country against somebody living in the West. It should, Dror believes, protect the author and itself against fundamentalist threats, which he terms a kind of aggression.

"Israel should have told the West that it must understand that Islam has a different tradition and should respect the right of Moslems to develop as they wish. It should also understand that Islam regards itself as a great historic success, broken by Western Christians who subdued them. The West should recognize that Moslems want their place in the world.

"The West has to demonstrate its overall respect for Islam and provide full protection for Moslems in the Western domain. That should lead Western governments to a liberal policy to those Moslems already living in their countries, as long as they do not endanger others. There should be a clear red line however, which one enforces strictly. The overall rules of the game should thus be that Moslems get a lot of free space, but they also get clear margins."

Unfortunately, Israel's neighborhood is destined to remain the scene of generations of turbulence. "The process of modernization of traditional societies is always turbulent," Dror says. He points to Saudi Arabia and says that in the long term, it has little likelihood of maintaining stability. "Windfall profits destabilize a traditional society."

Dror turns to Egypt. "The population will continue to increase. Some economic stabilization may be achieved by merging with Libya, though this would be a very partial solution. In the forseeable future, there is no overall solution for Egypt. It may become like Bangladesh—a type of ballast society with some islands of modernity—unless it adopts a very different socio-economic trajectory-changing policy."

This brings Dror back to the issue of democracy in such societies. "Egypt is a nominal democracy," he says. "What do we want to do? Introduce unnecessary norms into fighting fundamentalism. To prepare the Egyptian societal infrastructure for that will take a long time. Also, Egypt—like all Islamic nations—is fully entitled to prefer a path different from that chosen by Western Europe."

What does all of this mean for the peace process?

Dror supports the peace process, having suggested for some time that Israel should "throw surprises at history." But he is very reserved on the lack of deep thinking by Israel's top politicians, who he says show statesmanship in taking initiative but lack policy cogitation staff, and do not want them.

"The declaration by top Israeli politicians that many of the problems which arose during the realization phase of the agreement with the PLO were a surprise is a grave symptom of Israel's decisionmaking primitivity on fateful issues," he says.

"Let us realize the risks by looking at one possible scenario. There will be a Palestinian state in Jordan and part of Judea and Samaria. This state can become a regular or a fanatic one. As the Palestinians are highly frustrated, the latter probability is sizable. It may then radicalize the Middle East. This Palestinian state may support a new type of Saddam Hussein. All this will create a serious security problem for Israel, which will have a real Eastern front.

"This is not an optimistic scenario," he admits. "The Americans do not realize that such a Palestinian state will be a radical factor in the Arab world. It may also accelerate the destabilization of Saudi Arabia."

Dror continues: "If I could choose the future for the Middle East, I would prefer a stable, conservative Jordan, a weak Palestinian entity and Israel. However, I have no such choice, and the Palestinians will take over Jordan anyhow, so I want to ride on history and not be dragged behind it.

"By that, I mean that my only realistic option may be to support the Palestinian domination of Jordan, as far as possible within a constitutional monarchy and with peaceful transition, and get payment for it."

Reaching a compromise in Judea and Samaria would be much easier if there is a Palestinian state in Jordan, he says, maintaining that the Palestinian refugee problem can only be solved in Jordan, not in Judea and Samaria.

The peace process separates the Palestinians from the Israelis, he notes. It also aggravates the problem of the identity of Israel's Arab minority. This can be handled easily if there is real peace. If there are aggravated conflicts, this will enhance the cleavage in Israel's society between Jews and Arabs.

In the past, Dror made radical proposals on this subject. The chapter of his book in which these were launched has even been translated and published in the main journal of the PLO. He repeats them today: "In the longer run, if things settle down, we should permit Israeli Arabs to make a choice as to where to take their political rights.

"They can decide to exercise these rights in Israel, as is the case today. As full Israeli citizens, they will have all the obligations, including service in the army. If they want to take their political rights in the new Palestinian entity, then they will have full residential rights in Israel but no voting rights.

"Every Israeli Arab at the age of 18 should make his choice," Dror says. "This choice can even be reversible if the person changes his mind at a later age. In that case, becoming an Israeli citizen again would require a special procedure."

In the end, Dror takes the conversation full circle. Summing up, he returns to the importance of Israel's population. "Because the fundamental problem is such a long-range one, Israel's demographic base becomes so important as an existential requirement," he concludes.

MOSHE ARENS

Israel's Insurance Value
for the United States

FORMER ISRAELI DEFENSE AND FOREIGN MINISTER MOSHE ARENS came to politics from the business world, where he had been a vice president at Israel Aircraft Industries. Now he has returned to the business world, assuming the post of vice chairman and chief executive of one of Israel's largest holding companies, the Israel Corporation.

The Lithuanian-born Arens came to the United States from Riga, Latvia, at age 14 in 1939. In 1948, he immigrated to Israel. Arens developed a sharp sensitivity to the nuances of U.S.-Israel relations during his one-year stint as Israel's ambassador in Washington, the country's most crucial diplomatic post. Therefore, it seems natural to start a discussion with him on the subject of the special relationship that he worked so hard to maintain and enrich.

He views the American assessment of Israel and its value in terms of the American worldview. "The U.S. is basically an idealistic nation," he explains. "It is not unusual or unnatural to assist another country only because of common values."

In the early years following Israeli independence in 1948, he notes, little more than common values and ideals could bring the two countries together. It is highly unlikely, he says, that Washington perceived any tangible gains to be had from a relationship with the nascent state.

In fact, Arens recalls, when Israel was established, American officials—up to and including Secretary of State George Marshall—argued that support of the newborn country would be contrary to U.S. interests. "There were so many Arabs and so few Jews that Israel would lose the war in any case," he says. The irony is clear. "They felt that the United States should not back a loser."

These cynics, of course, lost the debate over the sort of relationship that should be fostered between the world's newest democracy and the world's largest democracy. What in the end brought the two countries together was the fact that Israel was the only democracy in the Middle East, making it very important to the Americans.

The U.S., which has long held a keen interest in the region, could hardly ignore the fact that one tiny dot on the Middle East map shared something of a common ideal with it. While Arens does not deny that the U.S. has been known to foster special relationships with countries that have no such common ideological base, he repeats that Washington could not resist the opportunity to help strengthen democracy in such a pivotal corner of the world.

Over the years, the number of Americans who felt that Israel and America shared common interests increased. Arens puts the number at near zero in 1948, but by 1967—following the spectacular victory of the Six Day War—the belief that Israel was living on borrowed time had been replaced by the notion that Israel was indeed a regional power. As such, it warranted a closer look.

Arens cites "mutually reinforcing factors where Israel became important both in the military balance and as a democratic ally." This perception evolved at a time when, he says, common values and ideals were seen as a key basis for common strategic interests.

The heyday of this special relationship seemed threatened just a few years later, when American interests in the Arab oil producing world grew so important after the 1973 Yom Kippur War. Despite the importance of oil interests, however, Arens says the Americans viewed everything through the perspective of the Cold War. Every issue and every region was measured in view of the East-West balance.

"In this context, the Yom Kippur War was perceived in the U.S. as a great Israeli victory," he says. "Washington saw Israel as an important ally in the Cold War—however strange that may seem in view of Israel's size."

Even after the end of the Cold War, Arens says, Washington continues to perceive certain common links between all democracies. "It is no exaggeration to say that many in the U.S. felt that while NATO was the bulwark against Soviet aggression in Europe, in the Middle East that role was played by Israel," he says with a touch of irony in his voice.

"Today, the US is no longer able to mount a Schwarzkopf-type operation as it did against Iraq," he adds. "Of course, the U.S. is very powerful, and it could do almost anything if it were given enough time, but it might take two-and-a-half years. It would mean mobilizing and training troops.

"For those people who consider the Gulf War the last major American intervention, this may not be important," Arens allows, but he leaves no doubt as to his assessment of that belief. "The objective observer sees that the Middle East will continue to be a very volatile area, and it will remain important to the US and the world. Most countries in this area are run by dictators. What happened in Iraq in 1990 can happen again both there and elsewhere."

If that does happen, Arens knows that the U.S. would do everything possible to avoid relying on Israeli force. "In strategy, however, you never put all your eggs in one basket," he says. "Having an insurance policy with Israel would be of considerable value to the Americans.

"That the Israeli capability is there means that whoever generates a crisis will have to take into account that our country is an ally of the United States," he says, quickly adding, "I find it difficult to see circumstances where Israeli and U.S. interests would be in disagreement with each other. It was no accident that Saddam Hussein—who was recognized to be an enemy of Israel for many years—turned out to be also an enemy of the United States. The interesting thing is that for a number of years the U.S. thought it could depend on him and do business with him."

Arens declines to term Israel somebody else's strategic asset. Instead, he cites common strategic interests. In today's situation, he says the U.S. may not even realize how deep these common interests run, and it's not a new phenomenon. Pointing again to the American belief in Saddam Hussein until shortly before the Iraqi conquest of Kuwait, he says, "We had common strategic interests there, but the U.S. found out late." Turning to the question of American changes at home, Arens points to the many problems that already affected the country at the time when Bill Clinton was elected president. Americans today are preoccupied with the state of the economy and with America's internal affairs, he says.

"Although America has gone through isolationist periods in the past, almost since World War Two it was considered obvious that the United States must take a responsible position in international relations, and that these problems were no less important than domestic ones.

"There is clearly an attempt to change policies, due to the apparent difficulties the United States is experiencing in the global economic sphere and the domestic social problems that seem to have arisen in the past few years," he says. "The general feeling is that the president has to concentrate on America's problems.

"This is justified by the consideration that you can be no stronger internationally than you are economically at home," Arens says. "So Clinton is concentrating a lot of his effort on domestic affairs. To some extent, this comes at the expense of international affairs.

"Add to this the fact that when Clinton was elected, he was new to international relations. He is still in the process of learning. Like all of us, he is a little averse to taking risks on matters he does not know too much about. There is a certain reticence to act, which may pass as he matures.

"It is difficult to foresee the kind of international problems which will appear and to what extent the American people will feel compelled to see American involvement. We have seen in the fighting in the former Yugoslavia, and even in Somalia, that the United States has been very sensitive to intervention. It has not been ready to commit major force or take serious risk by a major involvement.

"At first sight, it may be surprising that the great United States was not ready to make a major commitment against a local general such as Aidid in Somalia, whom nobody had heard of and who had no vast armies at his disposal," Arens says. "The United States certainly had the resources to wipe this guy off the map, but they were afraid of getting involved. In the case of Bosnia, this was even more clear.

"The U.S. is afraid of a long, active involvement in a conflict, or of entering some kind of morass. They have difficulty justifying an involvement and difficulty seeing how they will get out. This is an indication of what will happen in the future, when additional global problems emerge which may require intervention."

In line with this, Arens does not expect Clinton to assume a dominant role in the continuing Middle East peace process. "His administration's involvement was minor in the initial agreements with the Palestinians," he says. "Clinton does not seem to be a very confrontational person, and he is certainly not inclined to confront Israel, a country toward which he is very friendly."

"Those who think that America's contribution to the peace process should be elbowing and pressuring Israel will be disappointed, because we are not going to see that. I do not see Clinton trying to force Israel to do things the Israeli government does not want to do. To a large extent, the initiative will be with the Israeli government, as far as the American involvement in the peace process is concerned. I think that is the way it should be.

"The United States can be helpful to Israel at Israel's request, in terms of guarantees or some modest financial assistance that may be required, but this will not be the dominant factor in the peace process."

Arens says the Clinton era will be filled with budget cuts that are likely to affect foreign aid. "Assistance to Israel is a very significant part of the United States foreign aid budget, so in the long term there will be attempts to cut it," Arens predicts, adding that $1.8 billion out of Israel's $5.5 billion military budget comes from U.S. aid.

He says the fact that American aid to Israel was not cut through the 1994 budget year was a major achievement, and he terms it a strong indication of Clinton's feelings toward Israel, as well as his lack of desire to get into a confrontation with Israel and its friends in the United States.

Although such cuts would seem to conflict with America's perceived interests in the Middle East, Arens notes that every nation has a limited attention span. "The concentration on internal problems has to come at the expense of international relations," he says. "The tendency not to perceive the common interests with Israel on a potential Middle East crisis will increase, as the American people will prefer not to look at future problems in the world."

Even as he says these words, though, Arens knows that reality may overtake the American fantasy of looking inward. In 1992 and 1993, there were major crises in Bosnia and Somalia, and each future year seems sure to bring its own new crises.

The fact that the post-Cold War world is so full of conflicts does not surprise him, but he notes that it took the Gulf War to illustrate this for the Americans. "They learned that what might be considered a small crisis compared to the Cold War was not so small.

"President Bush suddenly discovered that Saddam Hussein had the fourth largest army in the world and that the great United States needed five months to put forces on the ground to deal with this," he says. "It is now clear that in order to deal with these small crises you require pretty big forces.

"It is not going to be easy for the United States to worry only about its internal problems," Arens adds.

Nonetheless, he seems convinced that the American people want to try, and he predicts that this inward focus will last at least until the country gets out of its present economic difficulties.

"Based on the little evidence we have so far, it is unlikely that the U.S. will cut itself off from all international obligations and will not want to spend a penny on them," he says. "We do not have to be concerned that the U.S. will cut itself off from Israel and end its aid, but military aid may not be $1.8 billion. It may be $1.5 billion."

Even that sort of decrease is likely to be temporary, Arens predicts, saying that when the American economy turns around, the country's idealism will prompt it to act on idealistic grounds once again.

"After Israel, the U.S. is the most idealistic country in the world," he says. "It will continue to do things because the public demands them for idealistic motives, within reason. The U.S. will do things which countries in Western Europe will not do."

Arens traces at least part of this trait to World War Two. "It did not express itself during the early days of Hitler," he notes. "The U.S. was not a party to the appeasement, but it did nothing contrary to it. Nor did it do anything to save the Jews in Europe, before or while they were being killed.

"They did not do for the Jews at the time what they recently did for the Somalians," he adds. On the other hand, he says that if the violent breakup of Yugoslavia had happened today in Mexico, the U.S. would not have stood by idly, as the Europeans did for the longest time.

Today, with large numbers of immigrants changing America's ethnic balance, Arens maintains that the newcomers will absorb American values and views, and says it is unlikely that their presence will change American commitment to certain central ideas.

This rising tide of immigrants could diminish the numerical significance of American Jewry, but Arens says they always have had importance beyond their numbers. He expects this influence will not be harmed, and that it will continue to serve Israel.

Returning to the U.S. interests in the Middle East, Arens reiterates the insurance concept. Anyone who takes out an insurance policy in a region as full of surprises as the Middle East understands that he may need to make a claim at some future date. Considering the presence of crazy states in the neighborhood, isn't it reassuring to know that Israel offers support in the event that it's needed?

Arens addresses this issue by referring again to Saddam Hussein and the Gulf War. "If Saddam Hussein had not invaded Kuwait, he would have had a nuclear bomb today," he says. "He went in to rob a bank, because he had run out of money. Had he been able to hang on for another year, we would today have a crazy man with a nuclear bomb in his hands. You can make some rationalizations as to why he makes certain decisions and not others, but his thought process is not similar to ours.

"One litmus test on how crazy these guys are is to ask, 'Would they use a nuclear bomb if they had it?'," Arens says. "The answer is yes. That goes for all of them, Saddam Hussein, the Iranians and Khaddafi." The field is ripe, he adds, for other dictators in the Moslem world to join the crazy state club.

While top priority must go to preventing these countries from obtaining nuclear weapons, it is natural to wonder aloud what they would do with them if they got them. Arens says that the Americans have little to fear from a crazy state nuclear threat, at least at this stage.

"The U.S. would not be in the first line of an attack by a crazy state, as they do not yet have the launching capacity," he says. "Someone may bring a bomb over in a suitcase, but that sounds far-fetched.

"A more pertinent question would be how the countries of Western Europe allowed the transfer of nuclear technology to Saddam Hussein," he continues. "France built a nuclear reactor in Iraq. They should not have had any illusions as to what would happen with the plutonium. There is only one answer. The French felt the danger this reactor would create would not be directed against them. It would only be directed against Israel, and that was not so terrible."

Arens also views many aspects of the peace process in light of the democratic values the United States and Israel share. "I am asked frequently what I think about the peace process and the deal which has been made with the Palestinians," he says. "I reply, 'Imagine for a moment that you go to outer space for ten years. When you come back, you need ask only one question to find out whether things have gone well or not.'

"That question is whether the Palestinian state, which no doubt will arise out of the autonomy, is a democracy or another Middle Eastern dictatorship. If you are told that it is a democracy, that is fine. If it is a dictatorship, then things have not gone well because we have another Middle Eastern dictatorship on the doorstep of Tel Aviv.

"I want to say with this parable that what Israel must do—and hopefully the United States will assist—is to try to promote democracy among the Palestinian population and among the neighboring countries to the extent that is possible. This is consistent with the most profound values of the United States.

"If the Palestinian state which will ultimately evolve as a result of the agreement with the PLO will be a democracy, it will influence countries like Jordan and Syria, as well as countries further away."

Arens voices deep optimism about the future of democracy. "When democracy comes to the Arab world—and I do not say 'if,' because I have no doubt that it is only a matter of time—it will be to a large extent the result of the democracy radiating out of Israel," he says.

"My view on the relationship with the Palestinians was that we should have gone for elections in the territories and then negotiated with the elected representatives," Arens says. "Democracy is a very pervasive idea. When it begins to take root, one cannot shake it off easily. One has only to look at the Israeli Arabs, who are Palestinians in every sense of the word. They know no other society. They have participated in so many national and municipal democratic elections that this has become part of their culture.

"The Palestinians living in Judea, Samaria and Gaza have also seen how the Israeli democracy functions. Arafat may ultimately be successful in imposing a dictatorship on the Palestinian state, but he will face many difficulties in doing so.

"When I was defense minister, I did my best to promote democracy in the territories by having elections for the chambers of commerce, industrial associations, student associations, etc. Thus democracy percolates into the social fabric.

"Democracy is the only weapon we have against fundamentalism. I do not know whether that weapon is strong enough to defeat it immediately, but democracy is the only viable alternative in the long run.

"Fundamentalism may rule the Arab world ten or 15 years from now," he says. "With the historical perspective we have, I cannot believe that it will rule the Arab world 100 years from now. Overcoming permanently the general trend toward progress is not something which seems likely. We have some pretty good indications that democracy is on the rise in the world, and is making good progress."

Drawing the conversation to a close, Arens says the role of personalities in the big picture is small, but potentially important. "The relationship between the U.S. and Israel is so firm and sound that it cannot be radically changed by personalities on either side of the ocean," he maintains.

"But from the Israeli side, the maneuvering margin is so small that even a very small change can be important to us. A minor change can certainly be brought about by personalities, and under certain circumstances a limited change may turn out to be very important. It has been a benefit to us that Clinton beat Bush.

"Clinton is a real friend of Israel," he concludes. "In the final analysis, he and Israel's many other friends in the United States will say that the Israeli government should know best what is good for the country. That is also a genuine test of friendship. In the crucial years to come, we still have enough backers in Congress as well as a friendly president, so the major support for Israel in the United States will most likely continue."

DAN SEGRE

Can Israel Ever Trust Europe?

D
AN SEGRE was born in 1922 into an assimilated Jewish family in the Italian village of Rivoli, where he grew up on his
mother's family farm. His father was the country's young-
est mayor in the village of Govone.

After Mussolini enacted anti-Jewish legislation in 1938, Segre fled
to Palestine, without any Zionist awareness. He has described this
period, in the bestselling first part of his autobiography, *The Memoirs
of a Fortunate Jew*, which has been translated into nine languages.
Segre has started work on a sequel, which will cover the post-World
War Two period.

He served in the British army during World War Two, and later
became a paratroop officer in Israel's War of Independence. Soon
thereafter, he became cultural and press attache at the new Israeli
embassy in Paris.

In 1952, he graduated in law from Turin University. Next, he studied political science at Sciences Politiques, and Oriental languages
at the Sorbonne, both in Paris. He served in various functions at

the Israeli Foreign Ministry until 1967, when he accepted a senior research fellowship in Middle Eastern studies at St. Antony's College at Oxford. From 1967–1969, he also was Ford Visiting Professor of Comparative History at MIT.

In 1972, he became full professor of international relations at Haifa University. Later, he assumed the post of Reuben Hecht Professor of Zionism. After his retirement in 1986, he was visiting professor at Stanford University for several years.

He has written a number of books in a variety of fields, most recently a biography of the Italian general Amedeo Guillet. Segre's other books include *Israel, Society in Transition* (1970), *The High Road and the Low, Technical Cooperation and African Development* (1974) and *Israel and Zionism, A Crisis of Identity* (1980).

Along with his teaching activities, Segre has always involved in journalism. For many years he was the Israeli correspondent of both *Le Figaro* and the *Corriere della Sera*. In 1974, he became a cofounder of the Italian daily *Il Giornale*.

"In order to understand how future links between Europe and Israel can develop in a more harmonious way," Segre says. "I prefer to look at how the roads of Europe and the Jews have crossed in the past."

The European position toward Israel has changed substantially over the decades. After Israel became independent in 1948, he explains, many Europeans were enthusiastic, because they saw in it the realization of an ideal state. They thought that it was a replay of the American revolt against Britain which led to U.S. independence. A second, not less important, reason for the positive attitude of many Europeans toward Israel derived from the shock of the Holocaust.

So why did this attitude change? Segre sees four reasons. The dream of the ideal state, unrealistic from the beginning, had to break down. Israel refused to be the only vegetarian state in a world of predators. To this came the sudden increase in Arab wealth as a result of the inept way the West handled the oil crisis in 1973. A third factor was the conjunction of Arab and communist propaganda against Zionism. A fourth factor was Israel's ties with the United States or, in leftist propaganda terms, American imperialism.

For Segre, the central thread running through European attitudes toward Jews—and today toward Israel—consists of long-held historical prejudices, complexes and frustrations. "Anti-Semitism has not disappeared," he says. To the contrary, Segre states that it has been broadened to include antizionism.

Segre sees in today's not-so-united Europe a modern version of the Holy Roman Empire, in which Jews always were strangers: first because they were different but not pagans, later because they were not Christians.

This European perception of the Jews as outsiders took different forms: traitors who opened the door of Spain to the Moslems; carriers of the plague in the 14th century; "quislings" for the Turks who threatened to lay siege to the Italian city of Ancona to help the Jewish community there; African slaves for Voltaire; dangerous revolutionary agents for Napoleon; liberal bourgeois, communists and capitalists; and "just bacteria" spreading social and racial contamination for the Nazis and their followers.

To many Europeans, Jews remain strangers to this day. To be an American Jew today is a legitimate way of being an American even if it is perhaps not the best way to be so in the eyes of that country's majority. For the Europeans, the perception of the Jew has remained that of a stranger, more so after World War Two and the creation of Israel.

Segre maintains that the predominant historical stereotype of the Jew in the eyes of the modern European is that of anti-Semitism, a word invented in 1874 by Wilhelm Marr, a German journalist and parliamentarian. This European attitude has profound motives. Jews have on many occasions been the test case of failed European ideas and ideals. The Dreyfus case, ending with the condemnation of the innocent French officer simply because he was Jewish, both symbolized and demonstrated the failure of the European enlightenment.

Segre contends that Jews also symbolize the European left's failure. They have shown its ideology's inherent contradictions as well as those between ideology and practice. For some of their precursors in the 19th century, such as the Frenchmen Proudhon and Fourier, the Jew and the banker are the same. According to a popular syllogism, since the Jew has the money and money dominates the world, the Jew dominates the world.

In the first version of *Das Kapital*, which was changed after his death, Marx wrote, "all merchandises are intimately circumcised Jewish money."

The second International and Lenin officially rejected anti-Semitism, but that didn't change the rank and file prejudice against Jews in the communist camp as shown, for instance, by the 1952 Slansky trial in Czechoslovakia and the "doctors' plot" engineered by Stalin in 1953.

Segre has no doubt that Marxist anti-Semitism has had a profound impact on the European left. "It accepted the principle that Third World peoples were by definition proletarian, while Israel was an imperialist stooge," he says. "Communism, which claimed that it had immunized itself against anti-Semitism, did not raise its voice against the delegitimation of Israel as a state by the Palestinian National Charter."

It did worse than that, he notes, when it used the whole arsenal of anti-Semitic weaponry against Zionism. "Thus, it upheld the principle, wrongly attributed to Hegel, that when facts do not agree with ideology they should be discarded."

The left and its opponents each had contrasting stereotypes: on the one hand that of the rich Jews, on the other those of the subversive anarchists, God's killers and world conspirators.

As far as European nationalism goes, Segre says that Jews have been both its promoters and its victims. For those familiar with the history of modern Italy, it is striking that between 1835 and 1870 the Jews were a considerable factor in the Italian Risorgimento—the fight for Italian unity—despite their small numbers.

People who demonstrate, through no fault of their own, the failure of the ideas of others are unlikely to be loved by those whose ideological balloons they have deflated. Segre says that Israel continues the Jew's traditional role as test case for the failure of European ideas.

Israel is effectively dealing with many problems Europe has difficulty facing, let alone solving. So, for instance, Israel confronts the challenge of integrating immigrants with reasonable success. Proportionately, it has absorbed more Third World immigrants into a Western-style society than any other country. Europe has a lot of good and bad experience in dealing with immigrants, Segre notes, but it lacks an adequate approach to the integration of non-Europeans.

It is subconsciously difficult for many Europeans to accept that Israel is dealing in a realistic way with the return of the "sacred" into politics, in the ongoing struggle between theocracy and democracy. This is an issue of vital importance for contemporary international society.

The element of the "sacred," which the French Revolution expelled from European politics, is returning in various ways with a vengeance in Europe. One example is Bosnia, which was part of a territorial national state and now is divided into religious enclaves. Segre expects other examples to follow in due course.

In this respect, Israel is the only country in the Middle East in which democracy and theocracy coexist, so far, without brutal confrontation between them. Yet it seems difficult for the Europeans to appreciate the universal value of an experience which no Third World country has been able to develop peacefully.

"Even worse," he adds, "Israel has shown in the 45 years of its history how an underdeveloped country can modernize, whereas many of the former European colonies are collapsing. This is another irritant for European leaders, though this is never explicitly said."

During its first years of independence, Israel embodied the only viable messianic socialist state in history, based on solidarity and voluntarism, Segre says. There are many examples in European history where attempts to establish such states failed. Among them: Bavaria and Hungary after World War One, and the republican regime in Spain.

"You cannot be liked by the leaders of Europe's leftist parties while rubbing in their faces successes in fields where they have failed miserably," he says with a note of irony.

Israel may even solve another problem Europeans have major problems confronting: the crisis between state and nation. The Italian nation today has difficulties maintaining an Italian state. The Basque countries do not want to be part of the Spanish nation. We are seeing an ongoing breakdown of the Belgian nation. The United Kingdom is in the process of becoming disunited. The disintegration of Yugoslavia is the worst example, he says, all the more so considering that the European Community has encouraged its breakup.

"While most European countries cannot solve this kind of problem, in Israel the state may create a nation from what is still a society made up of Jewish tribes," Segre says. "These 'tribes,' despite what many like to believe, have little common language or historical experience. Their language, Hebrew, started out mainly as an Esperanto.

"Still, these 'tribes' have created a state which most likely is creating an Israeli nation. Paradoxically, much of the credit goes to the Arabs. They have forced Israeli society to maintain unity in the face of hostility. Other societies have experienced external pressure, but they have not been able to translate this into creative internal unity. The case of European states faced by Soviet danger is a case in point. If Israel is not a miraculous example, it is at least spectacular."

To make matters continuously worse in the eyes of the Europeans, Segre says, Israel is a modern victorious state, whereas they would have been defeated in World War Two by an ideology of darkness had it not been for the military efforts of two nations that the Europeans regard as rather uncivilized—the Americans and the Russians. Modern European historians have begun to realize that the two world wars were, in fact, European wars which Europeans spread to the rest of the world.

According to a certain type of European historical determinism, a state like Israel, created by Zionism, the only national movement ever branded by the United Nations as racist, should lose wars against the Third World Arabs the same way the Europeans lost their colonies.

No Western power has been able to withstand wars of liberation, as the Indian, Indonesian, Algerian and Vietnamese examples seem to prove. In the case of Israel, many Europeans—obviously not all of them—who start with such a false premise are very disappointed if this does not lead to the expected false conclusion.

The prostration of the Europeans before the Arabs—and their oil wealth—in the 1970s and 1980s has blinded them to the dangers of justifying terrorism, mainly of Arab origin. Despite the facts, Israel was blamed for many of the West's major problems.

The United Nations, in one of its many perverse statements, declared Israel the main danger to world peace and the Middle East conflict the most serious one at the end of the century, Segre recounts. Israel was also blamed by its Western detractors for the entrance of Russian influence in the Middle East and Chinese influence into Africa to balance the success of Israeli cooperation policies.

"Nowadays the castle of mixed European, Arab, communist and United Nations lies has collapsed in an embarrassing way, resulting in a paradox," Segre says. "Israel, which was accused of threatening peace, is there, for everybody to see, as a major ally in the world fight against Moslem terrorism, a pluralist democracy in the midst of authoritarian, non-democratic, violent regimes.

"The Palestinian problem is certainly a severe test of Israel's moral and political values," Segre says. "It has caused many distortions to Jewish ethics and democratic behavior, for which Israel deserves criticism from both friends and foes. But this does not justify those critics who demand that Israel behave as a democracy in peace and not, for example, as a Western democracy at war. Furthermore, European foreign policy is far from ethical, and it is not inspired by purely progressive democratic principles."

He points to Europe's ongoing commercial ties with Iran as prime evidence that European governments have not learned much from the past. Although they could easily bring the Iranians to reason by cutting purchases of their oil—and thus strengthening their Arab allies—Segre says, the Europeans have made no such moves.

When one asks Segre where this all leads, he replies, "According to an ancient Jewish saying, since the Temple was destroyed prophecy is reserved for babes and fools. I am not a babe and do not want to look a fool. I cannot make prophecies. All I can do is indicate trends, which may or may not realize themselves."

Israel is the only modern state halfway between Washington and Peking. This has many implications and creates multiple opportunities.

"Until a new satellite was launched recently, a TV satellite farm in Herzliya supplied TV stations all over the world with recordings from central Asian stations," he says. "Now, following the political changes in Eastern Europe, a sort of new silk road has opened up for Israel to India and China."

One paradoxical result of the Arab boycott has been that Tokyo and Mexico City are closer to Tel Aviv than Damascus or Cairo, at least in economic terms.

He notes that the boycott has cost Israel billions of dollars, but has forced it to diversify its production and to enter competitive markets, while Arab economies have remained mainly either agricultural or oil-dominated.

Today, he says, the economies of Israel and the Arab countries are not complementary. One possible beneficial consequence of the agreements between Israel and the PLO may be to increase the present low flow of trade, manpower and technology between Israel and the Arab countries. Although a Middle East common market may not emerge tomorrow, Segre says, the breakdown of economic barriers between Israel and the Arabs may turn out to be an energizing factor for both sides.

The second trend identified by Segre is a political one. "There may or may not be peace," he says. "If peace comes, it will not be a lengthy process. It will have rapid, explosive results. Many foreign companies will open offices in Israel. Israel will fast become an international business center."

But Segre also sees reason for caution here. He quotes the hero of his most recent book: "An Italian ambassador, Amedeo Guillet, the Italian Lawrence of Arabia, told me more than 40 years ago that the Arabs are a body without a head and the Jews are a head without a body.

"The problem is how to get the two together," he continues. "Guillet is probably right even today. Arabs and Israelis are complementary in many fields. Their joining of forces will never put one in control of the other, but rather be beneficiary to both."

Segre points to one of many examples. "Just think of the Palestinians. They have two science teachers for every vacancy in their schools, while Israel is short of such teachers.

"In a true partnership, we must be very careful not to see ourselves as a potential new Venice, the Italian state which for many centuries was only interested in commerce. Money is not the only thing that counts. Israel should not act in the Middle East with a European approach. Rather, it should see itself as an integral part of the Middle East, and as a neutral bridge between countries."

The two trends mentioned so far combine as the opening of new Eastern European and Asian markets to Israel diminishes its dependence on Europe. In the past, he notes, the EEC has made many hostile declarations against Israel and even threatened it occasionally with sanctions.

It is again symbolic that the best-known of these declarations was one made in—of all places—Venice, in 1980. In it, Europe tried to impose its nonexistent strength on Israel to please the Arabs.

In recognizing the right of the Palestinian Arabs to a homeland, the Venice Declaration undermined the position of Jordan, which at that time was still the legal authority of the Palestinians—a fact the Europeans "forgot" to mention, thereby delegitimizing a country which had been a reliable European ally.

In the Venice Declaration, Segre says, Europe rewarded the PLO for terrorism at a time when it refused to accept the existence of Israel. Later, the Europeans did not support the only peacemaking event in the Middle East, the Camp David agreements.

Segre has even stronger words of distrust for Europe: "Europe does not seem to have renounced some aspects of its Shylock policy," he says. "It wants from Israel a pound of flesh in territorial concessions without paying attention to the damage these may cause to the whole body as far as the defense capabilities of Israel are concerned. To insist on unilateral concessions after the Yugoslav experience would look comic if it was not so tragic."

The third trend Segre sees is even more difficult to define. It concerns religion, ethics and morality, and is linked to what he calls "the Machiavellian dilemma." Machiavelli said that a Christian prince is a contradiction; either one is a prince or one is a Christian. Israel cannot solve this dilemma for Christian Europe, but Segre sees some light.

"Perhaps Israel can offer some suggestions," Segre says. "One is to invite the Europeans to follow with some humility the efforts of a small state which struggles with the problem of how to return to its sacred traditions without throwing away the modernization of which Jews have been major promoters in the last 150 years. One only has to think of Einstein, Freud and Marx.

"This is not just an Israeli problem," he says. "It is a vital problem facing Europe, and a common problem shared with the Arabs. They are confronted with the challenge to find ways to modernize quickly without breaking with their very strong traditions. In this area, Europe could help break new ground that could lead to understanding."

Only recently has Europe overcome religious and nationalistic wars and hate which have filled its rivers with blood for centuries. If Europeans wanted to make a genuine contribution to a stable peace in the Middle East, they could distill from their own experience certain useful elements.

Both sides could benefit by developing regional market institutions, he suggests. It could give preferential treatment—including full association with the EEC—to both Israel and the Palestinians on the condition that they cooperate in specific fields such as energy, water, science and banking.

More important, the EEC should see itself as the international organization replacing the old European Habsburg, Czarist and even Ottoman empires as an economic framework that could help many "tribes" find accommodation and reasons to cooperate by balancing traditions and modernization.

This may be difficult, Segre acknowledges. It surely will be less exciting for newspaper and TV journalists than what is happening today. It is, however, certainly a civilized way to compensate for all the damage Europe has done to Israel in the past and create a space in which the two can work together in the future.

He insists that there are better European traditions than those established by the Dominican monks when they burned the Talmud or by Napoleon, who wanted to civilize Egypt and proclaim a Jewish state to get easier supply for his army. The message of Europe, he says, should be that of Erasmus, which he sums up this way: "Rationalism, compassion, moderation and self-criticism, all of which have become scarce commodities in Europe."

MORDECHAI ABIR

Islamic Fundamentalism, the Permanent Threat

MORDECHAI ABIR teaches Middle Eastern and Islamic studies at the Hebrew University. He has published books on such diverse topics as Saudi Arabia, oil and Ethiopia. His most recent book, *Saudi Arabia, Government, Society and the Gulf Crisis*, deals with the background and impact of the 1990–91 Gulf crisis and war.

In a discussion that took place in Jerusalem, he surveys the likely impact of Moslem fundamentalism on Islamic states, global stability and Israel. He dissects and analyzes the various forces at work with a surgeon's precision. His matter-of-fact assessment offers cause for alarm, as does his warning that Israel's leadership must carefully examine every step it takes in the direction of peace with the Arab world, and the PLO in particular, in order to avoid possible disaster.

His survey of the Moslem world focuses on the rising impact of neofundamentalism; all the rest, he believes, is secondary. And any survey of trends in the Moslem world must begin with the Arab world, whose role is pivotal.

Despite the facade of fabulous oil riches, Abir notes that the vast majority of Arabs have remained poor and backward. Only a few of the more than 20 Arab states—mainly sparsely populated ones—enjoy significant oil resources, and none of these countries are inclined to share the wealth equitably with others.

Population growth, lack of development and a falling standard of living, set against the backdrop of oil riches that elude the masses, create a setting that is ripe for fundamentalism. That is the key factor in all changes that are likely to occur in the Arab world in the coming years.

Neofundamentalism, as Abir calls the current trend, differs sharply from the "modern" fundamentalism which emerged in the late 19th century, but it is not totally unrelated to its predecessor.

The "modern" fundamentalism of 100 years ago emerged as the Arab and Moslem world faced the bitter truth: they had lagged behind global development. "It was no longer an important part of civilized society," Abir says. "It belonged to the Third World. The despised infidel Christian societies had not only overtaken the Arabs in every field, but finally colonized them as well."

Abir stresses that fundamentalism has its foundation in the search for answers to problems posed by the new world impinging on the world of Islam. Jamal al-Din-al-Afghani, the father of modern fundamentalism, believed that Western culture and philosophy could be separated from technology, which he claimed the West actually had borrowed from the Moslems and developed further. His people, he preached, should take back that which was rightfully theirs, but reject altogether other aspects of Western civilization.

The message has undergone certain changes over the years, Abir says, but the basic rejection of Western values and hegemony remains essentially unchanged. What has changed are the tactics.

"In the circumstances of a future without hope, Islamic fundamentalists teach that the real answer for society's ills and people's personal problems lies in the return to the roots—the original teachings of Mohammed and his followers, the life they conducted and the success they achieved in the first centuries of Islam," Abir explains. What does this mean? He points to certain attractions of life in the early years of Islam: society was more egalitarian and people looked after one another when the Moslem world was led by pious righteous rulers.

"The old school of 20th-century fundamentalism, such as the pre-World War Two Moslem Brothers, sought to create a better society," Abir says. "They did not seek control of government. After World War Two, a major change took place: the Moslem Brothers resorted increasingly to militancy and terrorism to achieve their aims."

This militancy led to an increasingly blunt confrontation between fundamentalists and the successful secular nationalist pan-Arab movement championed by Nasser. "In Nasser's jails, in the late 1950s, some Moslem Brothers changed their approach totally," Abir says. "They no longer believed that any secular government could transform itself into a Moslem one. They considered government and society so corrupt that they had to be rebuilt from the bottom to adhere to the principles of true Islam."

In their quest for total change, Abir says, the neofundamentalists began to consider Jihad—holy war—to overthrow and replace their own corrupt governments. They compared the Arab states to the pre-Islamic idolatrous societies. The neofundamentalists rejected the secular Arab polity, which they associated with Western culture, its materialism and its philosophical foundations. Their leading ideologist, Sayyid Qutb, who lived for some years in the U.S., returned to Egypt around 1950, altogether alienated from Western culture, which he observed and abhorred.

Qutb called for using all possible means in the war against Western influence. His first target: the local Moslem governments that had permitted the corruption and decline of their societies. He held them responsible for introducing Western ills to Moslem society. He was also convinced that these governments were incapable of solving their peoples' social and economic problems.

Like many other Moslem Brothers who opposed Nasser's regime, Qutb was incarcerated in 1954. He was released in 1964, only to be executed by the regime in 1966. His books and letters from jail had a tremendous impact on changing the Moslem Brothers' outlook. They stimulated the emergence of neofundamentalism in the 1960s, its expansion in the 1970s, its further spread in the 1980s and the growing militancy of the early 1990s.

Bringing the picture up-to-date, Abir says, "The neofundamentalists want to change the societal system to a theocracy governed by jurists or religious leaders. We see now a militant Islamic fundamentalism that seeks to overthrow Arab and Moslem regimes in order to replace them by Islamic ones.

"Sayyid Qutb and his followers considered that the establishment and popular Islam, which was practiced so commonly in the Islamic world, had corrupted true Islam," Abir says. "In their view, it was worse than the teachings of the infidels. Qutb's followers felt that they had to remove themselves from the corrupt societies in which they lived to create a new circle of true Moslems. This is modelled on the *Hijra*, the prophet Mohammed's migration from Mecca to Medina. The thinking of the different neofundamentalist organizations is always based on the principle of Jihad, and that the end justifies the means."

The radical thought expressed in this approach finds a receptive audience among the intelligentsia and the masses throughout much of the frustrated Moslem world. Abir notes that only a few million Arabs actually enjoy the great wealth generated by oil revenues. "The Moslem have-nots number about 800 million, including 200 million Arabs," he says. "Their standard of living deteriorates continuously, because they reproduce so quickly. The growth of the economy of many countries cannot keep up with that. But, along with some intellectuals who joined them, the have-nots also are motivated by political frustrations resulting from the decline of Moslem power vis-à-vis the West."

He points to contemporary Egypt as a typical example. Poverty cohabits there with extreme wealth, he notes, and the standard of living of the masses continues to decline. Unchecked population growth and the limits to the number of people who can subsist on agriculture contribute to the increasing migration to the cities, which lack the infrastructure to accommodate them.

Since the 19th century, Abir says, some Western philosophers, such as Ernest Renan in France, have accused Islam of being reactionary and standing in the way of the modernization of the Moslem world. This, Renan said, was the cause of Moslem backwardness in modern times and the Moslems' inability to develop and improve their standard of living. Moslem reaction prevents the adjustment of its followers to the new world. The present reality, Abir notes, bears this out.

He cites non-Arab Iran, which underwent a total fundamentalist revolution under the Ayatollah Khomeini, as an example. "The lot of the average Iranian farmer improved temporarily compared to the Shah's days. This is no longer true, and the urban proletariat faces increasing hardship. Thus, the model fundamentalist state has not only failed to solve Iran's socio-economic problems; it has aggravated them.

"Iran has the potential of becoming a well-to-do society if it uses its oil revenues to develop its economy. However, it earmarks a large percentage of its income to build its military might by acquiring conventional and nonconventional weapons in its quest to regain the status of a major power in the Gulf, and possibly in the Moslem world.

"Shiite Iran sees itself as the vanguard of true Islam in the Moslem world," Abir continues. "The first target of its militant fundamentalist Islam is the Arab world. Iran has become the supporter of all Islamic revolutionary movements from Morocco to Afghanistan, including the Hamas and the Islamic Jihad movements in the territories, and to some extent even Israeli Arab fundamentalists.

Abir says that the Hamas and the Islamic Jihad both receive, directly and indirectly, financial aid from Iran, which also supports the Hizbollah in Lebanon. "Their cadres are trained in Iran, or Iranian revolutionary guards train them in Lebanon and Sudan. A lot of money is spent for this purpose," Abir says.

He notes that the Iranian government also finances training bases for fundamentalist extremists in Sudan and, indirectly, their activities against Egypt, Libya and North Africa. President Rafsanjani has hinted to the Egyptians that he will continue to undermine their regime as long as it collaborates with American efforts to advance the Arab-Israeli peace process.

"Iran aims to destabilize all secular Sunni Moslem-Arab regimes. They hope to achieve this directly or in cooperation with the Sunni-fundamentalist regime of Sudan, as well as the different militant Islamic organizations in the Arab-Moslem world and its affiliates in the West," he says.

Although it is widely believed in the West that there are two opposing political currents in Iran's Islamic regime, Abir maintains that they do not differ in their fundamentalist ideology.

"Rafsanjani is no less an extremist than his opponents, but he is also a pragmatist," he says. "He is ready to bow to circumstances, and wants to obtain Western technology and investments for his country in order to advance its economic power and military capability while improving the standard of living."

But his pragmatism is a tactic which coexists alongside the traditional trappings of a Shiite regime, propagated by his mentor, the late Ayatollah Khomeini. Its propaganda and indoctrination office, Da'wa, is responsible for all the shady operations. Iran uses it to "spread the word of Allah" through terrorism and subversion.

"Indeed, Rafsanjani's regime is behind major efforts in recent years to 'Islamicize' Moslem regimes," Abir says, noting that as long as a fundamentalist regime retains power in Iran the situation will not change dramatically.

"Iran's first target is to subvert the weaker pro-Western Arab governments," he says. "They assist domestic Sunni fundamentalist groups, through financial support, training of terrorists, helping guerilla fighters and supplying weapons and explosives.

"Rafsanjani still aims to achieve the goals of his mentor's Islamic revolution, but he is such a pragmatist that he endeavors to survive on the side of the West. He is looking for ways to achieve his ends but, unlike his opponents, he wants to avoid confrontation with the West.

"Many Western experts and some governments, notably Germany, are totally confused," Abir charges. "Many assume not only that Rafsanjani is a pragmatist, but that he is willing to adjust to realities and eventually allow Iran to rejoin the 'sane' community of nations. This is totally incorrect."

Abir points to a basic contradiction in Rafsanjani's philosophy: "One cannot insulate scientific and technological advances from the Western civilization which produced them. Yet the war declared by Moslem fundamentalists against Western culture is a war of civilizations."

He notes that long-held conventional wisdom maintained that highly populated, poor Third World countries with very high birthrates had no hope of improving their lot. India has disproved these gloomy forecasts. Despite its population growth, per capita income in India has risen meaningfully in the framework of its overall development. China is another outstanding example.

Abir maintains that China and India prove that Third World countries have hope and can develop. But Islamic society's apathy and hostility to the West prevent a huge segment of the globe's population from adapting to modern economy and technology, as well as from modernizing. Instead, they seek salvation in 7th-century Islamic models.

In adjusting to the modern world, the Moslems do not have to give up their basic cultural values. But unless they can overcome their xenophobic, anti-Western bias, Abir asserts, most Moslem states are unlikely to defeat poverty and chaos. "The have-nots are incapable of halting their economic decline without major financial aid from the oil producers or the West, which is unlikely to increase in the forseeable future," he says.

As if to demonstrate that irrationalism cannot coexist with the quest for development, Abir points to Iraq under Saddam Hussein. "Ironically, this was the one oil-rich country with a sizable population and a diversified economy which had significant economic growth due to oil revenue," he says. "But that was before it got involved in war with Iran in 1980, and before Saddam's Pan Arab anti-Western and anti-Israeli ambitions." Since that war, and Saddam's ensuing military forays, Iraq's economy has been almost totally destroyed and will take many years to rehabilitate.

After all of Abir's assessments and his survey of the situation throughout the Moslem world, the inevitable question arises: What does it all mean for Israel?

"The conclusions are very sad," he says. "The dovish elements in the Israeli government won the upper hand, and they are negotiating Palestinian autonomy with the PLO, which is likely to lead to the establishment of a Palestinian state. If this happens, it is questionable whether the PLO will be able to control a process which takes place all around in the Arab Moslem world: the rise of fundamentalism. Such fundamentalism, or ultra-nationalism, may even spread among Israeli Arabs, whose ties with their kinsmen will be stronger than ever.

"We see the beginning of a process," he says. "The power of fundamentalism in the territories is on the rise. It has spread from the Gaza

Strip to the West Bank and it brings newfound vigor to the battle against the Jewish state." He refers to a televised interview with Sheikh Yassin, the founder of the Hamas movement, conducted a few years ago, and to recent declarations by Hamas and Islamic Jihad leaders. All of them flatly reject the right of Jewish Israel to exist on land which they term waqf, part of a religious endowment. They continue to call for unceasing holy war—jihad—to destroy Israel.

"Sheikh Yassin said that he had nothing against the Jews and accepted them as *dhimmis*—a tolerated community with no political rights," Abir says. "They were always protected and treated well in the Moslem communities in the past. This dhimmi status is exactly what some old established Israelis can expect from a potentially fundamentalist Palestinian state, but newcomers will be deported to their countries of origin once the Arabs destroy the Jewish political entity. The people of the book can live in safety as a community, without political rights, in an Islamic state."

Although Sheikh Yassin may have intended his words to sound comforting—after all, he does not want to eliminate the Jews—Abir does not interpret them that way. Efforts to expand negotiations with the Palestinians, represented by the Arafat faction of the PLO, that will clearly lead to the establishment of a Palestinian state might prove a step beyond the point of no return, he believes.

Abir speaks openly of his fear that steps taken by dovish Israeli officials essentially pave the way to the establishment of a PLO state in the West Bank. He has little doubt that such a state will be taken over by fundamentalists and/or the rejectionist nationalists.

"Let us assume that for tactical purposes the Hamas will stand aside and let the Arafat-led mainstream PLO Palestinian state be established," he says. "In a second stage, the Hamas will take it over. The trend nowadays is that the masses—especially those who suffer economic hardship—increasingly follow the fundamentalists.

"Indeed, a Palestinian state may go through a very difficult economic crisis without the vast resources needed to solve the problems of its population and the Palestinians in the diaspora. It will be surrounded by unfriendly Arab regimes and Israel, unless it establishes some form of union with Jordan and receives substantial aid."

Moreover, he notes, only about half of the Palestinian people live in the West Bank and Gaza, many in refugee camps. "What will happen to the 2–2.5 million Palestinians who are outside and preserve their identity?" he asks. "They live in camps in nearby Arab countries, or in other parts of the world, rejected by their Arab brethren.

"For them, the war will not be over, as they will not have a place in the 6,000 square kilometers of the West Bank and the Gaza Strip —where the population will soon number a million people—and they will insist on the 'right of return' (awda) to Acre, Haifa, Jaffa, Ashdod and West Jerusalem. Can Arafat contain such demands? Does he sincerely want to? One can see the case of Lebanon and its political ramifications.

"I cannot consider such a solution being practical at all," he says flatly, "unless some magical formula is found to solve the problem of all the Palestinians. Otherwise, the pressure from within to overrun Israel when the opportunity presents itself will continue."

He does, however, see another alternative. "The best solution for the Palestinian people is that the Hashemite Kingdom will fall," he says. Jordan, which has a Palestinian majority, will become a Palestinian state with an offshoot in the West Bank and Gaza. Another, more problematic, alternative is a federated Jordan-Palestine.

"Israel has to look after its own interests, and therefore has to insist on security arrangements that will guarantee its existence," he says. "Once a Palestinian state is established—even an autonomous region—it will be protected by international law and organizations. Israel's ability to protect its population and its security will be constrained.

"The Jordanian solution will give the Palestinians a sufficient territorial basis," Abir continues. "Such a Palestinian Jordan could have joint water resources with Israel and common desalination projects on a very big scale. There could be many diverse major joint projects which would benefit both countries."

Even a Jordanian-Palestinian-Israeli economic confederation is possible, Abir says. It could attract meaningful Arab and international investment that would help solve the problem.

"The Palestinian-Jordanian entity would have a flag, army and air force east of the Jordan," he says. "It would have an outlet to the sea in Aqaba, which would also be meaningful for Iraq. It would also have an Israeli-controlled corridor to Gaza and other Mediterranean ports.

"The entity would have a much higher level of education than the Gulf countries and could become an important part of the development of the Arab countries and benefit from such connections. Many joint venture plans are already being proposed, and many more will emerge if the peace negotiations bear fruit and produce a Jordanian-Palestinian entity."

The country would derive significant revenues, Abir maintains, from oil and gas pipelines which could pass across its territory from Saudi Arabia, the Gulf, Iraq and Syria. It would also be a passage for trade from Israel to and from the Arab world, and a conduit to Israeli technology in various fields.

"Such a country could have real economic expectations and a realistic political chance of survival without having to resort to war again soon," Abir says.

This picture looks quite rosy, yet Abir stresses that only if a Palestinian-Jordanian federation emerges from the peace process, or if Jordan becomes a Palestinian home, can it become reality. While fundamentalism and other ultra-nationalist movements will persevere, he maintains that they may not acquire the power they will if an independent Palestinian state emerges in the territories.

"My opinion results from studying the Moslem world's history,"

Abir states." To a large extent, the success of fundamentalism is less an outcome of political discontent and more the result of economic misery. The Moslem world experienced waves of rising fundamentalism. There were and always will be fundamentalist tendencies in Islam. The only question is how powerful they will be."

Returning to the Iranian example, he says, "Paradoxically, fundamentalism did not provide an answer to Iran's socioeconomic problems. The standard of living of the Iranian population declined under the late Shah. Only 5 percent enjoyed the fat of the land. It was not surprising that the illiterate people, who were often tenant farmers, were seeking a fundamentalist solution.

"They are devout Moslems. In the same way, the misery in Egypt is generating support for militant fundamentalism. Yet 14 years after the Islamic revolution, Iran's economy is in shambles and the standard of living of its urbanized masses and rural population is even worse than in the past, and it is still declining."

Before Israel makes any final, binding arrangement with the Palestinians and its neighbors, Abir urges its leadership to keep in mind what is happening today to Christian minorities in "secular" Moslem states. Egypt—which he terms the most secular state in the Arab world, aside from the Christian parts of Lebanon—has been unable to combat the hate of fundamentalist Moslems for the Copts, who are true remnants of the original Egyptian population. The Christians in Lebanon have seen the writing on the wall since their failure in the early 1980s to establish a Christian-dominated Lebanon or a semi-independent entity in their part of Mount Lebanon.

"In today's secular Egypt, Copts and Moslems theoretically enjoy equal rights," he says. Nonetheless, the number of Copts steadily declines, due to emigration caused by widespread covert discrimination and, above all, because of increasing persecution by Moslem fanatics. "The Moslem masses refuse to accept a dhimmi community as being equal," he states.

"Sometimes, people from these dhimmi communities hold high positions in the public administration and elsewhere. Moslems work under them. This is totally objectionable to the average Moslem. In the Egyptian countryside, where the people are uneducated and backward, the situation is even more conducive to the success of fundamentalist propaganda against Copts. This increasing socio-religious tension in rural areas and provincial towns often erupts into pogroms and bloody clashes, which the government finds hard to control.

"As Moslem fundamentalism spreads in Upper Egypt, Cairo and the Delta, where many fundamentalists live, many Copts have come to the conclusion that the only solution is to emigrate. We do not know their exact numbers, as this is a sensitive political subject in Egypt, but they probably used to represent 7–9 percent of Egypt's population. There are sizable Coptic communities in New York, Chicago, Canada, and elsewhere in the Americas. The Lebanese Maronites also see the writing on the wall, and hundreds of thousands have emigrated to America and Europe over the last 20 years."

To Abir, the lessons are clear. Israel's leaders must be fully aware of the sad realities of the Middle East at present and in the fateful years ahead, he warns, and endeavor to avoid fatal errors in negotiations with neighboring Arab states and the Palestinians. Above all, Israel must preserve its vital interests and ability to defend itself.

"We have to keep in mind the risk of a PLO state in the territories which could eventually turn into a fundamentalist Palestinian state that openly rejects the very right of a Jewish state to exist in their midst," he concludes.

SERGIO MINERBI

Two Steps Forward, One Step Back
The Vatican, the Jews and Israel

S ERGIO MINERBI is a leading observer of the Vatican scene. Born
in Rome in 1929, he came to Israel in 1947 and lived in Kibbutz
Ruhama for nine years.

Minerbi holds a B.A. in economics and international relations
from the Hebrew University and a Ph.D. from the University of Paris.
He was a member of the staff of Israel's Ministry of Foreign Affairs
from 1961–1989, when he took a leave of absence to work as a private
consultant.

His last position at the Ministry was as assistant director general
of economic affairs. Before that, he was ambassador to Belgium and
Luxemburg for five years, during which he also headed Israel's mission to the EEC. Minerbi is married and has three children.

He has written many academic articles and encyclopedia entries
on relations between the Vatican and Jews and Israel. One of his
books, *The Vatican, the Holy Land and Zionism*, originally published in
Hebrew, has been translated in recent years into Italian and English.

Despite—or perhaps because of—the fact that Minerbi's specialty is Israel-Vatican relations, he believes that Israelis tend to over-stress the Israeli perspective on a wide variety of issues. It therefore comes as no surprise that he downplays the significance of the recent steps taken to establish full diplomatic ties between Israel and the Vatican.

"If we want to understand developments, we should focus on Pope John Paul II's attitude toward the Jewish people first, and on relations with Israel second," he says.

Minerbi says Jewish observers usually lack the theological and political understanding needed to interpret correctly the Vatican's attitudes towards Jewish and Israeli issues. "Without comprehending Church history, Jewish leaders may commit major mistakes in their present and future relations with the Vatican," he warns.

"We have to realize that whereas a Jew can define his identity without referring to Christianity, Christians have to identify themselves with reference to Jews. The issue is not symmetric."

Minerbi maintains that for as long as Christianity has existed, it has encompassed a fundamental contradiction in its attitude toward Judaism. "They want to be the only legitimate heir of Judaism so that the real accomplishment of Judaism is in Christianity," he says, adding that Christianity stresses its Jewish roots as a tool to gain legitimation from this past.

"Thus," he says, "Jesus became King David's successor. At the same time, Christianity sought to define a new religion, so it had to separate itself from Judaism. These two concepts don't go together."

From this dichotomy emerged the claim that the Catholic Church is *Verus Israel*, the true Israel, which left no legitimate place for the Jews in society. In the fifth century, Minerbi notes, St. Augustin defined Jews as the *popolo testimone*, the "witness people," whose very existence testifies to the truth of Christianity. Without such a justification, he adds, Jewish history could have taken a very bad turn indeed.

"Initially, the apostle Paul confronted the material commandments of Judaism with the good spiritual actions of Christianity," Minerbi says. "This is where the label of materialism was first applied to Jews, as opposed to Christians, who were spiritual. These generalizations are deeply entrenched in European culture, which is basically a Christian one. Even opponents of Christianity, such as Voltaire, accepted these Christian anti-Semitic stereotypes.

"As far as the attitudes of the present Pope are concerned, one has to understand that while he takes an interest in Judaism, he has far more important concerns. His thinking is centered on Poland and Eastern Europe. He is convinced that his help to the Polish Solidarity trade union in the 1980s was the main catalyst for the collapse of communism, including in the Soviet Union."

Today, the Pope worries that communism has been replaced by even worse values based on the consumer society and hedonism. Minerbi says the leader of the Catholic world blames the United States as the source of these bad influences on other nations.

The Pope is convinced that the answer to any breakdown of values must be a return to greater orthodoxy. Minerbi says that John Paul II sees this as the only way to keep the Church united in the face of today's modernism.

"This is a fighting Pope," he says. "He wants to return to positions from before the Vatican II Council, or at least not let the Council's ideas develop further.

"When he visited the United States, the Pope was confronted with important problems within his own church," Minerbi says. "Despite the fact that half of the American bishops have been appointed by him, he still faces substantial opposition to his policies concerning homosexuality, abortions and—above all—sexual relations. When he proposes sexual abstinence, when visiting the United States or Uganda, that sounds equally absurd to youth in both countries."

Of course, Minerbi points out that there are some friendly relations, and even some collaboration, between American Jews and

Catholics. Both groups are minorities in the United States, and both are comprised of people who came as poor immigrants and have done well economically.

"American Jews go by mistaken analogy," he explains. "They know the attitudes of US cardinals and are convinced that they can accordingly understand Vatican policies. The Jewish-Catholic dialogue, held mainly by American Jews, is based on a major misunderstanding of how the decisionmaking process in the Vatican functions, and incomprehension of its long-term policies.

"American Catholics are a minority in both the United States and the Catholic Church," he notes. "Their attitudes differ radically from those of the Vatican's Curia and of the Pope himself, who sometimes even surprises the Curia.

"Catholic authorities can be pleasant and tolerant towards Jews. There is more and more interest in Judaism in order to understand the roots of Christianism. They want to see how we do the seder in order to understand the gospel which explains the Last Supper. They want to get closer to Jews, yet they fear this closeness. I never understood why the Church has this ambivalent attitude."

But Minerbi doesn't need to understand why in order to see that the current Pope gives conflicting messages as far as Jews are concerned. He terms it a policy of two steps forward, one step backward.

What does he mean? Minerbi notes that in the 1965 *Nostra Aetate* declaration at the Vatican II Council, Jews were partially absolved of the killing of Jesus. "The change was not as big as I wished for. The responsibility for deicide was still there," he notes, "but it was limited to those who actually killed Jesus."

Minerbi gives another example of these internal contradictions in the Pope's position. "He has said that the old covenant—with the Jews—was never revoked by God. Two or three times, however, he has claimed that the old covenant could not continue because the Jewish people were not faithful to their God. Thus, there was a need for a new covenant to replace the old one. I would like to understand from the Pope clearly what he thinks is right or wrong doctrine.

"The Catholic Church has shown certain signs of sensitivity to Jewish issues," Minerbi continues. For example, Pope John Paul II calls the Holocaust by its Hebrew name, Shoah, and he even visited Auschwitz. In 1990, Polish bishops in Poland asked forgiveness from the Jews.

"With the agreement of the Pope, Cardinal Cassidy, who is in charge of the dialogue with the Jews, used the Hebrew word teshuva when referring to the Catholics' obligation toward the Jews. This statement, made in Prague, is very positive."

Notwithstanding the positive developments, Minerbi hastens to stress that all is not rosy. He characterizes the beatification of German-born Edith Stein, who grew up in an assimilated Jewish family, studied philosophy, converted to Catholicism, became a nun and ultimately was killed by the Nazis, as "one of the most negative signals from the Vatican in the past 20 years.

"In his beatification speech of May 1, 1987, the Pope said that she died for the glorification of God. He translated literally the Hebrew term kiddush Hashem. I am revolted when the classic formula for Jews who preferred to die rather than change their faith is used with respect to somebody who changed her faith to Christianity."

The Pope's words cut even further, Minerbi says, in the damage they did to Jewish-Catholic relations. "He compared Edith Stein to Queen Esther, who saved her people, the Jews," he says. "How could Edith Stein do this? She was killed and could not even save herself, let alone anybody else.

"The only logical interpretation is that she saved her people by showing them the right path, Christianity. What makes it even worse is that it is said about somebody who died at Auschwitz. At the supposed site of her tomb in Birkenau, a place nobody can know, there is—I am told—a Star of David together with a cross, a clear sign of syncretism."

Perhaps the worst thing about the Edith Stein beatification is that it is not the only such case. Minerbi says that the Catholic Church has long tried to expropriate Jewish symbols. This expropriation lies at the very origin of Christianity. Catholicism was born converting Jewish values and symbols to Christian ones.

"The wine of kiddush became the wine of the Holy Mass," he says. "The blessing of the bread on Friday became the Host. The Passover seder became Christ's Passion. The originators of Christianity took known symbols and gave them a totally different meaning.

"This expropriation of symbols continues to this day, and can take various forms," he continues. "At the road to Auschwitz, where most of the people murdered were Jews, nobody can miss the seven-and-a-half meter high cross. I have been told that there is a cross on the building of the *Kommandatur* at Birkenau, where all those killed were Jews. At Sobibor, where also only Jews were murdered, there is a church. In Dachau and Majdanek, where people from many religions died, the only place of prayer is a Catholic church. Why should one religion have the monopoly on remembrance?

"On the other hand, there are positive developments," Minerbi says. "The Jews can consider the fact that the nuns finally left the Carmelite convent at Auschwitz a success. This is particularly important in light of the anti-Semitic statements made by Cardinal Glemp of Warsaw. But nobody should be surprised that it has taken the Polish Church 25 years to translate *Nostra Aetate* into Polish."

Alas, despite the achievement, Minerbi points out that the nuns' departure took much more time than the written agreement called for. "They moved only because the Pope wrote to them and invited them to leave," he notes. "They are no longer within the perimeter of the historical site of Auschwitz, which the Polish government has agreed should not be touched."

Against this mixed bag of achievements and setbacks, Minerbi's criticism continues. The Jewish agreement to a compromise may have made the situation worse, he says. The nuns moved a few hundred meters away from the death camp itself. Instead of a closed convent where they sat inside and could not speak with anybody, he says there is now a Christian propaganda center at Auschwitz.

"It is called an interreligious center, but it is a highly Catholic institution," he says. "The difference with the previous convent is that the new one is much bigger, much more impressive and has much greater means at its disposal. Whoever visits Auschwitz is attracted to visit this center as well. Thus, in spite of the fact that the move is an achievement, I do not think that we have solved the problem."

History, Minerbi says, has been rewritten by the Church, but a larger issue overshadows this. "The real issue is that the Church still considers itself the true Israel," he says. "Another example of the Christianizing of themes is the Pope's speech at his Auschwitz visit. He stood before the inscription in Polish and spoke about remembering the six million Poles who perished. The number six million rings a bell. It is another Jewish symbol expropriated."

For all the importance of the Pope's visit to Auschwitz, Minerbi can't help but feel that the message of reconciliation was lost in the blurring of the Jewishness of the tragedy. During his entire visit, John Paul II did not mention the word "Jew" once. Minerbi notes that even when he stood before the Hebrew inscription there, he referred only to "the sons of Abraham."

"I guess that he meant to say that in Abraham we are all related," Minerbi says. "If we go back to Abraham, Jews and Christians are at the same level of heritage."

"When he visited Jerusalem, New York Cardinal O'Connor stated that the Jews have made a great gift to humanity through the Shoah," Minerbi says. "The Pope said in Mauthausen that the Jews in World War Two are like the grain which has to fall to earth in order to give life to a greater plant.

"That almost means that God did a bookkeeping exercise and when the sins were too great, the Shoah came. I am not willing to give legitimation to the Nazis as if they were the executive arm of God. Cardinal O'Connor thought he had said something good, but I am opposed to the idea that we have to give something to the world through our suffering. I prefer to make other gifts.

"Following a strange request of American Jews, the Pope is preparing an encyclic on the Shoah," Minerbi says. "This will force him to write all that separates us and all that unifies us. We can only hope that he won't do it. Otherwise, we will be helping to consolidate the extreme differences between us and the Catholic Church on the Shoah."

Minerbi maintains that any progress in improving Vatican Jewish relations has happened only because of the existence of the State of Israel. Catholicism has been forced to face the reality of Israel's existence, which makes it reconsider its premise that the Jews are punished and have to wander around the world forever because they did not recognize Jesus.

For instance, he says that John Paul II is the first Pope to mention the State of Israel by name. He points to the Vatican's Commission of Peace and Justice, which has called for eradicating anti-Semitism as well as antizionism, which it says is sometimes a form of anti-Semitism. These developments warrant guarded optimism on the part of Jews and Israelis.

It should come as no surprise that Minerbi is sceptical about the Jewish-Christian dialogue. "If we ever get to a discussion on the core of the problems with the Catholic Church, there is a border which they cannot cross," he warns. "We will get to a point where the Church will have to say that it defines itself as the Verus Israel. The problem is that they claim that the only true religion is theirs."

Minerbi states that Catholicism has other fundamental aims which Jewish leaders do not notice. "The Pope wants the unification of Europe to be done under the sign of the cross. He said this clearly a number of years ago at Santiago de Compostella, Spain. That is, not accidentally, the place where the reconquista of Spain and the Inquisition began. He returned to the same theme in Prague in 1990."

Minerbi says the Church bases its dream of a Christian Union of Eastern and Western Europe partly on the role so many Christian and Catholic politicians have played in promoting the EEC. Names such as de Gasperi, Adenauer, de Gaulle and Robert Schuman come to mind. The Church has started beatification procedures for Schuman, and claims that the only period in which Europe was united was under the Church in the times of the Holy Roman Empire in the Middle Ages.

"European Jews should feel some unease with this approach," Minerbi says. "I do not say that this European concept of the Catholic Church is a central one and has major influence. I think, however, that the idea of a Christian Europe puts the Jews aside, and we should not remain quiet."

The Church has had to overcome deep-rooted prejudices and long-held opinions about the Jews, Minerbi notes. In view of all these factors, he still expresses satisfaction at the progress that has been made.

In order to develop another perspective on Catholic-Jewish relations, Minerbi compares the Pope's attitude toward Islam with that toward the Jews. Christianity has a major pragmatic problem with Islam, which is growing quickly worldwide. Soon there will be three Moslems for every two Catholics in the world. There is a struggle between the two religions along the whole Atlantic Coast of Africa.

"Entire tribes descend from the Sahel to the coast in search of something to eat," Minerbi says. "They do not find any framework willing to deal with them except for the mosques. The Church is confronted with increasing conversions to Islam. It is powerless to do anything. Only in the last 50 years has it started to appoint African cardinals. Before that, the Church was identified with the white colonialists, and Islam was black. The nature of this old conflict is changing only very slowly.

"Despite Islam's successful competition, the Catholic Church views Moslems with much more tolerance and sympathy than the Jews," he says, noting that the Church has no major theological problem with Islam. Islam was founded after Christianity, and it recognizes Jesus as one of the prophets. The Christians do not claim to be true Islam, and Islam does not claim to be true Christianity.

The Church did not protest when the cathedral in Algiers became a mosque after Algeria gained independence. Likewise in Tunisia. Minerbi notes that the current Pope is very friendly to Islam, even to cruel anti-Western dictatorships such as those in Iraq and Sudan.

"The synod of Mid Eastern bishops, which came together in Rome in March 1991—after the Gulf War—lauded Saddam Hussein," Minerbi says flatly. "It linked the issue of the Palestinians with that of the Iraqi invasion of Kuwait. Before the Gulf War, the Pope condemned all use of force and spoke out against the war the United States had decided to wage. This is another expression of his anti-American attitude."

Turning to the issue of emerging ties between Israel and the Vatican, Minerbi says, "Israeli sources have been overly optimistic about the rapid establishment of diplomatic relations between the Vatican and Israel. I never believed these optimistic predictions.

"In July 1992, the Vatican and Israel created a permanent bilateral committee," he notes. "If it is 'permanent,' then it can work for a week or for 2,000 years. The move was necessary for the Vatican, in order to remain close to the Mideast peace process. In its July 1992 communique, the Vatican said it had decided to establish this committee with Israel because the Arabs also had started discussions with Israel. In this way, the Vatican struck Israel and pandered to the Arabs by saying that it did not do more than the Arabs do.

"This committee is supposed to identify the problems between the parties and determine how to deal with them," Minerbi explains. "Israel has agreed to a process that first clarifies all the claims which the Vatican has against it and only then will explore the possibility of diplomatic relations. Normally, there is no link between whether you agree or disagree with the policy of a certain government and the establishment of diplomatic relations with it.

"We should have said, 'Let us first establish diplomatic relations and then we will see what problems we have.' The current approach gives the Vatican a major instrument to raise the price, as the number of potential problems is unlimited."

As if to prove that his analysis is correct, Minerbi mentions that in December 1992, Cardinal Sodano, who is the Vatican's Secretary of State, a position similar to that of a Prime Minister, told the Italian daily *La Stampa* that the Israelis were preventing the establishment of diplomatic relations with the Vatican. He cited Israel's unwillingness to solve the problems of the Palestinians, Jerusalem, and the Church in Israel and the territories as the "barriers" to relations Israel has erected.

"If you have to solve two giant problems first, they can draw out the diplomatic relations issue at least until after a final agreement between Israel and the Palestinians has been achieved," Minerbi says. "The Vatican wants to be both inside and outside. As a matter of fact, after Israel and the PLO signed the agreement of principles in September 1993, there were rumors in the press that the Vatican would establish diplomatic relations with Israel shortly.

"Surprisingly, Israel has few claims against the Vatican. In order to have some symmetry, Israel asks the Church to fight anti-Semitism. The Church has already issued a decree labelling anti-Semitism a sin. A Christian who is an anti-Semite commits a sin against his Church, so Israel's sole demand from the Vatican is somewhat superfluous.

"Other things not mentioned are much more important. We

should not limit our discussions with the Vatican to political problems. We should deal with spiritual problems as well. We should have said, for instance, that we would appreciate it very much if the Church would not declare Spanish Queen Isabella, who drove the Jews out of Spain, to be holy.

"There are other issues. We should have asked them to check what is written in Catholic seminary texts on the Jewish people and Jewish history. There are many more issues which we should not leave to Diaspora Jews. Israel is the representative of millions of Jews who have the only Jewish government."

While progress has been made, Minerbi says much remains to be done. "There has been no progress on the question of Jerusalem," he says. "The Catholic Church still wants a special internationally guaranteed status for Jerusalem. It refers to the rights of the three monotheistic religions. Who has authorized them to speak on behalf of others?" For the time being, he notes that the question of Jerusalem has been left out of negotiations, but it is a central question for the Holy See, and it will be raised later.

Despite the difficulties, Minerbi remains convinced that good relations with the Vatican are of great importance to Israel. The Church has 800 million followers worldwide, and it has significant influence on European culture and politics.

He notes that the Holy See was preparing for diplomatic relations with Israel for a long time.

"On January 25, 1991, during the Gulf War, the Vatican's spokesman published a five page communique about relations with the State of Israel," Minerbi says. "It was one of the longest I have ever seen on a political subject. It explains that the Holy See—a more accurate expression than the Vatican—recognizes Israel fully but does not have normal diplomatic relations with it. It is almost a Talmudic pilpul reasoning, because if you have recognition, why not draw the full consequences?

"To prove that the Holy See recognizes Israel, the communique lists Israeli prime ministers who have been received by the Pope," Minerbi continues. "The reasons stated for the absence of full diplomatic relations are juridical and not theological in nature. This is important because the latter could pose eternal obstacles."

Minerbi lists some of the juridical reasons. "They note that the State of Israel does not yet have internationally recognized borders, Jerusalem has been annexed without international approval, and the situation of the Catholic Church in the territories and Israel is unclear. The latter argument, that something is wrong here, is a new one and a step backward.

"We have to doubt some of the other arguments as well," he says. "The Vatican was the first country to recognize Croatia. It even preceded the EEC, which was under great German pressure. Croatia was recognized in spite of the fact that it does not have recognized borders. The clear impression is that Croatia was recognized because it is Catholic.

"The Pope did not care that the Croatian leaders were the successors of the Ustasha of Ante Pavelic from World War Two, and that the present president of Croatia writes anti-Semitic books," Minerbi says in a sarcastic tone.

"The Catholic Church has a lot of concern about Catholics in the Arab countries and wants to have the best possible relations with Islam," he concludes. "The Church plays up the argument that these small Christian communities in Arab lands could be held hostage because of the Vatican's policy."

As the conversation draws to a close, Minerbi is asked to comment on the December 1993 agreement between the Holy See and Israel. He says it is yet another hesitant step in a long, hesitant process. "This long process is due not only to the Vatican's wish to be prudent," he says, "but probably to their decision to act in tandem with the peace process between Israel and its Arab neighbors."

DANIEL ELAZAR

The Future of
Israel-Diaspora Relations

W IDE-RANGING CHANGES in the global Jewish map and Israel
diaspora relations will take place in the coming two
decades. Early in the next century, Israel will have the
largest Jewish population of any country. Numerical dominance
will further strengthen Israel's undisputed position as the center
of Jewish life.

The role of the United States Jewish community is likely to
decline. This will be due in part to assimilation and intermarriage,
in part to the increased aliya of key members of the community.
Different trends will shape Jewish life in Eastern Europe, where
communal institutions will develop rapidly, especially in the former
Soviet Union.

There are other major forces of change as well, such as modern
technology and communications. In the coming decades, a significant number of a new type of Jews may emerge, those who take a
multicentered approach to life and will be part-time residents of
Israel.

These are among the central developments that Professor Daniel J. Elazar foresees when he looks to the future of Israel-diaspora relations. Elazar, a leading authority on Israel and the world Jewish community, is the founder and president of the Jerusalem Center for Public Affairs, the leading independent think tank devoted to the study of solutions for the fundamental problems facing Israel and the world Jewish community.

Elazar was born in Minneapolis in 1934. He received an M.A. and a Ph.D. in political science from the University of Chicago in 1957 and 1959, respectively. He became a full professor at Philadelphia's Temple University in 1967. He has held the Senator N. M. Paterson Professorship in Intergovernmental Relations at Bar-Ilan University since 1973, and is director of the Center for the Study of Federalism at Temple University.

He has held numerous positions in Israel and abroad, including the presidency of such bodies as the American Sephardi Federation, the International Association of Centers for Federal Studies, and the Israel Political Science Association. In 1986, President Ronald Reagan appointed him to serve as a citizen member of the U.S. Advisory Council on Intergovernmental Relations, the major government agency dealing with questions related to federalism.

He has authored or edited more than 50 books, including *Community and Polity*, which is considered a leading study of the American Jewish community. He is editor of the *Jerusalem Letter/Viewpoints* and the *Jewish Political Studies Review*. He and his family live in Jerusalem.

Before setting forth his vision of the future, Elazar sets the framework for the discussion based on milestones in the relationship between Israel and the diaspora. "Most of those who have analyzed the developments of the last ten years have come to the conclusion," he says, "that from the Lebanon War in 1982 until the Gulf War in 1991, there was a period of general erosion of diaspora sympathy for Israeli policies as well as of concern for Israel."

There was growing embarrassment among diaspora Jews at having to confront the media's reporting on Israel, he notes. Even if they knew that it wasn't all that accurate, they still were embarrassed by what was being presented to the non-Jewish world—"the world in which they live," as he terms it.

While the discomfort was widespread, the responses to it were as varied as the Jewish community itself. Elazar explains that some Jewish leaders vocally distanced themselves from the Israeli government's policies. Others reduced the amount of attention they paid to Israel, by getting involved in their own communities if they were interested or committed Jews. Others focused on different issues, and simply ignored Jewish issues altogether.

"I saw this on many occasions," Elazar says. "At one time, people would ask me, 'What's happening in Israel?, What's new?' During the period from 1982 to the summer of 1990, people assiduously avoided asking me about Israel, including some people for whom Israel had always been important in their lives.

"The Gulf War shifted Jewish attitudes toward a more positive view of Israel and a more hawkish view of the Arabs," Elazar says. While that was a good development, he was not thrilled by the main force behind this shift. "Israel behaved in the eyes of the Christian world the way they like Jews to behave. We were endangered," he says. "In the face of the blows against us, we were willing to turn the other cheek. The nations of the world that come out of a Christian heritage applauded Israel."

The Jews living in those nations were happy once again. Not only had Israel behaved well in the eyes of their neighbors, but many of the things that the hardliners in Israel's government had been saying suddenly took on a certain justification in the eyes of diaspora Jews. Maybe Prime Minister Shamir was not so wrong when he said that the Palestinians were not exactly to be trusted.

"Since then, there is every indication that the change of government in Israel has put many American Jews at greater ease," he says. "Policies are more in line with what they perceive that enlightened people in the West want. Unfortunately this may entail elements that are not necessarily good for Israel."

Then, in September 1993, from all appearances out of the blue, came the Israel-PLO agreement. American Jewry, like all of their brethren everywhere, were surprised and at first shocked. Then they lined up behind it, despite varying degrees of misgivings, responding to that very Jewish hope for peace that springs eternal in the Jewish heart.

Diaspora Jews also liked the apparent turnabout in world media coverage of Israel. In a moment—and perhaps just for the moment— Israel became very much of a "good guy," because it was willing to take risks for peace. However, taking too flexible a line in negotiations may make bargaining more difficult, Elazar says. Being too nice today for a short time may mean having to suffer for many years.

Elazar maintains that the West is more willing to take big risks for Israel than Israel can take for itself. "I am disgusted with diaspora Jews who are willing to defend Israel till the last drop of Israeli blood, and equally disgusted with those Jews who are willing to take inordinate risks for Israel's peace," he says.

Taking a moment to define terms, Elazar stresses that the diaspora is anything but a single, united front. "For these purposes, we have to talk about at least three distinct groupings," he says. "North America, Eastern Europe and the former Soviet republics, and the rest of the world, which means Western Europe and Latin America, as well as Australia and South Africa."

Turning to the question of future relations between Israel and the diaspora, Elazar stresses that each of these three realms must be considered on its own. "In Eastern Europe," he says, "We are speaking about a community estimated at between one million and two million people. Many are streaming out, most to Israel for reasons that are also affecting Israel-diaspora relations. In fact, neither diaspora Jews nor the countries they live in, no matter how enlightened they are, want more than a token number of those Jews who want to get out of what was the communist bloc.

"The Jewish communities can't afford to take them, and their countries don't want to take them," he says matter-of-factly. He adds that those East European Jews who emigrate to the U.S.—or to Germany, with its much smaller Jewish population—will not have significant impact on the communities there, because they are assimilated and not very Jewishly motivated.

Although he terms the U.S. "perhaps the most generous country in many respects," Elazar notes that its government quickly found ways to go along with Israel's urging that all such emigrants should go to Israel. All it took was the realization that hundreds of thousands of Soviet Jews wanted to get into the U.S.

"Many Jews in the USSR want to come to Israel," Elazar says. "They want to be in an environment where they are a majority. That is classic Zionism, without these people even knowing what classic Zionism is."

Despite the large numbers of Jews who have left the former republics, Elazar is realistic about the fact that many will stay there. "Unless there is a huge change in regime or in policies, the explosion in Jewish organizations and activities is irreversible," he says. Even if a big number of Jews leave the former Soviet Union, he estimates that at least one million will remain there. "They have organized themselves and will strengthen their communities from coast to coast, from the Baltic Sea to the North Pacific."

Elazar terms the ex-Soviet diaspora "an Israeli protectorate, or perhaps somewhat of a joint protectorate of Israel and American Jewry. The Jews in other communities outside the United States are not protectorates, but orbit around Israel, in their mindset in any case."

Turning to Western Europe, he notes that the most authoritative estimates put the number of Jews there at 1.2 million. He says that their host countries are coming together in various unions centered around the EEC, but the Jews remain separate national communities with only the least amount of unity across borders.

The two largest Western European Jewish communities are the French and the British, neither of which are noted for intercommunity cooperation, Elazar stresses. "European Jews have to start working together more between themselves. Moreover, European Jewry is rapidly assimilating, but it is quiet because, unlike the Americans, European Jews do not make much of a fuss about it."

He adds that, contrary to conventional wisdom, assimilation poses a threat to Jewish continuity in Latin America as well. Elazar says that we thought for a long time that Latin American Jews were immune to assimilation because of the gap between the 80 percent of Jews who came from Eastern Europe and the local population. By the third and fourth generation, however, that gap has disappeared, and the rate of assimilation is extremely high. Much the same is true in Australia, and a little less in South Africa.

After working his way around the periphery of the diaspora, Elazar focuses on the American Jewish community. He terms the US "the former bastion of hopes for the diaspora as an independent force." He recalls that it was the one community that could or would present a rival claim to Israel. American Jewry refused to accept the Zionist claim that Israel was the only center for the Jewish people. It talked about at least two centers.

"Only American Jewry could make a case for being a self sufficient, vibrant Jewish community," he says, noting that out of a population of some six million Jews, several hundred thousand were active in communal life.

Their case was well-made, and it was backed by empirical evidence. Elazar claims that it is no accident, for example, that many of the very best scholars in Jewish studies, including those in Israel, are

American Jews. They were born, raised and trained in the U.S. When the universities of Israel sought to hire the finest Jewish scholars, they found those people willing to come on aliya. Elazar, who happens to be in this category, stresses that, "they brought with them a breadth of spirit, understanding and knowledge, in many cases superior to anything done in Israel."

Elazar does not belittle the case that was built by American Jewish leaders. In his view, American Jewish leaders now realize and admit publicly that their community needs Israel, as they provide education through the Israel experience.

Elazar says that Israeli universities distinguish themselves in Jewish studies by having somebody to teach every period in Jewish history. "Even the best theological seminary or university in the United States may have three or four professors in Jewish history, but can't really cover in depth the range of 3,000 or 4,000 years of history," he says.

"But," he adds, "Israeli historians are taught to concentrate on their period very narrowly. American Jewish historians are not afraid to make broad comparisons, to take a larger sweep and to use newer methodologies to expand the historical analysis. The American Jewish community has a creative spark to it that frequently is missing in Israel, which tends to be a very conservative country."

Elazar is quick to point out that the creativity in the American Jewish community is not confined to the scholars. In the arts and other creative fields, the United States has a kind of culture that offers a flexibility and openness that allows all sorts of experimentation.

"There is a certain amount of exciting success in many places, not only in major centers." he says. "In rural New England, for example, Jews of the 1960s generation who settled in small towns have created an Association of New England Jewish Communities. They hold an annual conference retreat, they publish a lovely little newspaper and they have other activities."

"It's not unusual to find synagogues in many Colorado ski resorts," he continues. "They are called Bnei Evergreen, or Bnei Aspen or Bnei Vail. They identify with the place rather than choosing traditional congregation names. They have large services during ski season, when Jewish tourists reach out to one another on Friday nights."

Elazar points to modern Orthodoxy as another sphere in which American Jews have proven far more innovative than their Israeli peers: "There are women who create women's minyanim," he says. "There are people who try to find ways to accommodate new ideas in the realm of halacha, for good or for ill, but it's vibrant."

According to Elazar, the self-confidence of the American Jewish community rose to a peak in the last decade. Charles Silberman wrote a book, *A Certain People*, about American Jewry in which he launched an optimistic school of Jewish sociology.

Calvin Goldscheider, from Brown University, and Steven M. Cohen, formerly from Queens College in New York (who made aliya in 1992) and several others, took an optimistic view in spite of the huge diminution of Jewish knowledge, a diminution of Jewish observance even beyond that and a rising rate of intermarriage, Elazar says. They claimed that because Jews represented a certain stratum in society, associated with each other and were very creative, the creative elements would counterbalance the negative demographic ones.

"Many of us disagreed, but we were labelled Israeli pessimists," says Elazar. The 1990 nationwide demographic study commissioned by the Council of Jewish Federations confirmed the pessimists' fears; it showed that American Jewry is rapidly declining in numbers.

The study found that of a total of 6.8 million born Jews and converts to Judaism, 1.3 million are essentially practicing another religion, i.e., Christianity, due to formal or nonformal conversion or being raised in mixed marriages. And it gets worse. Another 1.2

million claim to be ethnic Jews only and are assimilating rapidly. According to Elazar, the American Jewish community is about to have a major crisis of confidence as its numbers are eroded.

This brings him to the conclusion that in ten or 20 years, Israel will be the largest Jewish community in the world. From there, he extrapolates that many more of those who are seriously Jewish in the United States will make aliya, reasoning along the following lines:

"As long as we thought we could live as good a Jewish life as in Israel, we preferred the comforts of America, but now that the chance that our kids will marry Jews is declining rapidly, we had better go to Israel."

Elazar forecasts that the numbers of American Jews making aliya will be twice or three times the current level, bringing a return to the figures of the 1970s, before they dropped to virtually nothing in the years after the 1982 Lebanon war. He predicts that this process will weaken the creativity and productivity of the American Jewish community. "These American olim will bring some of their vibrancy to Israel, as their impact has always been big relative to their numbers."

Partly as a result of American aliya, but also for other reasons, American Jewish issues will become worldwide Jewish issues. One example: Who is a Jew, once strictly an American problem, is now an Israeli problem as well, because of the influx of Soviet Jews.

The failure of secularization to ensure Jewish survival is now an American Jewish issue. Elazar believes it will become an Israeli issue as well: "We see the problems of secularization even with regard to the children of the kibbutz, so many of whom not only leave the kibbutz but leave the country or marry out."

Another important development on the horizon involves a decline in the dependence on American Jews for support of Israel and Israeli institutions. As a percentage of Israeli GNP, it already is small, though it remains important in certain fields.

His views are based on the assessment that if the most committed American Jews come to Israel, they will not be in the U.S. to give while those who stay in the U.S. and assimilate will stop giving to Jewish causes. Already, American Jewish giving has plateaued in real terms in the last 20 years.

The American Jewish community will feel this aliya through the loss of its leaders—those who led by giving and those who led by teaching.

He further points to the virtual demise of organized Zionism in the diaspora. The leaders of the American Zionist parties, other than the women's organizations, are in or close to their 80s. Soon, he says, even the fig leaf of organized Zionism will not exist.

Membership in the much larger women's organizations also is declining, due to declining interest in such movements in general. More women are working, and they are too tired to come to meetings at night. New institutions and new ways will have to be developed.

When asked to be more specific on these organizational changes, Elazar points to the experience with Project Renewal, in which American communities were twinned directly with Israeli communities, as an example for possible developments in the future.

"Project Renewal would have been a disaster, except for the fact that ways and means were developed for the diaspora communities to find out what the people in the neighborhoods really wanted, and to pressure the Israeli government on their behalf," he says. "People want to get away from overall, unidentified giving. They want to move to direct contact with Israel."

He continues: "They will find continuously that it is not so easy not to get taken in through the framework of direct contact. A lot of diaspora Jews who may be very intelligent are unsophisticated in this particular field. They can be taken in by attractive Israeli personalities. When they turn around, they may find they have not gotten exactly what they expected."

He elaborates on this issue to show that American Jewish influence on Israel is and will remain much more limited than many people think. "Americans who give a lot of money have certain esthetic preferences. For example, certain Israelis promise that some things can be achieved, in the name of improvement of democracy, American-style electoral reform, such as separation of religion and state and American-style pluralism. Most of this is not deliverable in Israel."

Elazar maintains that the limits to American Jewish influence on Israel stem from the fact that Israel faces a different situation, a different environment and different politics than the United States. The Americans who give money to make Israel a little U.S. are going to be disillusioned sooner or later, he says, like those who have invested in Israel unprepared for the business climate and have failed. "Some investment in Israel works well, if one knows the territory." he adds.

Elazar forecasts that this will lead to one of the two following alternatives: "Either people will stop giving, or they may say, 'Let us get together with others and hire expert representatives.' This is called federated giving, and it is a return to the federated community giving introduced in the U.S. 100 years ago. By the end of this decade, we will reach a judicious mix of hands-on giving and federated giving."

Elazar's vision of future Israel-diaspora relations can be summed up by stating that Israel will become much more powerful and much less dependent on American Jewry.

There is one other major development, seldom mentioned, which Elazar considers crucial for future relations between Israel and the diaspora. It derives from the impact of modern technology and communications on these relations.

Looking at transportation, Elazar says, "Even now, Israeli yordim in the United States fill the El Al planes before the holidays. Some of them come here several times per year.

"We may have a couple hundred thousand diaspora Jews and yordim who come to Israel a number of times a year," he says. "This will create a different constituency of Jews abroad. These are Jews who take a multicentered approach to life. They are part-time residents of Israel, and will obviously be people who have more money than less. Their relative importance as opinion leaders is greater rather than less. The same goes for their capability to support Jewish programs in Israel and the world."

He foresees a new trend: Many diaspora families may settle in Israel and let the breadwinner commute. There will be closer interpersonal communication, by fax and viewphone. This will also involve many non-Jews, because the families in the diaspora will include non-Jews in close relationships.

"This is already the case with Americans," he says. "It should become even more so with Europeans, who may have less of a tie with their country than Americans and are closer to Israel geographically." Increased unrest in Europe, especially if race riots were to become a regular phenomenon, will focus more of the attention of European Jews on Israel.

While all the forces are very different, Elazar maintains that they work in the same direction.

Lastly, Elazar sees great potential for change in the spiritual realm. Contrary to what some "progressive" politicians pretend, normalcy for the Jews in their own land is not becoming like all other people. "Normalcy for Jews is that we divide into three camps, and these interact," Elazar says.

During the Second Temple period, he recalls, there were indeed three such Jewish camps. The Pharisees wished to respond directly to God's commandments for their own sake. The Sadducees were interested primarily in the two major "institutions of reality," the state and the temple. The Essenes sought a collective holy community. Of these, only the Pharisees developed a system which was eminently portable. That is exactly what the Jews in the diaspora needed. Within a couple of centuries, they became the only Jewish camp.

Elazar foresees another spiritual confrontation between the existing neo-Pharisean halachic Jewry and what he calls neo-Sadducean Jewry, who define their Jewish identity mainly in terms of the existence of Israel.

"From the beginning of Zionist settlement, a need was felt for the spiritual dimension of this neo-Sadducean Judaism," Elazar says. "Its first start went down a false path, that of socialist Zionism, which has been a dead end. It also exhausted temporarily the energies of the neo-Sadduceans. A few of them discovered the religious dimension of their identity, mostly as a result of the Six Day War. Most have not, and the further we get from the Six Day War, the less they see it in this neo-Sadducean world.

"Instead of having some kind of authentic spiritual movement developing out of neo-Sadducean ranks, some hope that foreign imports like Reform and Conservative ideas will speak to the non-religious Israelis," he continues. "They will not, because they are not authentic and have not grown up from within Israel.

"The kibbutzim essentially created the same kind of Essean holy community in a secularized context which is still very religious in a Marxist or Tolstoyan sense," he says, completing the picture. "So we now have normalcy."

Elazar sees neo-Sadduceanism spreading to the diaspora too. "The American Jewish leadership, for example, can relate to a state they do not live in but which they see as the center of their existence. They have a calendar with raising money and participating in missions and doing all of these things, which are kind of Israel-centered in a Sadducean way."

Elazar concludes: "The amazing thing is that in the spiritually rich Jewish people there is not yet an indigenous Jewish movement that is neo-Sadducean. Instead, the debate is still stuck in 1890.

The village atheist is still arguing with the haredi. So until the neo-Sadducees restore enough energy to begin looking down a better path, we are stuck.

"I have to assume that it will come in the future, and then multi-camp Judaism in Israel will increase," he says. "This will also have a major impact on relations with the diaspora, although it is unclear what form this will take."

DAVID BAR-ILLAN

The Loaded Dice of the Foreign Media Are There to Stay

I N ADDITION TO HIS LENGTHY NEWSPAPER CAREER, DAVID BAR-ILLAN, the executive editor of *The Jerusalem Post*, is an international concert pianist and a recipient of the Liberty Medal of the City of New York for cultural contributions to America.

His articles have appeared in many publications in the United States and Israel. In 1985–1986, he hosted the weekly public affairs program "International Dateline" on American cable television.

Bar-Illan has been examining the foreign media's coverage of Israel from up-close for years. His popular weekly column on the subject in *The Jerusalem Post* yielded a book, *Eye on the Media*, consisting of selected columns, published in 1993. Bar-Illan is convinced that, despite Israel's massive concessions in its agreement with the PLO, the strong anti-Israel bias of most major print and electronic media will not disappear in the future.

He disagrees with the commonly held view that the world media are motivated by anti-Semitism, but he isn't quick to accept the oft-repeated explanation that Israel is expected to live up to higher standards, either. This, he insists, is nothing more than a trap from which Israel has no chance of escaping unscathed.

Despite the deepset biases, Bar-Illan says there may be a temporary lull in misreporting about Israel.

"There is likely to be a period in which some of the media, which deep down are concerned about the fate of Israel, will be more favorable in their reporting," he says, adding, "I do not expect that period to last very long. We have to keep in mind that the initial agreement signed in September 1993 is not the final one. The most tricky issues remain to be negotiated.

"What is happening now is an interim step," he notes. "The Arabs have made it very clear that there will be much bigger demands on Israel in the future. We will see this when the arguing about Jerusalem starts, and when the actual authority of the Palestinians in what is now known as the administered territories has to be defined."

Bar-Illan doubts that the world media will laud Israel for its bold steps. Rather than saying, "The Israelis have made concessions which nobody expected them to make; now it is the Arabs' turn to compromise on a few points," he predicts that most of the players will go right on doing what they have done until now: picking on Israel and urging it to make more concessions.

And when that doesn't happen, Bar-Illan expects the foreign media to attack Israel for not yielding further to the Arabs.

Israel has cornered itself in a very weak negotiating position, Bar-Illan says. "Once you establish peace as the ultimate goal, there is absolutely nothing which the other side cannot demand in its name," he says.

"Why should some old stones in the Old City Of Jerusalem be more important than the mountains of Judea and Samaria?" he asks rhetorically. "If you want to make peace and the only way to do so is to give up these mountains, then you'll give them up, as well as everything else." The implication is clear: once you've given up the mountains, what possible reason could remain to hold onto the "old stones"?

This approach may ultimately lead to what Bar-Illan terms "the peace of the grave." The other arguments used to pressure Israel into making concessions are equally chilling. For instance, Israel should make peace now because it is strong. "The result," Bar-Illan says, "is that we make ourselves weak by making peace after which we will not have peace at all. That is obviously very silly logic.

"If one can have peace by not having a country, then why not give it up?" he asks, bringing the situation to its extreme. "The Arabs offered us citizenship in a Palestinian country long ago.

"If one chooses to believe that by signing a piece of paper and by saying one will achieve peace instead of looking at facts on the ground, one will not get anywhere except into trouble, like many countries have before," Bar-Illan warns.

These prevailing views create an *a priori* difficult situation for Israel as far as its image in the media is concerned. When Israel is lauded for concessions, and when the majority of media outlets espouse views that may not truly be in Israel's best interests, he asks, what other outcome could anyone expect?

Against this background, Bar-Illan develops the multiple arguments on which his forecast about the future attitude of the media toward Israel is based.

"The assumption of most foreign media is that the Palestinian cause is a just one," he says. "Here is a people seeking liberty, freedom, self-determination, which is as good as motherhood. Israel should give it to them. If it does not, it is in the wrong."

But Bar-Illan says that this reason is not what truly motivates the media. "If it were, we would see the same clamor for the Basques, Corsicans, Bosnians or even Serbs in Bosnia. There are hundreds, if not thousands, of such causes. There are so many ethnic groups fighting for self-determination that if the media had wanted them to be treated like the Palestinians, the world would be totally fragmented.

"The true reason that the Israeli-Palestinian conflict is much more in the news lies in the complete disproportion between the two sides. On the other side, there are not only the Palestinians but all the Arabs," he says. "Their 22 states wield vast power and have major resources. They provide a big market for the West and are thus a strong force in world politics. If they did not back the Palestinian cause, people would care about it exactly like they do about the Basques in Spain, which is not at all."

He cites the late Billy Carter, brother of the former U.S. president, who put it bluntly: "There is a hell of a lot more Arabs than there is Jews." Bar-Illan puts it more eloquently: "The general mood in the West is that it cannot ignore what the Arabs want. Billy Carter was right as far as the figures are concerned. There are 120 million Arabs and four million Jews in the region. If you look around the world, you can add another billion Arabs and Moslems, but not even ten million more Jews. No matter how much immigration Israel has, these facts of life will never change."

Bar-Illan doesn't believe the anti-Israel bias began with the Western media. "I do not think it has anything to do with a paper's dependence on Arab money," he says. A general atmosphere and attitude toward a problem is created by governments. Western governments treat the Israeli-Palestinian issue completely differently from the way they treat any other self-determination issue for the reasons that I have recounted.

"The media are influenced by that. The press can claim that they are very independent, but once it becomes fashionable to think about the relationship between the Palestinians and Israel in a David-and-Goliath context, almost everybody follows the trend. The general mood thus created is an anti-Israeli mood."

But there's more to it than that, Bar-Illan notes. "We are Jews, and Israel is a Jewish state. There is something very newsworthy about Jews doing the kind of things we are doing.

"The fact is that Jews are doing things which they were not supposed to do, according to the stereotype, like shooting at demonstrators or chasing terrorists. Charles Krauthammer, a columnist for *Time* and *The Washington Post* who is a rare exception to the main trend, puts it succinctly: 'Jews is news.'

"This is a very charitable interpretation. One could assume that there is also an undercurrent of anti-Semitism in the media. I do not say that, because I believe that there are many other reasons for their attitude toward Israel. There is also an undercurrent holding Israel to what is called a higher standard. This means nothing but a double standard.

"I do not expect the media to hold us to the same kind of standards they apply to dictatorial states around us, like Syria, Egypt or Jordan," Bar-Illan stresses. "I do expect them to treat us the way other democracies are treated, but that is not the case.

"Once somebody else is in a state of war, many actions are understood and forgiven," he says. "Again, there is a double standard applied here. Everybody is talking about the transfer of populations in Yugoslavia without batting an eyelash. Even if Israelis wanted such a transfer today, it would not be possible."

This double standard has a deep impact on the media. Bar Illan says, "I have found it almost impossible to talk to foreign media about the justice of the Israeli cause. The conditioning of the media is more powerful than anything we can do. That is what I mean by the preference for the Palestinian cause; the mood in the West is very concerned about the Arab market.

"Israel's public relations effort is very bad, but I do not know whether a better one would affect the media the way we think it might. If we convince every single person in the media that we are the underdogs and the Arabs are the Goliaths, it will not make the slightest difference, because they want to believe that we are in the wrong. The underdog-overdog issue is just an excuse; the facts of life do not matter here.

"When the United States had to quell riots in Los Angeles in 1992, it took 55 dead in one day and that was it," he says. "Most were killed by the police." He doesn't even state the comparison. It is clear.

"A similar approach was taken in Somalia. The United Nations Army is supposed to be super-careful. They are not fighting for their land or protecting their homes. They are there to bring peace, yet when they are confronted with a demonstration in which women and children throw stones they shoot and kill. That has happened over and over again, and it is accepted. Such accidents happen throughout the world and nobody pays attention.

"If we had done what the United States did in Los Angeles or what the United Nations did in Somalia, it would have been a scandal forever," Bar-Illan says. "We would have been reminded of it over and over again."

He maintains that Israel takes great care in its approach because it fears world opinion. "The intifada began at the same time in Jordan as it did in the territories administered by Israel," he says. "The Jordanian police killed 12 people. Since then, there has not been a real disturbance in Jordan. Their system is really a life saver, except that Israel cannot apply it. We are constrained by democratic laws, and on top of that we worry about our image.

"Our judgment was wrong in assuming that if we behave nicely, people will like us," he says. "It does not work that way. In the end, you kill more people by being nice. The Israeli army has killed close to 1,000 Arabs in five-and-a-half years of the intifada.

"This is about the same number as that of Arabs killed by other Arabs during the intifada," he adds. "But that doesn't make any difference, because nobody in the world cares about those Arabs. When one speaks about the intifada death score, one only talks about people killed by Israel. In retrospect, it would have been much better had we used a much tougher method at the very beginning, and finished it right there and then."

Israel made other mistakes, according to Bar-lllan. "Allowing television cameras into areas of intifada disturbances was like waving a red rag in front of a bull. I believe that cameras are not part and parcel of the free press by some kind of law. You could have limited access to newspapermen without cameras.

"The cameras are what made the riots pay," he says. "They made the rioters believe that they could get to the world's consciousness. Later, the foreign networks supplied video cameras to citizens in the territories. This is not only wrong; it is professionally unethical.

"I used to say that the media are much less relevant than they think they are," he notes. "The media seem to think that they are God, or at least the most important estate in our life. Now that I have investigated the media for such a long time I tend to believe that we do not feel their impact on a day-to-day basis. Over the years however, they do have an eroding effect.

"The whole concept of the Palestinians being a small people oppressed by huge Israel, when the facts are the opposite, is at least partly, if not greatly, the result of day-to-day reporting by the foreign media.

"Many distortions about Israel have entered encyclopedias, textbooks and maps which must be ascribed to the long haul of year after year of media antagonism to Israel," he explains. "The foreign media have created a certain conventional wisdom which was never there before. The fact is that Israel has been in the media's bad graces more or less since 1967. The cumulative effect is very clear."

Bar-Illan quotes detailed studies which prove this media bias clearly. One study analyzed how much space four major U.S. newspapers devoted to the Sabra and Shatila massacres, in which about 350 people—mostly terrorists or men of fighting age—were killed, and for which Israel had, at most, indirect responsibility.

"The study found that more inches were devoted to this event than to all other worldwide massacres combined during the almost

40 years since World War Two," he says. "Thus, the issue of media bias against Israel is much more than just an impression. There are other studies similar to that one."

Bar-Illan also sees factors in Israel that strengthen the attitude of its external critics. "Nothing makes the conscience of a mediaperson —most of the time I believe that there is such a thing—easier than to be able to say, 'What do you want from me? Read what this or that Israeli writes. He says exactly what I say, if not worse.'

"It is very difficult to tell an NBC correspondent in Israel to be more Zionist than an Israel Television reporter," Bar-Illan notes. "Until *The Jerusalem Post* changed hands in 1989, many of the foreign media would say, 'What do you want from us? *The Jerusalem Post* wrote in exactly the same vein and tone.'

"There was even a journalist from the *Chicago Tribune* who almost got a Pulitzer Prize for a story he copied from *The Jerusalem Post*. He was caught, and deprived of the prize. The fact remains that he felt so close in his attitude to what *The Jerusalem Post* was then writing that he could copy a story, lock, stock and barrel.

"Every country has its ultra-liberals," Bar-Illan says. "The communists used to quote Americans like Ramsey Clark, Angela Davis and Jane Fonda and say that they reflected the real America. Everybody knew that was a joke, because they represented a fraction of a percent of the public.

"The Israeli case is more complex, because ultra-liberals represent a few percent of the population and are very vocal," he allows. "Also, intellectuals comprise a relatively large percentage of the ultra-liberal establishment. These ultra-liberals are already preparing the concept of Jerusalem as a divided city, one half of which will be the capital of lsrael and the other half will be the capital of Palestine."

How much do individual journalists count? Bar-Illan says they do, to some extent. "*The Washington Post* was notoriously anti-Israel for many years. Now it has somebody here who is not pro-Israel but is a very decent correspondent. He is different from his predecessors in that he believes that no matter how he feels about anything he must report the news as fairly as possible.

"The present correspondent of *The New York Times* is also much more professional than his predecessors were. In major newspapers like that, it is possible to find some decent people who believe in the tenets of journalism. They believe the ethics of the profession require them to say there is one side of the story and there is another side of the story.

"If, however, one takes the correspondent of *The Guardian*, an English paper, one hears only one side plus their propaganda. He always reminds one of the saying that no prostitute does anything without the approval of the madam of the brothel. One wonders whether the man was chosen because he was anti-Israel, or if he became anti-Israel because he knew that his bosses would love his work.

"In major newspapers, though a lot of editing is done, stories usually get printed more or less the way they are filed. In television, the anchorman sets the tone. Here one does not know whether the correspondent knows better or not, or just caters to the anchorman's wishes.

"The correspondent can take film for half an hour, but the editor chooses what you see. That is perhaps a minute and a half, which can be very selective and very tendentious.

"The BBC is by far the worst offender when it comes to Israel," Bar-Illan says. "There, everything I said before was extremely charitable. I shall only give one example of its malice. A few years ago a coffeehouse collapsed in Arab East Jerusalem due to structural problems. The most striking thing about it was that Jews and Arabs worked together to save lives.

"Even strong PLO activists like the deputy Mufti of Jerusalem were stunned by that cooperation. The BBC did not say one word about it. They only mentioned that Arabs suffered. They repeated the libel that a bomb had been put in there.

"This was a totally distorted report, leaving out the one phenomenon that should have made news all over the world: the fact that Jews and Arabs worked together to save lives at a time when the intifada was at its height. This is not a politically significant event. From the political sphere, there are hundreds of examples of BBC malice."

Bar-Illan offers another example of malice from a U.S. network. Before the intifada started, a fanatic Moslem killed two Jews who were more than 90 years old while they sat at a bus stop on Jaffa Road in Jerusalem. After stabbing them both to death, he was chased and caught by a crowd. Bar-Illan notes that the terrorist was a huge person with a big knife. The crowd was very brave to chase him. In New York, people would not have done that.

"The Peter Jennings show on ABC starts with a headline and a commercial," Bar-Illan says. The headline that day was that a lynch mob had almost killed an Arab in Jerusalem. Then came the commercial and then you heard the story of what happened. It takes malice to do that. I do not believe it has anything to do with whom you favor in this war between the Davids and the Goliaths."

Is there no way for Israel to get a better image in the foreign media?

"If the Arab purchasing power was not so great, our stereotype might change," Bar-Illan says. "There are, however, mainly bad scenarios of how Israel can get good press: if it looks like we are going to be defeated, or if we are in danger of being attacked in a real war. There is probably enough of a conscience around to worry about us in such a case. The reason I say this is that when we were showered by Scuds, the general attitude among the media was not bad.

"During these attacks, we somehow got back to our former role. We were sitting in sealed rooms like mice, waiting for the bombs to fall. This fits the world's image of Jews precisely.

"If one is very cynical, one could say that the media sympathy may have been because at that point Saddam Hussein was the bad guy. It is very possible that Saddam Hussein was the bad guy not because he attacked Israel, but because he was against the Americans and the other nations of their coalition. I feel, however, that at a moment of truth, if it came to an actual possibility of being endangered, more people in the media would treat us sympathetically.

"Jews are very sympathetic people, as long as they are victims," he repeats. "When they are not victims, they are not. If Katyushas fell on Tel Aviv, there might be a more sympathetic twist to it. At least more sympathetic than when they fall on Kiryat Shemona. That is my feeling, but I am not sure that I am right."

In light of all he has said, does Bar-Illan think that Israel should not have made any concessions to test the peace process?

"I did not say that Israel cannot make concessions," he replies. "Various arrangements can be worked out. I do, however, not believe that having a Palestinian state run by the PLO on the outskirts of Tel Aviv and Jerusalem is the solution Israel should want.

"From the Iranian border to such a state, there may be a large stretch of land controlled by radical Arab states," he explains. "Whether there will be three heads, two heads or one head to that mass of land is not the point. It is a landmass which is likely to be controlled by radical Arabs. I obviously do not believe that the Middle East has changed as much as Foreign Minister Shimon Peres believes it has changed."

But Bar-Illan does not despair of any hope for peace. He sees an optimistic scenario in the long term.

"There is the possibility that the Arab countries will become democratic," he says. "Then, Israel will not have the same image among the Arabs as it has now. Everybody dismisses that as an impossibility now. I think that in ten or 15 years it is a distinct possibility."

It isn't necessarily as much of a pipedream as it may seem at first. After all, Bar-Illan concludes, "In the past, anybody who said that the Soviet empire would become democratic would have been considered mad."

Section Two
Inside

PETER MEDDING

Democracy and Electoral Change

ETER MEDDING's two fields of expertise—political science and contemporary Jewry—give him a good vantage point on many key aspects of Israeli society. His book, *The Founding of Israeli Democracy*, published by the Oxford University Press in 1990, analyzes the values and conflicts which shaped the political character of the state between 1948 and 1967. Current projects include a sequel that will deal with the post-1967 period.

Medding was born in Australia in 1938, and has lived in Jerusalem since 1978. He received his B.A. and M.A. from Melbourne University and his Ph.D. from Harvard, all in political science. He is a professor in the department of political science and the Institute of Contemporary Jewry at the Hebrew University and has held visiting professorships at Brandeis, Harvard, the University of Michigan, the University of Washington and the Ecole des Hautes Etudes en Sciences Sociales in Paris. His other books include *From Assimilation to Group Survival* (1968), *Mapai in Israel* (1972) and *Jews in Australian Society* (1973). One of his current projects has a working title of *The New Politics of American Jews*. Medding has been an editor of the annual *Studies in Contemporary Jewry*, published by the Hebrew University's Institute of Contemporary Jewry, since the inception of the series in 1984.

In a discussion of the quality of Israeli democracy and the country's electoral system, Medding gives the system overall high marks. He says Israeli democracy is encumbered primarily by its own generosity. By allowing so many small parties to gain seats in the Knesset and thereby, under certain conditions, to gain a high degree of veto power over government formation and key decisions, he says, Israeli democracy allows itself to be held ransom to minority interests. The solution: a significant rise in the minimum number of votes required to gain admission to the lawmaking body. This would result in a smaller number of larger parties.

Medding shies away from the notion of total democracy, saying that few experts believe it can exist in reality. Democracy, he says, is rated in accordance with two criteria: who is allowed to participate in elections and be chosen for office; and how free people are to express and promote their views, and to organize around ideas that essentially oppose government policy.

With these two parameters in mind, Medding gives Israel very good marks, indeed. Despite occasional laments by some "experts" that Israeli democracy is endangered, he notes that serious studies of the situation in the country reveal a healthy and vibrant democracy.

"In the early 1970s, Robert Dahl, one of the world's leading scholars of democracy, ranked Israel among the 12 most democratic countries in the world," he says, adding that Dahl's assessment was based on the freedom to participate in the democratic process and to oppose government.

Back then, he notes, the main limits to democracy came in the form of censorship. Despite the fact that newspapers often appeared with gaping white holes where the military censor had banned a story at the last minute, Medding notes, "Overall, Israel ranked on a par with the United States and higher than the United Kingdom and Canada, even though it was a beleaguered country. Switzerland, highly democratic on many counts, gave half its population—women—voting rights only in the 1970s."

Considering that Israel's situation is hardly as idyllic as that found in the world's leading democracies, its achievements are notable. Medding points out that leaders of the Western world did not fare so well when they found themselves under threat.

"The most infamous example was when the United States interned Japanese Americans out of hysteria and fear during World War Two, without proof that they were enemies," he says. "Some of the people interned were second generation American citizens.

"Great Britain interned Germans, which meant mainly young German Jews," he adds. "After the fall of Dunkirk, the British shipped them out to Australia and Canada."

Medding recognizes that a lot has changed in Israel since Dahl did his research in the 1970s, but he maintains that the country would rank about the same today if another such study was undertaken. "By the formal criteria used then, Israel would be in about the same place now," he says.

Within the borders of the State of Israel, he stresses, the situation has actually improved. Levels of participation in the democratic process have grown, and emergency laws—while still on the books—are applied less than in the past. He notes an increase in liberalization.

"There is more press competition and more investigative reporting than there was back then," Medding says. "There is less political party intervention in the press. Israel now has a series of instruments which did not exist in the 1950s and 1960s. There are government-appointed commissions to investigate issues. The state comptroller has become stronger and more effective."

The country's Arab minority has fared better in recent years as well, Medding says, noting that the military government over Israeli Arabs was rescinded in 1966. "They participate more effectively in the political process," he notes. "The majority no longer votes for satellites of the Labor Party, as they did in the 1960s. They vote for Arab parties, joint Arab-Jewish parties or even Zionist parties, but they are not controlled by them."

Their situation is far from perfect, however. "They still suffer from a series of legal restrictions that prevent them from receiving treatment that is equal with that received by Jewish citizens," he says. "At the same time, they use the opportunities in Israeli democracy to protest the situation and press for greater equality."

Given the objective problems that Israel faces, Medding says the country has treated its Arab citizens well in the past. It is a plus for Israeli democracy that the Arab minority has been relatively restrained.

"Israel cannot chase out its Arab citizens, and indeed does not want to do so, for very good liberal democratic reasons," he says. "Although some Israelis would like to wake up in the morning and find that the Arabs had gone elsewhere, that's not on the agenda. Israel is not going to take action to drive them across the border."

Medding claims that even if, at some future date, many more Israeli Arabs were to engage in terrorist activities, public sentiment about transfer would not change. "If they became involved in intifada-type activities, then we would see more intifada-type solutions for Israeli Arabs. Israel would use its army to put down civil disturbances.

"The interesting point, though, is that the Arab citizens of Israel have been remarkably restrained since the intifada began in 1987," Medding notes. "The number of hostile acts perpetrated by Israeli Arabs is very, very small."

This lack of violence suggests that Israeli Arabs identify strongly with the Israeli political system, Medding says, and that they genuinely want to be integrated into Israeli society, but as Arabs or Palestinians. "Increasingly, the response of Israeli governments has been to try to find arrangements which make it possible to maximize integration of the Arabs into a Jewish state. Israel has moved very much in a democratic direction."

Israeli democracy got a little sticky during the period when the country controlled the territories totally. Although, according to Medding, experts agree that they were never a formal part of Israel —and therefore should be considered separately—he says there was serious concern that problems found across the Green Line would seep into Israel itself.

"If one were to include the territories, Israeli democracy had problems," he says. "The country had political and administrative control over a large number of individuals who are not participants in its political process and were subject to military administration. Maintaining such a situation permanently would have represented a serious blot on Israeli democracy."

As long as the situation was never deemed permanent, Medding says the litmus test lay in how well the "blot" was prevented from crossing into Israel proper. "There is no evidence that things like the methods of police, military or secret service employees, as well as the low level of tolerance for opposition and the minimum level of willingness to tolerate disturbances spilled over into Israel from the territories."

The current peace negotiations and attempts to disengage Israel as much as possible from the territories are likely to test the fiber of Israeli democracy internally as well as externally.

Internally, Medding notes that how the government mobilizes public support for its policy is critical for maintaining democratic legitimacy on such an emotional, ideological and crucial security issue. How the opposition to the process expresses itself is equally important. Will it overstep the limits of democratic protest? Will it resort to violence? How would the authorities act under such circumstances? These are all issues which could test the democratic resilience of Israeli society.

Externally, he says the key question is how Israel will handle extremist opposition among the Palestinians. An exacerbation of the problems from the intifada cannot be ruled out.

Medding points out that democracy is remarkably resilient, but he stresses that no one can predict its breaking point. "An unresolved internal problem bordering on civil war or a tremendous economic crisis have been conditions under which weaker democracies have folded in the past. We do not have many examples in the last 30–40 years of strong democracies going under. Israeli democracy is likely to hold up under most conditions."

He notes that as democracy survives, it grows stronger. "Age and practice do strengthen democracy," he says. "The extent to which the political culture is transmitted in the schools and a country's inhabitants accept this as being the norm are very important factors. In the last resort, democracy rests on the desire of the population to maintain it. It will collapse only when a large number of its citizens are prepared to use force to rip society apart."

When assessing political participation in Israeli society, Medding raises the issue of a law enacted by the Knesset in the late 1980s which bans parties that dispute Israel's raison d'etre as a Jewish state, negate democracy or preach racism. The law is a mixed bag, he says.

"On the one hand, excluding parties that do not accept Israel being a permanent Jewish state restricts minority rights," he says. "On the other hand, disqualifying parties which incite to racism protects the minority Arab population. So it goes both ways."

By its very nature, Israel's electoral system encourages many parties to run for Knesset—and it enables many of them to gain seats in the lawmaking body. In the U.S. and the UK, Medding notes, there are fewer restrictions on parties, but the countries' electoral systems effectively exclude most parties from entering Congress or Parliament.

Regardless of who is in power in Israel, some opposition voices always warn ominously of serious threats to Israeli democracy. Medding dismisses the doomsayers and assesses the facts.

"Government television has been politicized from the time it was instituted in 1969," he says. "The Labor Alignment had been in power for a long time, and it could politicize quietly by agreement in the government. Over the years, this politicization has become much stronger."

He says that every government has taken advantage of state owned TV. As soon as the faces around the government table change, he says, personnel changes begin to shake up the Israel Broadcast Authority.

"It's clear and naked politicization," Medding says. "Television is regarded as a power position which must be used. Because of the competition of the parties in the IBA one sees much more interference with programming, news, etc."

The other level is much more subtle: the extent to which television journalists regard their professional positions or advancement as being dependent on whoever the political masters are. Medding says the government has tried to muzzle TV reporters, but they seem to be able to evade the muzzle. At the same time, there are new and competing television channels, which makes for more pluralistic views.

Military censorship and self-censorship in the print and electronic media are on the decline. "Society and politics have become more open, and much more information gets to the public," Medding stresses.

"The blanket of censorship regarding the army has become much narrower over the past 20 years," he continues. "The army has begun to act faster to inform the public of disciplinary actions against officers who have been negligent or failed in duty."

As evidence, he cites an example of a military accident in which officers' negligence led to the death of a soldier. "The general heading the Southern Command immediately relieved the officers of their posts and made a public announcement to that effect. The soldier's mother was interviewed on the radio.

"Twenty years ago, nobody would have known how the soldier had died," Medding says. "His mother would not have been interviewed and there would have been no public response from the commander."

He goes on to cite other examples of openness in realms that once were strictly off-limits. For example, he says, the army voluntarily made public the fact that it operated units of soldiers disguised as Arabs in the territories. He acknowledges that the authorities may well use the media to spread both information and disinformation, as it suits their objectives, but he adds, "Once you seek to influence opinion via the media, it carries with it greater openness and scrutiny."

Compared to the 1954 Lavon affair, Medding calls today's openness striking. "Very few people knew that Israeli military intelligence was involved in misfired sabotage actions by Egyptian Jews in Egypt," he says. "Not many Knesset members or politicians were aware of it.

"When Defense Minister Lavon was effectively forced to resign, the reasons offered related to differences of opinion on the restructuring of the ministry," he notes. Five years passed before the true circumstances were revealed, and even then Ben-Gurion opposed releasing details of military matters.

Today's openness does not extend to every last detail, he adds. "There are still publication limitations, voluntarily maintained by the press," he says. "Moreover, Mordechai Vanunu is in jail for publishing evidence that Israel has an atomic reactor."

On certain issues, Israel simply refuses to comment. As an example, Medding cites the government's lack of acknowledgment of any role in the killing of senior PLO figure Abu Jihad in Tunis a few years ago.

Despite its limits, Medding seems satisfied with the country's progress toward achieving better, more open democracy. Any such discussion is not complete, however, without comment on what many see as the country's glaring hole in its democratic fabric: the lack of a written constitution.

"There are two opposing schools," Medding says. "American democracy is epitomized by its constitution. It determines how American democracy works. However, the 1992 Los Angeles race riots showed that American reality is different from the American dream encapsulated in the constitution, which promises liberty and equality to all citizens.

"In the former Soviet Union," he says, citing another example of a constitution that does not present a clear view of reality, "the constitution was beautiful, but nobody lived by it because political decisions determined reality."

Great Britain epitomizes the second school. "It has no formal written document called a constitution," he says, but adds that many constitutional concepts are encoded in written laws or unwritten norms.

Israeli democracy follows in the tradition of Britain. "The absence of a formal constitution reflects the inability of the Israeli public and political leaders to agree on certain fundamentals which normally appear in a constitution," Medding says, adding that *de facto* many constitutional norms have been adopted.

"Sometimes one reaches very untidy, uneasy and messy compromises," he remarks. "The vast majority of Israelis recognize that what unites them is much more important than what divides them. Many Israeli Jews have a common sense of national and Jewish identity and purpose that encourages them not to push to the extreme if they run into opposition from people who want the opposite of what they want."

These untidy compromises are typified by the religious status quo, which reflects the Israeli reality. Medding: "The majority of the population, according to surveys, does not want to do away with religious marriages and opposes separation of Judaism from the state. Even most of the Orthodox, despite what they say officially, do not want a theocratic state run by rabbis. They would not know what to do with those people who do not observe halacha."

If most people appreciate the status quo, then the inevitable question arises as to what changes should be made to improve Israeli democracy. Medding finds in the changed balance of power over the past decades the main reason for the change in Israel's political culture. "In the first years of statehood, about 60 percent of Knesset members belonged to the left. Today right and left are about evenly balanced, which gives much greater power to small parties."

Medding points to the disproportionate role played by small parties in the past 10–15 years on the Israeli political scene. "They seem to be able to get more out of the system than they deserve," he says. "It appears that the minority dictates policies to the majority because it holds the government to ransom.

"That raises other questions," Medding says. "Is the government able to implement a coherent policy? Is it able to govern effectively? Politicians are elected not only to rule, but to do so in a particular way. The government has compromised too much and become balkanized. Nobody at the ministerial level accepts personal responsibility for anything. In this field, Israeli democracy needs great change and improvement."

The solution is clear to Medding. If the problem stems from the power wielded by small parties in the coalition building process, then the first step must be to raise the entrance barrier to the Knesset. Prior to the 1992 elections, the barrier was raised from one percent to 1.5 percent of all votes cast, and that act kept one small party out. "It would probably be better to raise the floor gradually to three or five percent," Medding says, adding that such a step would probably reduce the number of parties in the Knesset to about six.

While the Knesset took a step in the right direction by raising the entrance barrier slightly, Medding believes that it must closely examine the relationship between the powers of the prime minister and the Knesset. In 1992, the Electoral Law was changed to provide for direct election of the prime minister, a move which inevitably will cause the relationship to change. Medding says the direct election law tries to have it both ways by providing for direct election of the prime minister and then reducing his constitutional powers, which makes no sense whatsoever.

One step enhances his mandate, which is his democratic legitimacy, but the other turns around and puts it at the mercy of the Knesset even more than before, as some aspects of the new law make it even easier to remove the prime minister, dissolve the Knesset, and bring about new elections, he says. "Too many elections in too short a time, due to the inability of the politicians to reach agreement, is destabilizing and likely to lower the public's faith in democracy."

But all is not gloomy. Medding does not believe he is the only one who sees the flaws in the new law. "I would not be surprised if the new law is amended before it is put into practice," he concludes.

Solving Israeli democracy's problems is not impossible. Trying to reduce the number of parties and increase the capability of the executive—especially the prime minister and the government—to make policy coherent is a tall order, but Medding believes it can be done. This means increasing the government's ability to act as a cohesive unit instead of a set of individual fiefdoms or balkanized estates.

A careful examination of the situation seems to point not to mandatory new powers for the prime minister, but rather a balance of power between the parties that enables the prime minister to knock heads together and impose solutions on coalition partners.

Medding says the reason government ministers do not abide by the laws regarding collective responsibility is clear: political circumstances are such that the prime minister cannot enforce the kind of sanctions permitted by law against those ministers who speak out against government policy.

These public differences of opinion may give individual ministers an advantage, or popularity, among the electorate, in their party or in a certain camp in their party. This makes the seductive forces at work very strong. In the final analysis, a lot depends on the prime minister's skill in marshalling the resources at his disposal.

Medding does not support radical solutions such as a change to presidential government and completely undercutting the power of the Knesset and the parties. "We do not know how it would work in Israel," he says. "If it was adapted, it would be extremely destabilizing, because it would give tremendous powers to the prime minister."

No assessment of the future of Israeli democracy can be complete without referring to a possible peace agreement. Medding suggests that solving the conflict with the Arabs may have surprisingly negative effects on Israel. "Resolving the security issue and eliminating most of the external menace may create much greater internal socioeconomic, ethnic and religious strains."

The external threat keeps the cap on the internal battle. It unifies the Israeli population and keeps a lid on the religious conflict. It also helps manage the conflict between Israel and its Arab citizens. Paradoxically, removing the external threat may create many other problems.

Medding concludes: "Israel has shown a reasonable degree of flexibility and high capability to resolve conflicts. Given the fundamental understandings Jews have in this country, I see no reason why other conflicts should not be manageable, even if the internal conflict may become more intense, provided that no groups seek to up the ante."

The last factor to consider is that anticipated economic development after peace may have a generally beneficial effect for Israel's democracy. "Economic strife and economic disadvantages are bad for democracy," he says. "Democracies do best when economic circumstances are good, because people tend not to go to extremism. In theory, that ought to work to strengthen Israeli democracy."

MIRIAM BEN-PORAT

Fighting the Administration's Abuse of Power

I N 1988, THE KNESSET ELECTED HIGH COURT JUSTICE MIRIAM Ben Porat to be Israel's State Comptroller and Public Complaints Commissioner. The latter function is more commonly known as Ombudsman. She has brought new vitality, new concepts and a new approach to the position, establishing new norms in many grey areas. In 1993, she was unanimously reelected for another five year term.

Ben-Porat was born in Witebsk, Russia, in 1918, and grew up in Lithuania. After finishing high school in 1936, she made aliya alone.

In 1945, Ben-Porat became a lawyer. In 1949, she served in the State Attorney's Office, becoming Deputy State Attorney in 1953. In 1959, she was appointed a judge in the Jerusalem District Court, and in 1975, she became its president.

In 1976, she became the first woman appointed to Israel's Supreme Court. By the time she retired from the bench 12 years later, she was vice president of the court. In addition to her judicial career, Ben-Porat taught law from 1964 through 1978 at the Hebrew University, where she was an associate professor of law.

She is the author of a commentary on the Law of Assignment, and has published many articles in the *Israeli Law Review* and various other Israeli professional journals.

In 1991, the government awarded her the Israel Prize, the country's highest award, for her special contribution to society and state.

Ben-Porat has used an activist approach to waging a never-ending battle against the abuse of power, and against the politicization of public administration. She considers this ongoing struggle essential in order to keep the process of improving governance in Israel on track.

She begins her remarks with the observation that Israel's legal principles and norms are of a very high standard, but notes that the way the public administration applies them leaves much to be desired.

In her words, "There is a gap between the real world and the theoretical world. If one does not apply the Supreme Court's norms, then they are only good for the very specific cases in which the court decided. We have many good laws, plus the norms of the Supreme Court, which compare well with those of any other democracy in the world. On the other hand, we have the grey reality that many of these norms are often not applied. This phenomenon has to be eliminated at the root."

She explains this concept in detail with examples from her experience in the Court and the State Comptroller's office. "On the High Court of Justice, I heard many petitions against the government and the public administration," she says. "The Court's decisions established norms and, in fact, a common law constitution, as Israel does not have a written constitution. We operate according to these principles and norms, which are very effective.

"As a state comptroller and ombudsman, one has to apply the same careful norms," Ben-Porat stresses. "The ombudsman acts *de facto* as a popular court to which the citizen can appeal against the administration if he thinks he has been wronged. As ombudsman, we do part of the work of the complaining citizen. We investigate and serve as his mouthpiece even if he has not brought up all of the relevant facts and arguments, or did not state the specific remedy he seeks."

In her desire for greater integrity in public administration, Ben-Porat has confronted systematically the problem of political appointees. "One must see the civil servant as the public's trustee," she says. "Citizens are entitled to benefit from his services. Political appointees, especially in key positions, may feel they owe their loyalty to those who appointed them, rather than to the public which it is their duty to serve.

"If the government appoints an official for political reasons, he will be expected to serve the interests of those who appointed him. Even if the person is competent, there is a serious problem which is difficult to address. He may be talented, but he might not have been appointed had he not been a member of a certain party. If he is competent, he should be neither favored nor discriminated against. A lot depends on the person's integrity."

The public has a right to expect to be served by public employees for its benefit, without any foreign considerations, and with due dilligence. Therefore, Ben-Porat says, the most suitable persons should be appointed, regardless of their political views, which should be a neutral factor. If the connection to a certain political party or the political views of a candidate constitutes one of the factors in his nomination or appointment, then the appointment is flawed. Ben-Porat points to a well-known corruption case to illustrate how complex the situation can get when political appointees do not separate their political interests from the public function they hold. She reads from the court ruling in this case:

"A politician in a high government position or in the public administration should be aware and sevenfold prudent not to confuse his political status with that of a public servant. The citizen who needs service from the public administration cannot discern the intentions of the person who requests a political contribution. If he refuses the request, he has to fear that this may harm him in the future. Thus, the prestige of the administration and the trust of the public oblige a total separation between the political party interest, which the civil servant has according to his convictions, and the actual interest of the government office or body where he works, as well as his commitment to the public, which is entitled to his services."

Ben-Porat explains that the ruling is from a Supreme Court case involving a land dealer named Shmuel Einav. "For his business, he needed, like many others, the good services of the Ministry of Agriculture.

"Before the 1988 elections, those in power were looking for contributions for their party's campaign," she explains. "They called a meeting, and Einav and others were present. The others left before they were asked to make a contribution. At the meeting, there were clear hints that if those who wanted the ministry's good services would make contributions to the party, both sides would benefit. That was how Einav understood the matter.

"Now an odd thing happened," she continues. "Initially, a suit was brought against the land dealer, who was found guilty. No effort was made at the time to press a suit against the official concerned or lift the parliamentary immunity of the deputy minister involved. Only much later was a suit brought against those who had received the contributions. This shows the difficulty and the reticence to bring suits against civil servants and public appointees.

"There is even more reluctance in those cases where one has to request the removal of parliamentary immunity," she says. "Maybe that will change now. In any case, I never stop preaching that."

Ben-Porat insists that change is essential for bringing greater integrity to the public administration. She alludes to specific cases when she says, "If one would press more charges against people in key positions, this would be the best deterrent. It would prevent others from doing the same things."

She expresses full confidence in the court system's ability to apply proper norms in such cases, but reiterates that the problem is that too many cases never reach the courts.

"There has been a significant number of cases of betrayal of the public's confidence or abuse of authority by highly placed officials," she says.

"This abuse of authority derives from the fact that both power and special interests corrupt. Here again, the problem of conflict of interest emerges; the obligation to serve the public conflicts with the obligation toward the party which got you your position.

"If an outsider hands out cash from the state's treasury to whomever he wants, everybody will agree that this is theft. If a minister or civil servant abuses his competence and transfers money to those who are not entitled to it, I do not see in this anything less criminal. They, however, do not run the same risk. So far, their fear to be brought to court has been minimal.

"Even if a politician were to claim that he only wanted to correct an injustice, this would not justify his acting contrary to the law," Ben-Porat adds. "If he thinks that the law is wrong, he has to try to change it, but he cannot take the law into his own hands."

Admitting that the situations are not identical, Ben-Porat nonetheless draws a parallel to Dostoevski's character Raskolnikoff. Although he wanted to correct an injustice, she says, society still sees his deed as highly criminal.

Ben-Porat took the fight against the intermingling of political and business interests in another direction. "I was appointed in an election year," she says. "I realized that the names of the major contributors to the various parties were not made public. I investigated whether that was permitted by law. If that were the case, then the most I could have done would have been to say it seemed to me a bad law, but it is not my role to control the Knesset, which elects me.

"But when I looked into the matter, I was told that nothing in the law guaranteed contributors' anonymity," she says. I found that it was based on a silent understanding. As the names were not published for so many years, this was interpreted as if there were an agreement that if somebody made a contribution to a party his name would not be mentioned in the State Comptroller's Annual Report. Nor would the State Comptroller disclose it in any other way.

"I knew that Knesset Member Amnon Rubinstein had proposed a law which fixed a maximum amount per contribution," she continues. "I faced a dilemma. I did not want to be seen as wanting to take the place of the legislature. That would have meant an abuse of my authority. On the other hand, I considered this an important area where I should watch out for the administration's integrity, which is my role as written in the law.

"The proposed law did not progress in the Knesset," she says. "Finally, after consultations in our office, I reached the decision that the names of those who contributed more than NIS 10,000 would be published.

"We disclosed only contributions which were received after a period of grace of a few weeks, having given prior notice of my intentions to the parties. Also, if somebody brought forward good reasons to remain anonymous, such as that he would incur risks in his country of residence abroad if his contribution were known, we would consider his request.

"Then another strange thing happened. In the framework of the discussion of an unrelated financial law, a proposal was made to change the State Comptroller's law in such a way as to give the Knesset chairman discretion over which parts of the State Comptroller's report would remain secret.

"By chance, one of our staff members saw this proposal before it came to a vote. I asked to appear before the Knesset Finance Committee. I must say, to their honor, that its members were quite ashamed about the proposal and cancelled it. But that only happened because I intervened in time."

This brings Ben-Porat to another of her favorite themes: the importance of intervening in a timely manner. By embracing an activist approach, she tries to prevent mistakes before they happen, rather than criticizing them after things have gone wrong.

"I intervene if I see that a project is proposed which is not economically sound," Ben-Porat says. "That makes much more sense than reacting after it has already been completed. What can I say then? That it is not a good idea to build unprofitable plants? Everybody knows that. I want to prevent them from being built in the first place.

"The government can be of another opinion," she admits. "I have to express my opposition in time—not when it is too late—provided the facts at my disposal support my opinion. There are many countries which have not reached this level in their approach to the function of the state comptroller; even the most enlightened ones hesitate."

Before discussing concrete examples to illustrate the need for a precautionary approach, Ben-Porat offers a hypothetical one. "Let us assume that the government wanted to sell military equipment which contained confidential technology. The sale would reveal lifesaving secrets to a state which is not very friendly to us. Should I remain silent and let the sale go through?

"Should I only investigate after this has happened, and conclude that we have all been put in danger? In my opinion, that is forbidden. I say this to support my approach that one—only in exceptional cases and in a prudent way—has to use this instrument of interference before the damage is done and before the state has taken on a legal commitment."

But the examples are not all hypothetical. Ben-Porat lists several situations in which her office intervened to prevent mistakes. In one, the government had decided to privatize several state-owned companies, in line with global trends. One of the companies up for privatization was the Jerusalem Economic Corporation, which had major land holdings, mainly in the Jerusalem area.

"I asked myself, 'Do I have the right to say, privatization is fine, but why start with a company which holds significant amounts of government-owned land?'

"When we looked into the matter, it turned out that some of the company's land holdings were very depressed in value. We had reason to believe that this was a temporary situation. We said that if the government needed money, why not sell the valuable land holdings of the company? That could have brought in a lot of cash, while retaining in government hands the land which was likely to increase in value."

Ben-Porat says that her office's investigation indicated that this approach would prove more effective than selling the company outright. Her staff had the company's landholdings appraised, and found that the holdings were worth far more than the proposed selling price.

"I then suggested that the government keep the company and sell part of the land," she explains. "We said very carefully, 'Why not consider this option?' We did not say that we wanted to decide instead of the government; we merely asked them to reconsider."

But there is more to the story. Ben-Porat's office discovered that the government had not consulted the company's board about the proposed transaction. "According to the law, one of our tasks is to check the legality of the public administration's actions," she notes. "When we queried this, we got as answer: 'Why should we ask the board of directors? They do not want to lose their function, so they surely will oppose the sale.'

"If one pushed this kind of argument to the extreme, then a judge in a court case would not hear the defendant at all, because he would probably deny the charges," Ben-Porat says. "In this specific case, we said, 'Perhaps the board of directors will bring convincing arguments that the company should not be privatized. The board members may indeed have an interest in the company not being sold, so they will probably bring the best arguments against the transaction. It seems logical that before the government decides what policy to follow, it should hear all the relevant arguments.'

"I therefore decided to raise this issue in a letter to the Minister of Finance, using carefully worded questions aimed at drawing his attention to arguments against the transaction. Despite my questions, the transaction was completed.

"What should I have done?" Ben-Porat muses. "Should I have waited until they sold the company?" By then, she says, the country would have incurred a loss.

She cites yet another example of the need for intervention in a timely manner. "The previous Minister of Housing intended to sign an agreement for the construction of 20,000 housing units—a huge contract for a small country—with one developer without a public tender. The terms of the agreement seemed to us very onerous for the state. When the Ministry agreed to issue a tender, we examined it and found that it had been tailor-made for that developer. It barred smaller companies from participating. We commented on this during the negotiations.

"Then the Minister reduced the tender to 10,000 units, and later to 5,000," Ben-Porat says. "Finally, he abandoned the whole project. If we had not intervened in time and the agreement had been signed, we could only have cried over spilled milk and calculated the damage, part of which could not even have been measured in financial terms."

One of the most famous cases Ben-Porat has handled concerned the gas masks distributed to the public before the 1991 Gulf War. "During the Gulf War, we heard that some of the gas masks did not fit the people who wore them," she says. "A significant number of people were not protected while they thought they were. Should I have said, 'I have not written a report, so how can I raise the question?'"

To Ben-Porat, the answer was clear. She decided that she could not delay action on such an important issue. The potential damage was so great, she reasoned, that her office was entitled to intervene. She wrote a letter to the Minister of Defense, discussing the issue. The letter was leaked to the press.

"I am very much against leaks such as this, even if sometimes they have positive results," she says.

"I then brought the issue before the State Audit Affairs Committee of the Knesset," she continues. "The first discussion was held before we had issued a report."

Although this order of things was at variance with standard procedure, Ben-Porat justifies it because of the severity of the matter at hand.

Active monitoring of public administration is a cornerstone of Ben-Porat's approach. "Let us assume that somebody who participates in a public tender finds out that his bid is the cheapest, but the tender is awarded to a competitor," she says. "If he wants to prevent this, he has to appeal to the High Court without delay.

"He certainly must do so before the competitor starts to carry out the work," she says. "If he comes later, the court will say, 'We're very sorry. You can file a civil claim against the public administration and try to prove that you have suffered damage, and—quite naturally— conflicting views of a problem can arise. Your competitor, however, is innocent. He has signed a legal, valid contract.'"

Generally, she notes, when someone wants the assistance of a court, such assistance should be sought before damage is caused to a third party. She is adamant that the same approach should guide the state comptroller's office.

The state comptroller's fields of activity often coincide with those of the attorney general, Ben-Porat says, noting that certain tensions between various authorities are unavoidable. Nonetheless, she feels that many of these tensions damage the objective of good government.

For example, she says, a conflict exists between two parallel court systems that deal with issues of personal status: the rabbinical court and the general court. Neither will hear an appeal of a decision by the other, and they often issue decisions that conflict with each other.

"What is the competence of the state comptroller?" she asks. "The law states that the state comptroller has to examine the legality of the actions of the public administration. If he or she decides that a certain action is not legal, this may conflict with a prior opinion of the attorney general.

"This puts the executive branch in a very difficult situation. It sees itself—rightly so—bound by an opinion of the attorney general. Many years ago, a committee headed by Supreme Court Justice Agranat decided that where there is no court ruling, the attorney general's opinion is binding.

"That committee addressed a more limited issue: the relationship between the Minister of Justice and the attorney general," she explains. "It did not discuss the position of the state comptroller. The latter should be free to decide whether the actions of the public administration are legal or not. When the state comptroller, in his function as ombudsman, expresses his opinion, it would not be correct to appeal to the attorney general, because that would undermine the state comptroller's position."

She says that a citizen who seeks the aid of the ombudsman in effect is saying, "I did not get what I was entitled to." Determining what the citizen deserves requires an interpretation of the law. If the ombudsman were to be bound by the attorney general's position, Ben-Porat says, the situation would be intolerable.

The conversation turns, quite naturally, to an issue which has occupied Israeli public opinion extensively in recent years: The relationship between the High Court and the government.

Ben-Porat underscores the many nuances of the issue: "It is very difficult to determine where the High Court can express its opinion, because the case is not political, and where it cannot, because the issue is political. Even if the case is political, but has general public aspects as well, the High Court can express its opinion. I cannot say whether that is necessary, right or wise. The only question I can answer is whether the Court is allowed to do so."

Ben-Porat says the High Court has great discretion here. It should avoid dealing with those issues which concern the political world and the public at large when the result would be that the court would lose credibility in the eyes of the public. This, she says, is the crucial issue.

"If somebody comes and says he wants to see norms established, or that he has been harmed by the public administration, then the court has the competence to deal with it," she says. "In each generation, the High Court has, however, to determine the borders of its intervention. A major consideration here has to be that public trust in it will not be harmed."

For similar reasons, Ben-Porat turned down a Knesset request for the state comptroller's office to write an opinion on the politicization of the army. She thought it would be unwise to express herself on what generals could and could not say. The Knesset, she said, should address the issue and set the norms that will guide top army brass.

While these issues are important, Ben-Porat is most concerned with pragmatic collaboration between institutions. In the struggle against the abuse of power by the public administration, she often has to bring matters to the attention of the attorney general, so he can take any necessary action. "Of course, he has his own discretionary power to decide," she notes. "But I am allowed to do all in my power to convince him to act against abuse of power.

"The same goes for the police, which I want to encourage not to be reticent to investigate highly placed people. My idea of what a public figure should be is somebody who acts correctly and not somebody who abuses his power in a highly placed position for which he apparently is not suited. If the attorney general and the police were to take this approach, I think that we would make a major step in the right direction against abuse of power."

MOSHE SANBAR

More Impulses for Economic Growth

B ANK LEUMI CHAIRMAN MOSHE SANBAR was born in 1926 in Kec-
skemet, Hungary. In World War Two, he was sent to several
concentration camps, including Dachau. He described his
experiences there in his 1961 book, *My Longest Year*, which was translated into several languages. After the war, he came to Israel.

After studying at the Hebrew University—he earned a Master's in
economics, statistics and sociology in 1951—Sanbar worked at the Israel
Institute of Applied Social Research, eventually becoming deputy director. In 1958, he moved to the Ministry of Finance, where he held a number
of top positions, the last of which was budget director. From 1968–1970,
he was chairman of the board of the Industrial Development Bank.

In 1970, Sanbar ran the Ministry of Commerce and Industry. The
following year, he was appointed governor of the Bank of Israel, a
post he held until 1976. Since then, he has held a variety of chairman-
ships of public companies. In 1988, he became chairman of the board
of directors of Bank Leumi.

Sanbar's published books include a volume called *The Local Gov-*

ernment in Israel. His many awards include the Yad Vashem prize for Holocaust studies (1958), the Herzl prize for public service (1973) and the prize for extraordinary contribution to the development of local government in Israel (1986.)

Sanbar characterizes the Israeli economy today as a "stream of new momentum." He explains: "There is always something new. One impulse follows another. It started with the big aliya from the former Soviet Union and has continued with American loan guarantees, the hope for peace, peace talks and the agreement with the Palestinians. All this leads to enlarged foreign interest in the country, and in the region as a whole." But Sanbar does not expect any dramatic leaps in Israel's economic development as a result of peace. "Peace is very important," he says, "but not as far as structural changes in our economy are concerned. The Israeli economy has done well in recent years, and peace will act as a catalyst for a continuation of that positive trend. Peace brings a new wave of foreign interest and adds additional momentum."

Contrary to what some people want to believe, Sanbar states, "exports to countries in the Middle East cannot change Israel's development in a major way. The economic aspects of dealing with the Palestinian entity will be of a secondary nature. The same goes for economic relations with the Arab countries bordering on Israel. They all have a very low standard of living, and their import needs are not particularly well-suited to what Israel manufactures.

"Israel's economic development depends mainly on the expansion of its exports to developed countries," Sanbar says. "Peace will help that trend, but it requires additional investments, which is another reason why the process will take time." He puts the issue in perspective by using a European comparison: Holland imports more than all of Israel's Arab neighbors combined. "The Netherlands is a more advanced country, so there is greater economic logic to trying to increase Israel's exports to the Netherlands rather than to its neighbors."

Setting aside the issue of peace and its potential benefits, San-bar focuses on an equally interesting question: Why has the Israeli economy developed strongly since 1990, while all the world has been in recession?

"Since the end of 1989, about half a million immigrants have come, mainly from the former Soviet Union. Increasing a country's population by ten percent in such a short time creates major additional demand for primary needs such as food, housing, schooling, clothing, etc.

"Even if the immigrants have below-average incomes, they still create additional demand for goods and services," Sanbar explains. "Industry met demand largely from existing production capacity, without additional investments, so it sold more products at full price while producing them at marginal cost. This increased profits substantially, and the whole economy benefitted.

"A second major factor for the economy's expansion has been the monetary policy," Sanbar notes. "The abundant money supply was intended to keep interest rates and inflation down while devaluations were small. This flow of additional money was not used for consumption; it went to the capital market, which prevented an increase in the inflation rate. All told, a number of good things came together, and they led to a positive economic climate in Israel.

"The ample money supply and low interest rates made it logical to invest in the stock market, and this trend was strengthened by increasing corporate profitability," he continues. "This led to a major increase in share prices. In turn, this caused greater foreign interest in the Israeli stock exchange."

Sanbar notes that the 1992 elections, which brought Labor to power, convinced the public in Israel and abroad that the time had come for peace. Then the American government finally authorized $10 billion of loan guarantees for Israel, which it had not reached an agreement on with the Likud government.

"The importance of the guarantees is not that they enable Israel to get money," Sanbar explains. "The main message to the international financial and business community was that Israel has a significant amount of foreign currency available and is not in economic danger. Israel's internal discussions as to whether or not to use these guarantees do not touch the heart of this issue.

"The business logic to foreigners was that if the country has reserves it does not need, it must be a safe place to invest. This gave a push to foreign investment, which was no longer limited to the capital markets or real estate.

"Now, more new money will flow into this part of the world. In the framework of the $2.5 billion to be made available by foreign donors to the Palestinians, there is talk about some very big projects.

"Many people think that if a Western company is a main contractor for such a project, nothing will remain for Israel," Sanbar says. "That is a mistake. Both Israelis and non-Palestinian Arabs will benefit. Despite the fact that this money is meant for the Palestinians, much of it will be spent here in the neighborhood."

He uses an example of French contractors who may win a contract to build new roads near Nablus, saying that they will not bring many engineers and laborers from home; much of the work will go to Israeli and Palestinian subcontractors, and local engineers—who cost less than those brought from France—will get a large piece of the pie.

Furthermore, Sanbar predicts that the Palestinians will use a fair share of the money they receive in aid to buy Israeli products. "This has been the case since 1967," he says. "The French may cream a project's income and transfer its profits out of the region, but the main flow of money, that for the work done, will go to local people."

These examples all contribute to Sanbar's thesis: that peace will cause new impulses for further development, even if structural changes in the economy will not be forthcoming.

Despite the optimistic outlook, Sanbar warns that not all is positive. "Macro-economically, there are some negative developments," he says. "Israeli consumption is increasing, as are imports. In the past, we considered this totally bad. The country's economic history is characterized by its lack of foreign currency, which was always the sensitive point in its economic thinking. Today, we have to change our mindset, at least partly, because foreign currency is available.

"It is a basic economic rule that if demand for goods exceeds supply, the result is either inflation or an increase in imports," Sanbar says. "In the past, we preferred increased prices to increased imports. Today, the greater imports help reduce inflation to levels which are low by our standards. This policy is a luxury we now can permit ourselves."

This new policy is a direct outgrowth of one of Israel's major achievements of the past decade: reducing inflation from 20 percent per month in 1985 to about 1.5 percent, where it remained for several years. Rising imports helped bring the level down even more, to about one percent per month. Sanbar notes that other countries which lowered hyperinflation rates only held them down temporarily, while in Israel the levels of the early 1980s have not returned.

Contrary to what many people believe, Sanbar insists that Israel has done quite well in the employment field. "Unemployment went up from nine percent in 1989 to almost 12 percent," he notes. "Then it came down again to about ten percent. This seems high, but the fact that such a major factor as the aliya caused only a limited rise in unemployment should be considered another great economic achievement.

"Of the 200,000 olim who came here in 1990, half entered the job market and at least 80 percent have found work." Of the 100,000 potential workers 40,000 had an academic background, leading Sanbar to say, "This was a windfall for Israeli society, as somebody else invested in their education and training."

In Western eyes, increased unemployment usually means less people are working, Sanbar says. That stands in stark contrast to the Israeli situation, where more people work and more people are without work than a few years ago.

"In view of the substantial increase in population, the latter should not surprise anybody," he says. "Israel's ten percent unemployment rate is still lower than that of some Western European countries, and that is a major achievement."

All of these positive factors will get several boosts from the progressing peace process, Sanbar believes. In addition to the factors already mentioned, he says that large foreign companies which have ignored Israel in the past—in part because of the Arab boycott—may now decide to establish regional headquarters or offices here.

"We have a very big advantage over our neighbors in the professional services we can supply," he says. "These big foreign companies will come here for regional business, not just Israeli business. They will explore ways to participate in some of the projects which will start in our neighborhood. They will send people to Israel, and these people will gradually become familiar with what goes on in the country.

"One of the first things they will realize is that Israel has highly qualified manpower which is cheap by their standards, especially in high-tech fields. Many immigrants are not yet employed in their professions; they do less qualified work, and they represent significant manpower available for new projects."

The reservoir of professional manpower is much larger than the unemployment figures indicate, and Sanbar believes that if immigrants find appropriate work, the whole country will benefit.

"This may lead to another interesting, positive development," he suggests. "It is reasonable to assume that when job opportunities increase and unemployment falls, aliya will rise again.

"Many Jews want to leave Eastern Europe, where the bad economic situation affects most of them," he continues. "When they see that Israel can provide employment, they will move, thereby providing still more momentum to our economy. Of course, that may cause unemployment figures to go up again, but that will be temporary."

Returning to the peace process, Sanbar lists several developments which he believes should occur. Some concern Israeli government policy, while others depend on the approach of the international bodies which will allocate funds for regional development projects.

"President Clinton has succeeded in mobilizing significant funds for the Palestinians, who will receive about $500 million in each of the coming five years," he notes. "Of this sum, the Americans have pledged $600 million."

This international aid is earmarked for development projects. The Palestinians have set as a priority projects that lessen their political and economic dependence on Israel, but Sanbar maintains that peace and economic independence are contradictory.

"Peace must mean interdependence between people," he says. "We saw that clearly after World War Two. When Germany put up a power station near the French border, France did not put up a competing power station on the other side. Today, many European power stations feed into a common network. Common networks link multiple European countries for supply of resources ranging from natural gas to such specialized products as ethylene."

Sanbar notes that economic interdependence is a cornerstone of the EEC model. It was, he recalls, the very basis for early discussions about European institutions, and it led to what eventually became the single European market, which will lead to a single currency.

Against this frame of reference, Sanbar is understandably not pleased with the Palestinian concept of economic independence. "They want to erect an electric power station in the Gaza region," he says. "There is already an Israeli power station 20 kilometers to the north, in Ashkelon. The Ashkelon station supplies electricity to

Gaza, and steps already have been taken to double its capacity.

"If the Palestinians want to build their own power plant rather than use power from Ashkelon, then the West should tell them, 'We will give you money to accelerate the peace process. Projects which have the opposite effect should not be financed by our money,'" Sanbar suggests. "The donor countries should give a clear message that such independence projects contradict the spirit in which the aid money was pledged."

Although he believes it is in Israel's interest, too, to foster economic interdependence, Sanbar does not think that Israel should raise the issue in the context of aid to the Palestinians. The countries that are giving the money should set the rules; the reason is based at least in part on self-interest.

"The small part of the European taxpayers' money sent to this region has been made available to let peace progress," he says matter-of-factly. "From an economic viewpoint, the independence projects are a waste. If that is how the aid money will be spent, then the Palestinian standard of living will go up less than it otherwise could, and the donors can rest assured that they will be called upon to give more very soon."

Projects which foster peace will cause Palestinian income to rise faster than it otherwise could, and such a rise would mean that the Palestinians will be less likely to come back to the Europeans and Americans looking for more aid money.

"Many Palestinian leaders cannot believe that $2.5 billion is all the aid they will receive," Sanbar says. If they begin to spend on the assumption that more money will be forthcoming, he warns, then the international body overseeing aid allocation will need to assess Palestinian development projects with an eye to their contribution to advancing peace.

Sanbar stresses that he does not oppose a Palestinian power station, *per se*. If the Palestinians were to establish a major power station for regional use, and if neighboring countries were to agree to buy electricity from it, he would back the plan wholeheartedly.

If such a plant also met Israeli demand, he says, it would create economic interdependence and thus make a contribution to peace. And, he sums up, if Israel and the Palestinians both benefit from such a development project, then the project will give a boost to peace.

"If there will be no peace," he points out, "then Israel can hardly be expected to purchase electricity from a Palestinian station." If, on the other hand, the Palestinians cut off the supply, Sanbar notes, they too will suffer, as their own cost of electricity will increase.

He believes that, in the spirit of peace, Israel should be permitted to participate in the execution of development projects in neighboring countries, just like any other country.

"One might even say that in order to promote peace Israelis and Arabs should get a certain priority," he suggests. "The donor countries may be shortsighted enough to want the money they give to create work for their own companies. It would be a very bad omen if there were no equal terms for Israelis."

Yet another condition for real peace lies in the end of the Arab boycott. Sanbar notes that the boycott began when the Palestinians asked the Arab states to create it, and says that they must now ask them to end it, given that they have achieved peace. Without such a step, he says, there will not be real peace.

Genuine peace also requires open trade between Israel and Arab countries. Sanbar says that Israeli companies must be permitted to sell their goods in Arab countries, initially in Jordan and North Africa, and eventually in Syria, Saudi Arabia and the Gulf states. Demand will not be great, he acknowledges, but the political importance exceeds the economic value.

He maintains that Israeli politicians who have lobbied mainly for abolishment of the secondary boycott—that of Europeans who refuse to work with Israel—erred. Perhaps, he allows, industrialists who were hurt by the secondary boycott could have spearheaded such a campaign, but Israeli politicians must insist on seeing Israeli products appear in Arab markets. "This is a basic principle of free trade, and peace also means free trade," he states.

"We have to realize that Israeli products will never be able to compete in Arab markets with products the Arabs can make themselves," he says. "Their labor costs are much lower than ours."

"Some Israeli companies may even establish plants in Arab countries. The Israeli textile firm Delta is already setting up a plant in Egypt, with plans to export its production to Europe. This is a good alternative to investing in Eastern Europe. Before such investments can be made, obviously, the Arab boycott must be abolished."

Sanbar believes that the potential for Israeli exports to Arab countries will be limited to those goods which those countries already import. He says that Israel will need to compete with other countries that vie for Arab market share, and that Israeli companies should understand that their market share will never be large. The political significance of such trade is crucial, he says, despite the fact that Israel's economic future will not be determined by it.

Another important factor in the implementation of true peace has to do with open borders between Israel and the Palestinian entity. Sanbar stresses that "open borders" means free travel for goods, capital and manpower. The interest of peace will be served, he says, by open borders.

"That means that even if a Palestinian factory which competes with an Israeli plant is built, we will not protect our products," he says. "From a macro-economic point of view, our economy is strong enough to meet the competition of Palestine, or even Palestine and Jordan together. Such a policy may pose a problem for Israeli company owners who will face competition, but these things have to happen.

"If Israel has open borders with the autonomy, then third party imports on the autonomy's outer borders will become a problem," Sanbar warns. If Israel and the Palestinians reach a long-term agreement delineating similar customs duties and quality control, the problem could be minimized—at least in theory.

"In practice, it is likely to fail," he says. "Copying European common market concepts would be an error. The EEC reached this advanced stage only when the individual countries were more-or-less on equal economic footing, and the countries' interests were broadly similar. They certainly did not start after World War Two, when the German economy was totally destroyed.

"Clearly," Sanbar says, "this is not the case in the Middle East. The gap between the Israeli and Palestinian economies is very wide. If the Palestinians were to apply existing external Israeli customs duties, they may not have adequate customs protection for their own products. Furthermore their population may have to pay higher prices for some products to protect Israeli interests."

By adopting Israeli customs levels, he notes, the Palestinians could indeed generate some income from imports, but he notes that customs and duties do not exist solely to raise money. If the autonomy and Israel sign a customs union, he says, there will be a very real risk that Palestinian border controls will not be sufficiently strict.

"One cannot send Israeli customs officials to check, as Palestine will be an autonomous entity," he notes. "Even if the Palestinian authorities would like them to adhere to the joint rules, who says that their officials will want to do so?"

There are so many potential problems, Sanbar predicts, that customs controls will have to be erected between Israel and the Palestinian entity, regardless of what agreement is reached at the outset.

"We do not like to confront this issue, because it means we have to ask where the border is," he notes, adding, "A transition stage will be necessary to get from today's situation to the final one, as in the fields of security and defense.

"The autonomy process proceeds in stages, so we can try the customs arrangements initially in the Gaza region," he suggests. "It would be a mistake to commit ourselves to abandon customs controls immediately. We can assume that we want to give freedom of customs duties to all Palestinian and Jordanian products. Then we still will need to check carefully whether the product is indeed made there and has not been imported from elsewhere. Thus, we will have to define what are genuine Palestinian and Jordanian products.

"We should apply the same concepts which rule Israel's exports to the United States under the free trade agreement," Sanbar suggests. "The Americans check each product to determine whether or not it can be considered Israeli. They require a 35 percent added value in Israel, as well as substantial transformation. This rule is designed to prevent us from exporting goods that have been assembled from imported components to the U.S. without customs."

He maintains that Israel's customs system has been designed for the country's economic reality, and it should not be changed in the framework of the peace agreements merely to avoid administrative complications at the Palestinian borders. Solving this problem in an intelligent, practical way without hurting the Israeli economy need not be impossible.

But there will be problems, to be sure. As an example, he points immediately to the field of agriculture. "We have to decide how much we are willing to sacrifice, and at what speed," he says. "We need a transitionary agreement in this field, and we need to consider our macro-economic picture, but there is no doubt that Israel must make sacrifices regarding agriculture.

"Transition arrangements will also be necessary in the field of transport," Sanbar predicts. "Israeli operators will face major competition from Arab trucks and tour buses. Already, many tour buses operate in eastern Jerusalem. The difference in taxes actually paid will create competitive advantages for Arab operators. If the macro-economic considerations of promoting peace are important, then we have to make sacrifices here, too, as long as there is fair competition."

Not every sector will be threatened by peace. Sanbar points to tourism as a field which is likely to boom. He predicts that tourism between Israel and her neighbors will not be major, but that Westerners will flow to the country in the era of peace.

If quiet is maintained, he says, religious tourism will accelerate, and he notes that Jerusalem is the natural focal point of such tours. Likewise, he says, business tourism will grow, as conventions will take place in Israel in far greater numbers than happened in the past.

"Many of these conventions did not come to Israel for two reasons," Sanbar explains. "First, because many organizations have Arab members, and they opposed Israel as a venue. And second, dates for large conventions are fixed a few years in advance, and organizers rarely wanted to run the risk of political or military unrest, so they usually avoided Israel altogether."

He predicts a flood of conventions coming to Israel now. "Israel is an interesting country," he says. "The weather is nice. There is a good tourism and communications infrastructure. People here speak many languages. New tourist facilities will be built."

Another area that has been touted in the context of peace projections is financial services, but Sanbar does not show great enthusiasm. "One has to differentiate between becoming a financial service center and a financial center," he says. "We will be the first, but are unlikely to be the second.

"We will be able to provide financial services to those multinational companies operating in the region," he adds. "Israel may be able to draw more private financial deposits than it has today, but this will give us more the nature of a financial service center than of a financial center.

"Israel will not be a financial center, as we will not be able to attract large amounts of capital. We will not be able to compete with London or Singapore. The only real money in this neighborhood is that of the Gulf states, and they are not about to invest heavily in or through Israel."

He stresses that the barrier is not due to lack of technical ability; Israel, he says, is capable of providing the services of a financial center, but the rich countries of the region already get good service in the West.

"If they will come here at all, it will be for a small part of their money, and it will take a long time until they are convinced that peace is really stable," Sanbar predicts. "Then it may be in their interest to diversify and also operate through Israel. If this happens, there will be ferocious competition because this money will have to be withdrawn from elsewhere."

The picture is not all rosy, but neither is it all gray. Sanbar sums up by saying, "We will have to make sacrifices for peace, not only in the political field, but also in the economic field. These sacrifices make sense if the other side also makes some." Sanbar foresees a bright future for both the Israeli economy and its society. "I see the possibility of continuous progress in the coming years, but all of this could change if the peace process does not progress or if it suffers a major setback."

ISRAEL KATZ

Changing Social Policies

D
R. ISRAEL KATZ has played a major role in shaping Israel's social welfare policy for decades. The secret of Katz's success lies in part in his readiness to adjust his views over time. He has exhibited a flexible pragmatism and willingness to adapt to the many changes that Israel has undergone in its brief history.

Katz was born in Vienna in 1927 and came to Israel in 1938, after the Nazis took power in Austria. Even as a young man, he could not be satisfied with one pursuit. While he studied physics, chemistry and mathematics in Jerusalem in 1946–47, he also participated in one of Palestine's first outreach projects in a slum area, where he worked with juvenile delinquents.

In 1952, he completed a Master's degree in psychiatric social work at Columbia University in New York. A decade later, he received a doctorate in social administration from Case Western Reserve University in Cleveland. Upon returning home in 1962, he served as the first Israeli dean of the Paul Baerwald School of Social Work at the

Hebrew University. After taking time out for a visiting professorship at the London School of Economics, he spent four years as director-general of the National Insurance Institute, between 1969 and 1973.

In 1973, Katz was elected to the Knesset on the Mapai ticket. He gave up his seat to be the founding director of the Brookdale Institute of Gerontology and Adult Human Development in Jerusalem, a post he held until 1977. That year, he became Minister of Labor and Social Affairs on behalf of the Democratic Movement for Change, a new center party. From 1982 through the end of 1992, he was director of The Center for Social Policy Studies in Israel, a Jerusalem think tank.

Katz assesses the changes that must be made in the country's social policies. He calls for better monitoring of social needs, greater voluntarism and increased efforts to make people pay for social services. But he stresses that nobody can advocate change without understanding the ideas that guided the country's founders as they set up the national social welfare institutions.

Katz points out that the Histadrut trade union and the quasi-public Vaad Leumi had created a social welfare infrastructure before Israel gained independence in 1948. Some of these functions were assumed by the government, which expanded them through the 1950s.

"By and large, Israel modelled itself on what Beveridge had done in England as it developed the postwar welfare state," Katz says. "Sweden was another welfare state model."

He stresses the need to remember what was happening around the world in the 1950s. It was a period in which many socialist thinkers in countries such as the United Kingdom contrasted the bad "economic man" who represented the marketplace, mainly interested in profits, with the good "social man" who was concerned with humanitarian values.

The notion of the modern welfare state, Katz says, has become a relative issue, as most countries—democratic and otherwise—provide for a vast array of public needs with money generated by taxes. "They differ in the degree of providing services," Katz notes. "Saudi Arabia even provides free telephone services. Some states provide many universal services to all, free of charge; others provide more free services, but only to the poor."

In the early days of statehood, Katz says, Israel provided some services on a universal basis, while others were provided only on the basis of need. It wasn't at all uncommon, he says, for social workers to peek into people's ice boxes during home visits to determine which families needed free foodstuffs.

The reality of mass immigration from so many disparate cultural backgrounds posed countless challenges for the fledgling country. Katz, who was working as a psychologist at the time, notes that problems cropped up in nearly every imaginable sphere. "We tested children from European and African countries," he says. "The differences were so great that some experts thought there were genetic differences between Moroccan and European children."

It took time for the experts to realize that one standard test could not assess children from so many backgrounds. Until this became clear, however, many children were deemed to be mentally retarded.

"For instance, we showed a Yemenite boy a picture of a head without ears," Katz recalls with amusement. "He said that something was missing. When I asked him what, he said, the payot, the sidelocks."

That answer did not sit well with the testers, and the child was deemed mentally retarded. The situation continued, Katz says, until a non-Jewish expert from Geneva who had experience testing Moroccan children came. "He said, 'I do not think these children are mentally retarded,'" Katz recounts, "'but I think your psychologists are.'"

It was quite a blow to the basic assumptions of the Israeli Establishment. At the time, even Ben-Gurion believed there were fundamental differences between Moroccan and European children, though he did not term them genetic differences. Today, no serious observer would claim that genetic differences exist between Ethiopian and sabra children.

Nonetheless, Katz predicts that the color of Ethiopian immigrants' skin will play a major role in their difficult integration. "We have to recognize that it will pose a barrier between the Ethiopians and white Israelis," he says. "I have never thought that Jews are better human beings than non-Jews. Beyond that, there are great differences in customs; the status of women in general, and divorcees in particular, is terrible in Ethiopian society."

Katz predicts that even after Ethiopians make inroads into Israeli society, the color barrier will remain an issue. Many veteran Ethiopian immigrants have been absorbed in local industry, the army and institutions of higher learning, he notes, yet the barriers remain in place.

While he says color is the main issue, Katz says that major gaps separate all immigrants from Israeli culture. He predicts that the multiple objective problems facing Russian immigrants will cause many of them to leave the country in the coming years.

"The majority will remain," he says. "They will show their strength, in politics and other fields, much faster than other immigrant groups have done in the past." It remains to be seen if their political activity will take place within the existing political frameworks, or if they will establish their own parties. "Within ten years, we will see their potential," he predicts. "In the long term, Israeli leadership may come from their ranks."

The trauma of absorption has slowed any signs of the immigrants taking a leadership role, but Katz stresses that they are better-educated than the average Israeli. "They have higher motivation to have their children study," he says. This human investment will yield rewards in the future."

Katz says that decades ago, he and his colleagues speculated about what would happen when "the children of Stalin" would come to Israel. Today, he says, the answers are becoming clear: "These people have tremendous potential. Their skills and talents have been suppressed for a long time in the Soviet Union, but they quickly rid themselves of these past limitations. Look, for instance, at how many daily newspapers are published in Russian."

Katz notes that the marginal groups among Israelis of Afro-Asian origin watch the influx and absorption of Russian Jews with trepidation. It took them 30 or 40 years to see their children break into mainstream Israeli society, he says, and now they fear that this educated, intellectual new immigration may push their own success stories aside.

Katz has not studied the subject formally, but he has discussed the situation with people of Afro-Asian origin, and they speak openly of their fears. They claim that the current wave of immigrants gets benefits that immigrants never got 40 years ago. They note bitterly that Project Renewal, which was aimed at helping the underprivileged strata of Israeli society, was all but cancelled to free money for Operation Exodus, which funded the immigration and absorption of immigrants from the former Soviet Union.

The Afro-Asians realize, he says, that the Russians' education will enable them to adapt much faster to Israel's prevailing Western culture than they themselves did. "You hear them say things like, 'We are the victims. We served in the army. Our children are victims, look at what others are getting.'"

They may not use those precise words, Katz says, "But that is what they mean. It is taboo to say it publicly, because all Israelis are supposed to support aliya. You cannot leave Jewish people abroad to their fate. People do not dare speak against aliya, but the feelings of jealousy undoubtedly exist."

Beyond the social tensions created by the Russian immigration, Katz notes that another very real problem will be accelerated due to the influx.

"About ten percent of Israel's citizens are 65 or older," he says.

"When the State was founded, the figure stood at three percent. With the influx of the Russian immigrants, who have very few children, the percentage will increase further."

He points to the need to confront the reality created by a sharp increase in the number of citizens who are more than 75 years old. "It is wrong to put people in institutions too quickly," he warns.

"If possible, people should not live detached from society. We need more community support services to enable older people to live in their homes as long as possible."

Important as it may be in the medium and long term, Katz says the issue of an aging population is less urgent than the potential powder keg of culture clashes between different segments of society.

In the state's early years, Katz says, the question of cultural dissimilarities inevitably came to the fore. He has no illusions, however, that the hard work of the social services community brought about important changes. That helped, to be sure, but it took the political echelon's interest to give the issue a real boost. Katz says matter-of-factly that things could only change because they became political issues.

"In the 1950s, 1960s and 1970s, there was a high correlation between being poor and deprived and coming from an Afro-Asian background," he says. "Sad as it was, this correlation became a political fact and was politicized. In the first years of the state, Ben-Gurion was almost a messiah for many, but the 1977 elections, which brought the Likud to power, reflected a backlash against Labor, rather than a vote in favor of anybody else."

Katz cites figures showing that total outlay on social services in Israel today exceeds that for defense. While social services have increased their weight in the Gross National Product since the state's early years, he notes that the increase has been greater in other Western countries.

"In 1980, we spent almost 36 percent of all public expenditures on defense and 31.7 percent on social services," he says. "In 1990, defense was 29.6 percent and social services accounted for 43.7 percent of the budget."

These figures include income maintenance payments from the National Insurance Institute, as well as fiscal benefits, health, education and culture, housing and environment, labor-employment and personal services, such as services for the elderly and the disabled.

Ironically, these changing expenditure ratios, which reflect the social policies of the modern welfare state, have contributed to welfare but have done little to decrease inequalities. Katz raises the possibility that too much power and responsibility may have been delegated to large state-run bureaucracies. "We have relieved citizens too much from their public and social responsibilities," he says.

Other lessons have come in the face of the reality of Israel's heavy tax burden. "We have learned that there is a limit to taxation," he says. "In the years to come, we may not have adequate resources to provide the services that will be needed. The goals for building a better society have not changed, the means and instruments have."

Katz counts himself among the supporters of the welfare state, but he admits that the system is not perfect. "When you detach the human being from the community," he says, "you deresponsibilize people." By letting people pay taxes and think this absolves them of any responsibility to care for their fellow citizens, he says, the public develops a dangerous apathy.

This problem is not unique to Israel. Katz points to Sweden, the most outstanding of all examples of the welfare state. Citing fairly precise statistics on voluntarism around the world, Katz notes that Sweden has very low levels. Israel, on the other hand, has a higher level of voluntarism than that found even in Britain or the U.S.

In the mid-1980s, Katz says, Sweden set up a commission to study the country's future needs. The findings: there would not be enough money to satisfy the country's growing welfare needs if they continued to be met by paid workers. The conclusion: every young

Swede should be compelled to give a number of hours per month to voluntary services in his community, for instance in hospitals. Katz finds it interesting that this notion of compulsory volunteering emerged in a nation which had always favored professional services over volunteering.

"They know that the resources for ever-increasing public and social services will not suffice," he says. The public, which enjoys increasing amounts of leisure time, may have to start committing a part of that time to public service.

It took years to reach the conclusion that the longstanding confrontation between social man and economic man was harmful and misleading, but Katz says the message has finally gotten through around the world. "Social man now understands that without economic growth, there are not enough resources for social policies. Austria and Sweden may have advanced their welfare states mainly because they developed more consensus between employers and labor."

Choice, productivity and efficiency are basic needs of both economic man and social man, he says. The economy and the welfare of the public face many common dangers. Among them: big bureaucracies, too much central planning, monopolistic behavior of public services, lack of efficiency, the monopolistic behavior of professionals such as psychiatrists, doctors and lawyers, as well as strong adherence to political ideologies.

Ironically, Katz says that decades of adherence to the social welfare system has proven that the main beneficiaries have not been the poor; the middle classes have reaped the greatest rewards.

"Thatcher and Reagan did not destroy their respective welfare states," he says. "In some areas, they even strengthened and reinforced services to the middle classes, but they penalized and deprived the poor and weaker in their societies."

In both the U.S. and Britain, the main political backing comes from the majority, he says, noting that in modern states the middle class is the majority and the deprived are a minority.

"In Israel, many of us are conditioned to the thought that the more social services we have, the better for the poor," Katz says. "That is nonsense. We must find out how we can better serve the weaker sectors of our society, without making the services stigmatize them."

He admits that this is a tall order, but he has ideas about how to achieve it. First of all, Katz stresses the need for better information about the true state of social affairs in Israel. He calls for the production of an annual social report, or accounting system, to provide information on the condition of geographical regions in the country and population subgroups. Such a report would provide the information needed to understand the reality in which social services must operate, thereby allowing aid to reach the people who need it most.

The idea isn't as revolutionary as it may sound. Katz notes that Sweden and other Scandinavian countries already produce such reports. This tool would allow Israel to bring true social problems to the Knesset and put them on the national agenda in the order of their urgency.

"We must increase the accountability of public and social services," he says. "If we have no information, such accountability is not possible. Bureaucrats do not like to be made accountable for what they do or fail to do.

While he directed The Center for Social Policy Studies in Israel, it worked with the Central Bureau of Statistics to develop a National Social Accounting System. He notes that the Swedish system is based on ten indicators: economic conditions, education, employment and hours of work, health, housing conditions, leisure and recreation, political resources and activities, safety and security, social relations—i.e., whether a person is isolated—as well as transport and communication.

That model offers a good start, but Katz suggests adding three more indicators: religious practice, military service—compulsory service and reserve duty—and voluntary activities, i.e., donating time and money. This list of indicators would enable researchers to pinpoint the true state of the nation at any given time.

Part of the reason that such a system is so crucial is that the nation's social problems are as diverse as its population. Katz says that no single risk region or group dominates the scene. Some problem groups stand out—such as parents on drugs, alcoholics, mentally disturbed or emotionally deprived people—and social workers understandably notice the problems in their immediate surroundings, but the big picture gets lost amidst all of these local reports.

"Tomorrow, sociologists may or may not find eighth graders who don't know how to read or write," he says. "We do not really know how big these and other problems are and where they are located. Once one has the information on a continuous basis, one sees what social programs and services achieve. One also has to search systematically to sense social problems.

"When the National Health Service in England was established in 1948, studies showed that doctors spent more time with people who spoke good English or with good-looking ladies than with a simple London Cockney, irrespective of the diagnosis," Katz says, adding that the doctors did not realize that they were discriminating.

The same thing used to happen in Israel. Katz found that in the 1950s and 1960s social workers spent more time with attractive women and Yiddish speakers.

Another important factor is the opportunity for advancement. Growing up with parents who both are "social cases" influences a child differently than growing up in the home of a Nobel Prize winner. Social honor is another important factor; people behave in accordance with their self-image and that which society attributes to them.

Katz illustrates this by telling a story about his maid, Esther, who immigrated from Fez, Morocco. "One day, she said to me, 'You must meet my brother. He is wonderful. He is a rabbi in a development town. You will not believe that he comes from Morocco.'"

The next factor is closely related: control over political resources. The extent to which people are represented in the power centers of the country and in the political reality influences their social standing.

This has changed over the years, as illustrated by the fact that when Katz took over at the National Insurance Institute, his agency had 16 regional offices. Of them, 15 were directed by Ashkenazim. The 16th, in Nazareth, had an Arab head. Today, he says, the picture has changed significantly.

While many things have changed, Katz says the basic structure of social services remains flawed. He calls for greater efforts to charge for social services and for progress toward introducing competition in the social services market.

"When I was Minister of Labor, I was against competition for the National Labor Exchange," he says. "Now I know that unless we have private exchanges in addition to the public one, people will get poor service.

"We feel strongly that we should indeed provide many universal services for all but the better off, who should be made to pay," he says. "Another important issue is to recruit people to provide services who are not paid for providing them. Compulsory army service is not only important for defending the country, but also for providing social services."

Katz points out that Germany allows people who refuse to do military service to devote themselves to voluntary service to the community instead. It has worked well and attracted many conscripts. This may be a good option for Israel, too, Katz says, provided that the country's defense needs permit it.

Beyond channelling soldiers into social service functions, Katz stresses the need for greater voluntarism. When speaking about hungry children, he says that people who volunteer to help them can become better people by reaching out.

In Israel, many people volunteer, he says. In fact, twice as many people, per capita, as in England or the United States, but he calls for more. "Voluntarism is not only altruism," he says. "People are rewarded by the satisfaction they get. Our rule should be not to use professionals in areas where we do not need them."

While Israel's overall philanthropy figures look good, Katz notes that cultural differences color the picture. Israelis of Ashkenazi origin, he says, are much more active in philanthropic endeavors than their Sephardi counterparts, he says. He concludes that Ashkenazi sensitivity is much greater due to the persecutions they suffered.

"I asked my Sephardi brother-in-law, who lives in Turkey, why this is the case," he says. "He said that the Sephardim had historically focused on the needs of their own extended families. After the Inquisition, he said, many Jews went to Turkey, where philanthropic activities were largely limited to buying the freedom of Jewish prisoners who were brought from Europe."

In summing up the social problems Israel will continue to face in the coming decade, Katz quotes a Chinese curse: "You should live in interesting times." He adds to it: "We live in an interesting society at an interesting time. That is why the most important challenge for us Israelis is to strengthen the social fabric of our society."

URI MARINOV

Peace Promotes
Environmental Awareness

D ECADES OF WORK on environmental issues earned Uri Marinov the name "Mr. Environment." He headed the country's
Environmental Protection Service for 15 years, and when
the Environment Ministry was established in 1988, he was chosen
as its first director-general.

In July 1992, he moved into the private sector, where he became a
partner and director in an environmental engineering firm, as well
as a consultant. He enjoys worldwide respect, as reflected by his
receipt of the prestigious United Nations Environmental Program
Global 500 Award for Environmental Achievement in 1989.

At a time when peace has become a distinct possibility in the
Middle East, Marinov believes that Israel may be moving toward an
era in which the environment will move from the periphery toward
a more central place in Israeli society.

Hopefully, he says, this will express itself in a more systematic
approach to key environmental problems. At the same time, peace
would foster collaboration with Israel's neighbors on a number of

major transnational problems concerning the environment.

Marinov, who was born in 1935, is married and has three children, earned a D.V.M. in veterinary clinical sciences from Iowa State University in 1965. He later served as a research associate in the department of physiology at the Hadassah Hebrew University Medical School in Jerusalem. From 1969 until 1973, he worked in the Prime Minister's Office as head of the life sciences division of the National Council for Research and Development.

Marinov was a member of the National Board for Planning and an acting professor in the Technion's faculty of architecture and town planning. He is a member of the Council of the World Resources Institute in Washington, one of the most prestigious international environmental think tanks, and of the editorial advisory board of the World Resources Report.

He has published extensively. Marinov opens a discussion on the environment by defining his terms. "Everyone has his own definition," he says. "When I was at the Environment Ministry, I would joke that if officials at another government ministry wanted you to deal with a subject, they would say, 'It is an environmental issue,' and if they didn't want you to deal with it they would say, 'It isn't an environmental issue.'"

He identifies three main environmental problems facing the country in the 1990s and beyond. Far and away the most important one is the water situation. This is followed by toxic chemicals and air pollution caused by vehicular exhaust. In a lengthy discussion, he focuses on these three issues.

In broad Israeli terms, he says, from the government's point of view, "environment" refers to two things: protection of natural resources, including water, air, land and sea; and providing the population with quality of life as it relates to the physical environment.

"From a national point of view, the first priority is human health, but 'physical environment' also includes the protection of vegetation, landscape and structures," Marinov says. "Air pollution, for instance, affects vegetation. Some flowers are more sensitive than humans to air pollution, and we have to protect them."

Marinov traces Israeli concern with the environment back to the early 1970s. A long period of annual economic growth exceeding ten percent left the environment in a sad state. That period of rapid industrial advancement brought the environment to a state of near-collapse.

As awareness began to grow, however, the picture improved, according to Mr. Environment. "This can be demonstrated by examples such as the construction of sewage treatment plants and reducing the air pollution from stationary sources," he says. This progress was offset by other problems, such as the country's rapid population growth.

Marinov says that the 1980s saw an overall improvement in the environment, but adds that the mass immigration of the early 1990s has brought with it some backtracking.

"If you bring half a million people within a relatively short time, the government seems to have the justification to circumvent the planning and building laws," he says. "Planners are not very popular, and they are accused of bureaucracy that delays projects. Building a great number of housing units rapidly was approved without a proper investigation as to where they should be located.

Some units were built on former landfills, Marinov says, while others were located too close to airports and still others were built without proper sewage facilities. From the environmental point of view, the mass aliya of the early 1990s saw the government fall back into an approach from the 1950s. The economic and environmental damage was enormous, Marinov says, adding that if a new wave of olim came tomorrow, the leaders might choose the same approach all over again.

Marinov then moves to his main concern: water. "Those who

think that two years of ample rains in 1991/1992 and 1992/1993 improved Israel's water supply structurally are totally wrong," he says. "These rains filled the reservoirs a little bit, but the country's most serious environmental problems continue to lie in the realm of water—quantity and quality."

As quantities go down, Marinov notes, so does quality. "Israel has been overpumping for 10–15 years, and quality declines fast. When we overpump, seawater intrudes in our underground aquifers, increasing the salinity of our water supplies."

Marinov notes that Israel's Water Quality Law, enacted in 1971, gives the Water Commissioner ample authority to prevent water pollution. Nonetheless, successive water commissioners have neglected the issue.

"They have done nothing," he charges. "No regulations, no prosecution against those who pollute and overpump. They were answering the immediate demands of the farming community, which was not concerned with the future."

This lax enforcement is responsible for the country's water quality problems. Marinov notes with dismay that government officials are among the major violators of environmental policy. "Our mayors will prosecute you for closing your balcony without a permit," he says, "but they disobey the water and sewage laws on a daily basis."

In accordance with national law, municipalities charge residents and businesses a sewage fee, which is supposed to be used to build and operate sewage treatment plants. Instead, Marinov charges, many of them use the money for other purposes, and dump their sewage into the country's rivers. As an example, he cites former Jerusalem Mayor Teddy Kollek. In nearly 30 years in the city's top job, Kollek oversaw the construction of excellent facilities improving many other aspects of life, but at the same time he allowed most of the capital's sewage to flow untreated into the Kidron and Sorek valleys.

"Politicians and mayors have a different set of priorities than we do," Marinov says, reflecting on why public officials blatantly disregard the law of the land. "Sewage is not visible. They can get their picture taken with a new museum or a school, but not with a sewage plant or a solid waste disposal facility."

As if this wasn't bad enough, Marinov adds that much of the sewage system built in the 1970s and 1980s has collapsed under the strain of a growing population, which means that freshwater supplies are being contaminated by sewage.

In 1990, responsibility for water quality was transferred to the Environment Ministry, and Marinov boasts that his people did "more in one and a half years than the Water Commissioner did in 18 years."

As is so often the case, Marinov says that money—or the lack thereof—lies at the root of the problem. "With half a billion dollars, we could build, within the Green Line, all the sewage treatment plants we need," he says. As time passes and damage is done, however, all the money in the world won't remedy some of the damage being caused. He adds that, if sewage treatment would be privatized, finding money to build adequate facilities would not pose a problem.

"Nothing can clean an aquifer when it gets polluted," he says flatly. "The damage is irreversible. The problem stems from the fact that the Ministry of Agriculture was in charge of water quality for years, but neglected its responsibilities."

The aquifers are not the only focus of irreparable damage, but they pose the most serious threat. Marinov notes that building new towns and cities causes irreversible damage to the environment, but he stresses that the greatest threat posed by such developments is in the sphere of water quality. "If there is air pollution, a good rainstorm will clean it up," he says. "Noise is a matter of minutes or seconds until the airplane passes." Damage to water resources stands alone at the pinnacle of environmental threats.

Even as reckless behavior causes irreparable damage, those in the know calculate how solutions may be found. If the aquifers become irreversibly polluted, as Marinov warns they could, then desalination could always take center stage. The main problem, though, is the high cost of this high-tech solution.

Another potential remedy lies in changing the agricultural sector's use of water. By implementing "closed systems" on the nation's farms, output per liter of water could be increased by a factor of ten or 20. Again, though, the problem is money. Transforming a small family farm to a closed system could cost upwards of $100,000, and who would foot the bill?

"The peace process will have an impact as well," Marinov says. "Palestinian per capita consumption of water is about a third or a quarter of that of Israelis. Their consumption will grow rapidly. In the Gaza Strip, where the population has increased fast, practically all sources have been penetrated by saltwater due to overpumping. In Judea and Samaria, there is also a shortage of water. Jordan's water shortage is even more severe than Israel's."

After peace, the whole issue of supply of adequate quantities of water and the maintaining of water quality will become even more central. Marinov says there are many ideas and plans on how to solve the water problems of both Israel and the Palestinians. "We will have to be very innovative to produce additional water in great quantities and to store it," he says.

"This can be done in part in the Sea of Galilee and the Coastal Aquifer. There is no doubt that one of our great challenges is to live in a rather barren area that often will have years of drought.

"We will have to take daring initiatives," he stresses. "One alternative is to bring water from other Middle Eastern countries by pipeline. Egypt is a possible source. Another is a 'peace pipeline,' from Turkey via Syria, which would supply Jordan, Saudi Arabia and Israel.

"A second possibility is to produce water by desalination. There are also ambitious plans on paper to bring water from the Mediterranean to the Dead Sea. For instance, to let two billion cubic meters of water flow through a pipeline to the Beth Shean valley and desalinate 400 million cubic meters for Israel. This water would go straight to the National Water Carrier to improve water quality."

Under such a plan, Marinov says, the Palestinians and Jordanians would take another 400 million cubic meters, and the remainder could be used for making electricity, if this were economically justified. While the idea seems attractive, Marinov says such an ambitious plan would be very costly and would need to be studied carefully in conjunction with neighboring countries.

"In the meantime, Israel will allocate less and less fresh water to agriculture," he says. "More and more will go to households and industry. Agriculture will have to limit itself to other water sources. We have 200–250 million cubic meters of effluents flowing from sewage systems available, and we will have to use this resource in a more intelligent way."

Although he now works in the private sector, Marinov is still widely acknowledged to be the country's Number One expert in setting national environmental policy. What would he suggest if the government was to allocate half a billion dollars to the environment?

"I might use a little bit toward some of our solid waste disposal areas, because these affect water quality," he says matter-of-factly. "I would use another little bit to help municipalities move sanitary landfills away from the coast. Industrial money should go to air and noise pollution problems. Government money, however, should mainly be spent on water problems.

"In 1993, the whole subject of treating effluents water, which then can be reused, was given a new impetus by the government, which began to give 25–30 percent grants for investments in sewage treatment plants," Marinov says. "Private entrepreneurs are considering investment in such plants, as local authorities are willing to give them long-term contracts on the basis of a fixed fee per cubic meter treated.

"Israeli water consumption at present is about 500 million cubic meters annually for household use, which gives us 350 million cubic meters of effluents," he continues. "The remainder evaporates, or goes to irrigation in homes or gardens. There are also leakages in the pipe system and other losses. Outside the Dan region, there is no adequate sewage treatment. We just seem to have other priorities.

"The greater Dan area, which includes Tel Aviv, produces about 100 million cubic meters of effluents per year, and these could be used for agriculture. Cities such as Jerusalem, Netanya, Hadera and Ashdod have plans to do the same and others are likely to follow.

"Hopefully, within two or three years this process will lead to the construction of another 15–20 sewage treatment plants, which will supply us with 200–250 million cubic meters of water for reuse."

Despite these potential positive developments, Marinov stresses that it will take more than a few years to fix the damage caused by more than 40 years of neglect and abuse. "We like to think that we are part of the Western world, but in the environmental field we are far from it," he says.

While water issues pose the greatest risks and challenges in the environmental realm, Marinov is not blind to other issues. The manufacture and use of toxic chemicals ranks as his second concern.

He notes that the past few years have been marked by several major chemical accidents, including a fire in a Herzliya pesticide warehouse and several traffic accidents in which bromine was released. "Now we have an emergency system that operates the moment an accident occurs, and people are trained for emergencies."

In the last few years, Marinov adds, new prevention measures have been adopted. Drivers need a special license to carry chemical payloads, and only specially licensed agencies may ship chemicals.

Marinov remains more concerned about day-to-day operating procedures than the ability to deal with crises and accidents. Despite all its achievements, the Environment Ministry still has less information about potentially dangerous situations than its counterpart in the U.S., the Environmental Protection Agency.

"Toxic chemicals are stored and transported without scrutiny of any regulatory agency," he says. "We have to put some order in this mess. The Environment Ministry must publish a whole set of regulations to control the use, production and storage of toxic chemical waste."

Part of the problem lies in double standards regarding foods for local consumption or for export. Marinov notes that the Agriculture Ministry checks the level of pesticide residue in produce destined for foreign markets, but not in produce for local consumption. He attributes this inconsistency to the fact that foreign countries occasionally reject produce that does not meet their standards, while nobody looks over the Agriculture Ministry's shoulder on the local scene.

He cites one specific example: grapes. A few years back, lab tests revealed pesticide residues, including some chemicals which farmers are not supposed to apply to grapes. In protest, Marinov declared publicly that he would stop eating grapes. His one-man show of defiance prompted some grape growers to announce plans to control pesticides more carefully.

"Recent studies, undertaken jointly by the Environment and Health ministries, provided additional data pointing to higher-than-permitted pesticide residue levels in food. We still continue to export food to Europe which is clean, and market in Israel food that has high pesticide residues.

"Israelis get too many residues in almost all their food products, including eggs, meat, milk, fish, vegetables and fruit," he says. "I stopped eating strawberries for that reason.

"It's more than a matter of principle," Marinov insists. "Israelis may be paying for this lax enforcement with their health. We know that residues of pesticides in food are bad for us and should not be there according to the law, but we cannot say that if you eat two kilos of a specific product you will get sick.

"In 1993, however, the Academy of Sciences of the United States came out with a new report showing heavy damages to children under the age of five from pesticide residues in food products," he notes. "This report is one of the most encompassing ever. It convinces me again that until we apply the same strict rules for food destined for local consumption as we do for food destined for export, this problem will not be solved."

Marinov acknowledges that tracking epidemiological claims to pollution is difficult. "We have more cancer and asthma in the Haifa Bay area than in other Israeli cities," he says. While Haifa is home to the country's petrochemical industry, he says that no direct links to environmental causes have been made. In the environmental field, cause and effect are very difficult to demonstrate. That's part of the reason that it is so difficult to set legal standards.

Marinov identifies air pollution as the country's third most pressing environmental priority. While there is still room for improvement in the environmental records of the Israel Electric Corp. and the Oil Refineries, great strides have been made in minimizing their pollution. After dealing with the reduction of sulfur oxide emissions, nitrogen oxides should be next on the agenda.

There is slow progress as well, Marinov believes, in reducing pollution caused by automobiles. Since 1993, all cars imported into the country must have catalytic converters. Such cars use lead-free gasoline. As old cars slowly disappear from the roads, air quality should improve, unless the number of cars on the roads continues to increase rapidly.

More and more lead-free gasoline, which reduces the emissions of this toxic metal, is being sold in Israel. Another positive step is that

Israel now imports crude oil with a much lower sulfur content than it did a few years ago. These are all changes in the right direction.

These steps cost money, and every Israeli will have to foot his share of the bill, Marinov says. "It will cost more to live in a clean environment. It will cost more to produce electricity and drive cars."

He favors a sharp rise in gasoline prices as a tool to reduce consumption. "With the increasing number of private vehicles, we will not be able to maintain the quality of the environment in the metropolitan areas, even if everyone has a catalytic converter," he stresses. The answer: more public transportation.

Ironically, the reality of outdated collective wage agreements actually exacts a heavy toll on Israeli air quality. Marinov notes that when an employer hires a new worker, he often recommends that the newcomer purchase a car. "Salaries can be doubled by the money workers get as a car allowance," he says. "Sometimes, public officials buy very old cars just so they can collect the upkeep money. This is insane and needs change."

Another area where progress has been made concerns recycling. In July 1993, the Knesset passed a recycling law which can force those who generate waste, including households, to separate it into various types. A major problem of recycling, however, is that one often does not know what to do with the secondary materials produced.

Recycling will be stimulated as landfill costs in Israel, which are ridiculously low by international standards, increase. They will rise as a result of the Ministry's decision to close most landfills and concentrate disposal at a few sites.

"I hope that the Environment Ministry will enforce the recycling law sensibly," Marinov says. "Pushing too hard may be counterproductive and lead to anti-environmentalist sentiment, as has happened elsewhere. When I was in the public service, I always said that we have to deal with environmental issues in a rational way, as environmentalism is neither ideology nor religion. The greatest enemies of environmentalism are the irrational environmentalists."

One of the big challenges that Israel faces in the 1990s is the need to educate its populace about environmentalism. Marinov notes the difference between inside and outside environment: "Our apartments are beautiful and clean, but people perceive the outside as belonging to the municipality," he says. "We need to change people's attitude. First they need to understand the issues, and then we need to teach them how to behave differently."

Marinov sets an example in his own daily behavior. He never writes on fresh paper, preferring the back side of a used sheet. He sends his wastepaper for recycling and encourages others to do the same. When he was in the public service, he selected a very small car for his personal use. "Everyone in the government thought I was crazy, because I was entitled to a bigger car," he says with a laugh.

Marinov notes optimistically that the local population has proven that it can be educated on environmental issues. The Society for the Protection of Nature in Israel and the Nature Reserves Authority have enjoyed great success in teaching the public not to pick wild flowers. When he was in the public service, Marinov enlisted the help of psychologists and sociologists in his efforts to understand why the same methods have not put an end to public littering.

"Israel has invested more in nature conservation than in any other environmental issue," he says. "The government has expropriated thousands of dunams from private people to create a national park.

"I sometimes joke that when there is a dying bird in the Hula Valley, ten or 15 people with jeeps and radios are mobilized," he says. "If a toxic chemical is dumped in the Jordan River or the Kinneret, no one says anything."

As always, much of the issue comes down to budgets. The Nature Reserves Authority has a staff of inspectors who track abuses of nature, and its lawyers make effective use of the courts to further its causes. Their concern, however, is limited to very specific environmental issues, and other organizations lack the resources that they have.

"The Water Commissioner has just one person to protect the water quality in this country," Marinov says with a sigh. "So how can he compete with the Nature Reserves Authority?"

In conclusion, Marinov takes a final look at the meaning of the peace process for Israel's environment. It goes far beyond collaboration with neighboring countries on environmental issues, he insists. From a macro-economic point of view, the reduction in defense costs may facilitate greater investment in environmental issues, if the population presses for it.

Another aspect is that the army, which controls about 25 percent of the land area of Israel, will free some of it for other uses. Such a move will make additional areas of the country available to the population, but it is not without risk. The army's control has prevented the irresponsible development of some seacoast areas, Marinov says. We have to be careful that these will not be destroyed when they are freed.

"Pollution knows no frontiers," he says. "As far as collaboration with our neighbors is concerned, the number one issue concerns the Gulf of Aqaba. This is a closed area with a unique nature. Both Jordan and Egypt plan major tourist developments there. Saudi Arabia's plans, if any, are not very clear.

"For the Jordanians, Aqaba remains a crucial location even if Israel provides access to its Mediterranean ports. Aqaba is the only place where Jordan can build a large power station and cool it with seawater."

Marinov predicts that the countries that border the Gulf will establish an Aqaba Gulf Authority that will maintain statistics and data to be exchanged in case of disasters. As the area's future is mainly in tourism, its unique coral reefs have to be kept intact, which requires international collaboration. Corals are very sensitive to pollution, he notes. "Either we all collaborate or nobody will have a reef.

"Similarly, a Jordan Valley Authority will have to be established. One cannot deal with the problems of the eastern or the western side of the Jordan separately. First of all, the river has to be cleaned up and more water has to be brought in. Then both sides can be converted into resort areas.

"Some collaboration already exists around the Mediterranean," Marinov says, adding that it must be stepped up. "One prime target is to put an end to dumping raw sewage into the sea. All countries that border on the Mediterranean dump waste into the sea, although Israel dumps the least."

Marinov sees many more issues on a common regional environmental agenda. Twice a year, he notes, one billion birds pass over the area, and they have to be protected. On a totally different front, he says that Israel is the only country in the world which has demonstrated its ability to prevent desertification. For obvious reasons, this knowhow is of great interest to the Arabs.

With new issues emerging all the time, Mr. Environment is convinced that the common environmental agenda of Jews and Arabs in the Middle East will only grow as the years pass.

ABRAHAM B. YEHOSHUA

New Components of Israel's Identity

ABRAHAM YEHOSHUA is one of Israel's best-known and most successful writers. His novels have been translated into many languages, and he has received such prestigious Israeli literary prizes as the Brenner Prize (1983), the Alterman Prize (1986) and the Bialik Prize (1989).

In 1992, he received the Prize of Israeli Literature—for his most recent novel, *Mr. Mani*—which is given every two years for the best prose book. This novel, considered by most critics to be Yehoshua's best work ever, uses five different characters' viewpoints to tell a story about a Sephardi family over the course of 150 years.

After graduating from the Hebrew University, where he studied philosophy and Hebrew literature, Yehoshua went to Paris in 1963 and became secretary-general of the World Union of Jewish Students (WUJS). He returned to Israel in 1967, taking the post of Dean of Students at Haifa University. He has been a full professor of comparative literature at Haifa University since 1972.

In 1975, Yehoshua was a guest writer at St. Cross College in

Oxford, England. He also has served as visiting professor at a number of American universities, including Harvard, Chicago, Stanford and Princeton.

If the peace process bears fruit, Yehoshua believes that Israel will face many new identity problems. "Peace will create both new challenges and new risks for Israeli society," he says. "Automatic solidarity against a common enemy will no longer be our main binding element. The common front of solidarity against outside hostility will have to be replaced by a more substantial identity.

"Time and again, questions arise about the main ingredients of Israeli identity," he says. "Whenever I'm abroad, I'm always amazed that I can identify Israelis from afar, based on their body movement and the way they are dressed. That proves to me that there is an Israeli identity, even if I cannot define its components very well."

Yehoshua believes that the end of hostilities may open the door for many new alliances between groups within Israel, which had been divided on issues related to territorial concessions and Greater Israel. In the era of peace, freed of the old conflicts, he says, Israelis will be able to reach out as a people to help the world in significant ways for the first time.

Before launching into an assessment of the impending changes, Yehoshua defines his views about Israeli identity until now. "Israelis are the most genuine Jews there are," he says, "regardless of whether they practice religion or not. Only Israelis are 'total Jews.'

"The Jewish people were born under the name of Israel," he adds. "When the Bible details the exploits of our national heroes, they are called 'sons of Israel,' not 'Jews.' They did not even know what Jews were. It is of more than formal importance that 'Israel' is the authentic and first name of our people. "Only in one of the Bible's last books, the Scroll of Esther, is the word Jew mentioned for the first time," Yehoshua says. "It tells us about Mordechai the Jew, who lived in the Persian capital of Shushan. It is not incidental that a man living outside the land of Israel is called a Jew. He was, by the way, a rather despicable character; he married off his niece, in a mixed marriage, to King Ahasverus."

Yehoshua notes that when Ezra and Nehemia led the returnees from the Babylonian exile, they reinstated the name of Israel, a support from history for his conclusion that Israelis are the authentic Jews.

"Our biblical tradition also says that the name Israel was given by the Lord himself to the forefather Jacob, after his struggle with an angel," the writer notes. "It was not by chance that when the modern Jewish state was founded in 1948, it was called Israel, rather than something with the name Jew, Judea or Zion in it."

Yehoshua sees a clear difference between Israeli identity and citizenship. "Today, if you say 'Israeli,' you refer not only to Israeli citizenship but also to an Israeli identity," he maintains, adding that the difference is important: Israeli Arabs are Israeli citizens, he notes, while their identity is that of either a Palestinian Moslem or a Palestinian Christian.

He describes the relationship between Israelis and diaspora Jews as the relationship between a total Jew and a partial Jew, or what he says could even be called a partial Israeli.

"I live in Israel, in a reality which is entirely Jewish and which is being constructed and developed by Jews," he says. "All of its major components are Jewish.

"That is why, as an Israeli, I am a total Jew. As far as being Jewish is concerned, I have a clear advantage. The Jews abroad are diluted Jews of various degrees depending on the society they live in and how they interact with it.

"Religious observance is not a precondition for being a Jew," he continues, putting forth ideas that seem obvious to him but which are nonetheless revolutionary for many diaspora Jews. "Many Jews are not religious at all. Being a Jew is defined—even by the religious authorities—as a national, not religious, identity. Halacha considers nonreligious Jews to be Jews, as long as they are born to a Jewish mother.

"Diaspora Jews are considered Jews regardless of whether they are religious or not," he adds. "The chief rabbi of Vienna was an Orthodox Jew, while Theodor Herzl, the founder of Zionism, who lived in the same city, was not. Nobody would contest the Jewishness of either man. In Israel, both religious and non-religious Israelis are total Jews.

"We Israelis did not start from nothing in building our identity, as the Americans did at the time of George Washington," Yehoshua says. "What we have brought from the diaspora, where we lived for 2,000 years, is part of that identity. It includes our culture, history and language.

"I can explain this concept to Americans with ease. Were George Washington or Thomas Jefferson any less American than John Kennedy or Bill Clinton in our time? Washington's American identity was totally new, but that was all there was about American identity at the time. Nobody can claim that Clinton is more of an American than Washington just because more than 200 years of history have passed.

"The fact that Americans lived in a separate territory and were part of a population which organized around an identity center gave them that identity," he explains. "The black man who stood next to Washington—who might not have been a Christian and certainly was not an Anglo Saxon—had that same American identity. Washington was no different from an Englishman living in North America, but the Declaration of Independence and the formal fact that he created an independent country made him an American."

In comparison to America's beginnings, Yehoshua says, Israel had a much richer starting point as a modern state. The diaspora experience was only part of the new country's identity; before that, there was the history of the people when they had lived in their own land.

"Today, we continue to add to this identity," Yehoshua says. "We face challenges in the total Jewish reality of Israel. We also have to find answers to issues such as how to establish an economy, what Jewish foreign policy means and how to create a Jewish social policy.

"Being Israeli means having a very strong, multi-layered identity," he says. "The reality of our new state required rapid on-the-spot answers to many problems, unlike the French or the Dutch, who had hundreds of years to let their values develop gradually into a national tradition."

Yehoshua believes that traditional Jewish sources should be important reference points as Israel determines its values and policies. One example: what does the Talmud say about unemployment?

Though Yehoshua is far from the religious community, he stresses this historic link. "Even when the Jews lived outside their country and were no longer judged by Jewish courts, the Talmud continued to deal with theoretical problems of Jewish justice and questions concerning the agriculture of the land of Israel," he says.

"Israel's decisionmakers should absorb more of these traditions and values," he adds. "The ancient sources have to be a cultural authority. In France, it is obvious that one should not build a new branch of the Louvre without studying the national architectural tradition and applying it to a modern situation. Whoever wants to open a French restaurant in Paris with a new menu somehow seeks to continue the French culinary tradition.

"What is nowadays termed international style often covers up for American style. I am not against foreign influences, but there is a difference between being influenced by foreign traditions, which has happened throughout history, and copying them.

"When I write a novel, I do not start from zero, without a link to the past. I write in a language which has existed for thousands of years and has a literary tradition which goes back that far. I may also be influenced by foreign writers; the two things merge.

"I maintain that my works are no less Jewish than a poem by our medieval classics, such as Yehuda Halevi or Shlomo Ibn Gvirol. It cannot be that a homosexual poem which Ibn Gvirol wrote in the diaspora is Jewish or that a wine song of Shmuel Hanagid is Jewish while a wine song of contemporary Israeli poets such as Yehuda Amichai or David Avidan is not considered Jewish."

He describes as absurd a claim that what Franz Kafka wrote in German, without any Jewish content, is Jewish, while his own work might not be considered Jewish. "To the contrary, I do not consider Kafka's work Jewish, because of the absence of Jewish themes," he says. "Had he, however, written in Hebrew, then his oeuvre would have been Jewish literature by definition.

"Pornographic books in Yiddish sold thousands of copies at the end of the 19th century," Yehoshua adds. "They are Jewish works, written by Jews for Jews in a Jewish language. The same goes for pornography written today in Hebrew.

Yehoshua uses the example of democracy to illustrate how foreign ideas become part of a culture. "Democracy is not a specific Jewish value, nor is it a specific German value," he says. "To some extent, it may be a specific French value. To countries such as Japan and Russia, democracy was irrelevant for many years. Today they function as democracies, and that is part of their identity.

"While the Jews did not create a formal democracy like the Greeks did, they operated according to many clearly democratic principles. The Bible contains many examples of democratic attitudes. The opinions of the opposition to the kings get a more central place than what those in power had to say. The prophecies are the protocols of the opposition's statements.

"The Talmud consists of discussions, and the minority opinions are included," he adds. "This gives legitimation to discussion and opposition. The decisions in the courts were taken in a democratic way, based on a majority vote.

"The same goes for the rabbinate through the ages. There was no Chief Rabbi whose opinion was binding for other rabbis. Each rabbi was autonomous in his territory. If some rabbis had great authority, they earned it because their knowledge was recognized as superior by others. The reasoning with which they arrived at their opinions legitimized the authority, which the others voluntarily bestowed upon them.

"There are other elements of identity," Yehoshua says. "The Yishuv was faced with crucial decisions on which there were major ideological differences of opinion, yet internal violence was minimal. It is remarkable that in the 100 years of our national struggle very few Jews killed or wounded other Jews. There was always a common enemy, so everybody was careful not to go too far."

While it is too early to define in detail the new challenges to identity posed by peace, Yehoshua lists a number of controversial issues as well as a number of sources which may contribute to the discussion of Israel's identity.

"Americanization is an important challenge," he says. "Cable television has been an important instrument in promoting it. Foreign media programs cause major problems of cultural identity, even in big countries such as France and Italy, which have more than 50 million inhabitants and enough economic resources to create original programs."

Despite the fact that Americanization is a problem worldwide, Yehoshua believes that with the passing years, more Israelis will realize that the country's society cannot be built solely on the pillars of making money and becoming Americanized.

"At the same time as the international American influence moves in, a certain orientalization of Israeli society is taking place, in view of the greater Arab influence," Yehoshua says. "Both may develop to fill the vacuum."

Another challenge concerns the relationship between religion and state, Yehoshua says. The problem has been minimized today, he says, because the country is so divided between those who are willing to make territorial concessions to the Palestinians and those who are not. In order to create viable governments, both Labor and the Likud have needed the support of Orthodox parties, he notes, so they have strived to minimize conflicts with them.

"Once the future of the territories and peace are no longer the central dividing issues between the major parties, new avenues for coalitions will open up," Yehoshua forecasts. "Lawyer parliamentarians from Likud and Meretz, such as Dan Meridor and Amnon Rubinstein, can easily find a common language. Socially oriented parliamentarians such as Meir Shetrit of the Likud and Amir Peretz of Labor also can team up together.

"The 1993 municipal elections are a good indication of this crossing of voters between the two main political blocs," he says. "Many Labor supporters voted for Ehud Olmert as mayor in Jerusalem and for Ronni Milo in Tel Aviv, even though both are prominent Likud members. The electorate did not think that this party affiliation was particularly relevant for the competent running of the cities."

He terms the change in character of the National Religious Party one of Israel's great political tragedies. "In the first decades of the country's existence, it was a loyal partner of the Labor Party," he says. "It emphasized religion but was always willing to share total responsibility for Israel's future. The children of its supporters still serve in the army, but it has become a right-wing party.

"Once the conflict with the Arabs will cease to be the key issue in Israeli politics, the NRP will return to its traditional place in the center of the political map," Yehoshua predicts. "It will again be a party which will emphasize the religious aspects of the state within the framework of total responsibility for its future. Maybe, for the first time in many years, a new type of alliance may be possible between the non-religious and the religious."

He stresses that this reconciliation will not include supporters of Shas or Agudat Israel, with whom he says no ideological alliance is possible. "All you can do is make political deals with them in the Knesset. I see, however, a beginning of a new dialogue between the intellectuals of the Labor and modern Orthodox camps. One finds the latter not only in the NRP but also in the Likud and Labor.

"Obviously, the ultra-Orthodox Jews will fight in their way for their views as to what the Israeli identity should be," Yehoshua says. "Shas and Agudat Israel see in the state only an instrument for building their own closed societies. They feel responsible mainly for the future of their own communities, not for that of the state.

"The ultra-Orthodox will fight to bring the more moderate Orthodox over to their camp," he forecasts. "They say, 'If you already are Orthodox, you should go the whole way.' But, while the ultra-Orthodox are increasing their numbers, they will not wage battle on the total identity of the state, as their main interest is to increase their share of the cake."

Shifting focus, Yehoshua says that after the end of Arab Israeli hostilities, the enormous difference in the numbers of Israelis and Arabs will become visible. Yehoshua illustrates this with an example. "With open borders, a million Arab tourists can come on any given day to Israel.

"They may sit peacefully on our beaches or walk through our cities and suddenly, the real proportion in numbers, which has been hidden, will become clear. The visual confrontation with these numbers will force Israeli society to think more about its own identity.

"I have often said to the Jerusalem Arabs, 'If you would go out of the Old City dressed in your typical clothes on a Saturday morning for a walk on Jaffa Road or King George Street, the main streets where the American Jewish tourists can be found, you would show them how many Arabs there are in Jerusalem.'

"More challenges will emerge as the Israeli Arabs will claim equal status as citizens in Israeli society," Yehoshua says. "At the same time, they may link up culturally with the Palestinians across the border."

What elements will contribute to the new identity? Yehoshua does not exclude the possibility that nothing new will emerge from within, while the unifying factors will disappear. This, though, is the most pessimistic scenario.

"One nucleus of response could be the rebirth of the ideological center," he suggests. "In the past, it consisted of Mapai, the Progressive party, part of the General Zionists as well as the NRP. The search for a better-defined identity will force us to rebuild the political center.

"Once society senses the increasing Americanization and the orientalization, there will be a reaction. The issue of Israeli identity will concern many more people once Jews are not being murdered by Arabs.

"Israeli intellectuals will benefit from peace and the search for new elements of identity," he says. "Key figures of Zionism, such as Herzl, Nordau and Jabotinsky, were both writers and intellectuals. They created the building blocks from which the nonreligious identity of this society was built, which was accepted by those who did not want a religious identity.

"I do not think that the big sales of books in Israel result from the fact that literature proportionately attracts more people in Israel than in France or England. The fact that writers were the builders of our identity plays a major role here.

"Intellectuals and academics can give direction to the new ideological process which is required," he continues. "That will happen once we no longer size up each other according to whether we are for or against territorial concessions and Greater Israel.

"In the last 20 years, this was the sole ideological criterion on which one judged people before deciding whether to ally oneself with them. The change of alliances is going to be one of the great changes in Israeli society.

"Efforts will be made by many groups to influence the Israeli identity. Meretz supporters will crystallize around the human rights issue. There will also be a revival of Canaanism. People will claim that in the absence of enmity with the Arabs, the Israeli identity must be determined by the Israeli nationality. "Such a movement will not be limited to Jews," he adds. "It will look for a common identity for Jews and Arabs. There is already an Arab writer, Anton Shamas, who writes in Hebrew, and there will be more."

Yehoshua raises many other questions concerning Israeli identity. What will be the attitude of world Jewry toward Israel in the post-hostility era? Will there be a decline in anti-Semitism? A new definition of Israel-diaspora relations will have to develop.

"Israel will no longer be able to say to the Jews abroad, 'Please lobby for us politically, please help us in our struggle.' The major issue is whether we can find new positive contents for the collaboration of Jews and Israelis.

"In an article I wrote for the *Ma'ariv* daily in 1993, I suggested that we try to develop some kind of a common mission toward the Third World," Yehoshua says. A specific suggestion: a joint Teaching Corps.

"There are many unemployed Jewish intellectuals in the world," he says. "Why not send them to Third World countries for a year or two to teach music, history, science, technology or computers? Jews and Israelis can participate in such a project, which will make these people available, free of charge, to the Third World. If 1,000 or 1,500 of these teachers take up posts, they will make an impact. It is also another way of bringing Jews and Israelis together for a common purpose.

"Now that we have an established state, the image of the cosmopolitan character of world Jewry should no longer worry us,"

Yehoshua says. "We can now address the world as an integral part of it. In the future, Israelis may serve in United Nations forces, just like Norwegians or Swedes. Even such activities can contribute components to a national identity."

Once their own immediate wellbeing is secure, Yehoshua stresses, Israelis will be free to consider what they can do for humanity. Such undertakings will please a certain group of Jews, he says, who feel that Jews should act as a people to give to the world at large.

He stresses the break from the contributions of individual Jews in past centuries. Many Jews, such as Freud and Einstein, have made important contributions to the world, he says, but they have made their contributions as individuals. Many Jewish professors at universities around the world have ideas which enrich the world, but their contributions are made outside of any firm Jewish framework.

"Switzerland's image is based on neutrality, in addition to chocolate and banking," he says. "Through the Red Cross, Switzerland gives services of neutrality to the world. That neutrality is part of its identity. In the same way, the Teaching Corps will be part of Israel's identity.

"Jews always had more of a problem of defining their identity than others," Yehoshua says. "I think that when peace frees our mind somewhat, a whole range of new ideas will emerge. It may be a question of small groups getting together.

"One additional type of search for identity I see is renewed interest on the part of non-religious Jews in traditional sources. This will not be done for political reasons, but will reflect a genuine search to understand their content.

"We may start to ask ourselves about the meaning of Shabbat in the state of Israel," he says. "Such a question is very relevant, as we cannot avoid defining our role in the Middle East and in the face of the wave of orientalization that will engulf Israel. Where do we participate in Middle Eastern culture, and where do we separate ourselves from it?

"Israel is not an amorphous entity. A lot is going on already. A new ideological center will have to be born. We will have to develop new codes of what is and what is not permitted. In politics, the end often justified the means. Almost anything was permitted. Here, too, there will be an evolution because norms always were overshadowed by the security issue.

"But we always had moral codes," he says, drawing the conversation to a close. "Even in war against the Arabs, there were moral lines we did not cross. When dozens of Arab civilians were killed in the village of Deir Yassin during the War of Independence, a broad range of people with radically different political ideas united to condemn it. There were also clear norms on the behavior toward hostages. Now we must develop moral codes for many new fields."

MENACHEM FRIEDMAN

Impending Changes
for Ultra-Orthodox Society

Menachem Friedman is professor of sociology of religion at Bar-Ilan University, where he heads the Institute for Judaism and Contemporary Thought. He has been a visiting professor at Oxford University, and also has taught at the Hebrew University, Harvard, Berkeley and Yeshiva University. He was awarded the Warburg prize by the Hebrew University and the Ben Zvi prize by Yad Yitzhak Ben Zvi.

Born in Israel in 1936, Friedman studied sociology and Jewish history at the Hebrew University, obtaining his Ph.D in 1973. In 1974, he became a faculty member at Bar-Ilan University. Years of work have earned him a reputation as the leading expert on Israel's religious communities. His main fields of interest include the relationship between Orthodox and non-Orthodox Jews, the social history of the Jews, the sociology of Halacha and the sociology of ultra-Orthodox-communities in Jewish society.

His books include *Society and Religion: The Non-Zionist Orthodoxy in the Land of Israel 1918–1936*, published in 1978, and *The Haredi Commu-*

nity: Sources, Trends and Processes, which came out in 1991. *The Poster People*, due out in 1994, will study the Haredi—i.e., ultra-Orthodox—community as seen through its wall posters.

In a lengthy conversation about the direction of Israel's ultra-Orthodox community, Friedman says that the system—and very way of life—which has evolved in recent decades is doomed to collapse. He stresses that the ultra-Orthodox community has many positive attributes, including a very cohesive nature. Nonetheless, he believes it will have to change its social behavior more drastically than Israeli society at large, and that this change will come about in a dangerous, explosive fashion.

The reasons for this impending change do not have their roots in religious issues, he stresses. Rather, the force at play is purely economic. Haredi society has experienced a rapid increase in its ranks, but its income base has not expanded commensurately. "It has adopted social patterns which are economically self-destructing," Friedman says. "I am convinced that big problems will emerge soon, and these problems will make major changes inevitable."

Friedman states that the way the Haredi community has functioned until today—as a community of those who learn in yeshiva and kollel (yeshiva for the married)—is economically unsustainable in the long run. In order to prove his point, he analyzes the community's social situation.

"Before World War Two, only a few married youngsters continued to study in a kollel," he says. "Now all do."

This basic change impacts every aspect of Haredi community life, and Friedman traces its evolution as follows. "Its origins lie in feelings which developed in prewar Eastern Europe," he says. "The problem which frightened the leaders of ultra-Orthodox communities there most was religious erosion. Many youngsters who studied at yeshivot left religious practice.

"After World War Two, during which the Eastern European Jewish communities were largely destroyed by the Nazis, the center of Jewish learning moved gradually to Israel," Friedman explains. "A complex of factors made it possible for the ultra-Orthodox Ashkenazim to develop a system which ended, to a large extent, the phenomenon of their children dropping out from religion.

"The heads of the yeshivot had understood for a long time that the failure of the social system of their community in Eastern Europe derived from the economic problems which were always on every yeshiva student's mind.

"The students were saying to themselves, 'I am learning now; but how can I make a living in order to marry and support my children?' When they married, young men had to earn their keep, so they left the yeshiva. The few who stayed on knew that they would have difficulties finding a wife. They remained at the yeshiva until they finally found somebody who was willing to marry them. There was a well-known phenomenon termed by the Yiddish phrase, *alte buchrim*, which can best be translated as 'old boys.'

"Eventually, the heads of the yeshivot understood that in order to convince most of their pupils to continue their Jewish studies on a full-time basis, they had to neutralize the economic consequences of marriage," Friedman relates. "They probably do not explain it this way, but that was the essence of their conclusions. They had to find a way to turn marriage from a traumatic economic event into part of the normal social process without major economic penalties."

The rabbis succeeded. Many things changed in the life of a newly married young man, but his Jewish studies barely noticed. Men married and continued to learn. This led to major expansion of the network of kollels. Before the war, only a few had existed in Eastern Europe, Friedman says, but as policies changed, money became available to support more of them.

"When the economy improved significantly, many more people

could afford to let their sons study full-time," Friedman says. "There was no need any longer, as in Eastern Europe, to have one's children go to work at a young age to help their father earn a living. In Western society, the middle class does not need income from the work of its children.

"The development of the welfare state played an important role in stimulating social change in the ultra-Orthodox community," Friedman says. "It helps the economically weak in various ways and provides security to its citizens. In case of need or catastrophe, there is a social safety net provided by sick funds, pension funds and other institutions.

"Modern society is characterized by a flowering of middle and higher education. Elementary and high school are free of charge. Parents keep contributing money for the education and upkeep of their children in high school, university or yeshiva. These support mechanisms have made a marked change on society.

"Parents often continue to support their children for many years, long after they marry," he notes. "In the Haredi community, this led to another change in the social process: the significant lowering of the marrying age. Given that the youngster is financially dependent anyway, why wait with getting married? Young men marry between age 20–23, but this age is likely to decrease further, to 20 or 21. Girls marry at 18 or 19.

"The Haredi community saw this transition to 'the society of learning' as a miracle," Friedman says. "It had discovered an effective way of stopping religious erosion. Parents could now be reasonably sure that their children would follow in their footsteps. The community is no longer shrinking; to the contrary, its population is growing fast, due to high fertility rates."

In the past, he says, cases of children leaving Orthodoxy usually involved unmarried people old enough to provide in their own needs. Today, youngsters who do not have to leave the yeshiva remain in their social environment and continue to belong to a community which exerts strong social pressure against deviation.

"The combination of the economic safety net and social pressures has changed the system markedly. Exit roads from ultra-Orthodoxy have essentially been blocked. Students cannot support themselves, and they tend to have the added responsibility of a wife and children at an early age. Young couples are very dependent on their parents for financial support while the husband continues to learn in a kollel. All of this interlocking responsibility and dependency create a situation from which few people can flee.

"When the beneficiary effects of the system became clear, heads of yeshivot and Haredi parents wanted to apply it to all the male children of their community," Friedman says, adding that this has led to a major social change over the past 15 years. "Everyone who learns in a yeshiva gets married there and automatically goes on to the kollel. For Haredi society, this system has been a great success.

"In the meantime, students stay longer at the kollel," he continues. "Not because they have become more religious, but primarily because finding work outside the kollel becomes more difficult, so they stay where they feel secure."

Increasingly long stays at kollelim—the average today is 7.5–10 years—have become a socially acceptable answer to unemployment problems. Friedman notes that some people remain there for their entire lives. By the time young men leave this environment, they tend to have several children, and leaving religious life has become nearly impossible. In the few cases where a spouse does decide to change his or her way of life, Friedman says, divorce usually results.

"Those few who drop out from religious practice have a feeling of great loneliness," he says. "They have no substitute. There is no easy way to fit into modern non-religious society. It is an alienating environment, without a social structure to receive you, as opposed to the warm society you come from. You are thus cut off both from your original society and from the one you want to join."

While the kollel has been a key pillar in the changing reality of ultra-Orthodox society, Friedman notes that other factors have also been involved. Among them: an ever-rising fertility rate, which only exacerbates the economic woes created by continued studies and lower marrying ages. Parents who can provide financial assistance to one or two children cannot help five or more, he explains.

"A basic given of Israeli general society is that marrying is linked to the purchase of an apartment," he says. "This means a very big financial outlay. In the modern community, parents can help because they have few children and the newlyweds can pay their mortgage from the money they earn from work.

"If one has only two children, there are usually a few years of age difference between them," he reasons. "Parents help the first child when he marries, and if the second one also wants their support, he either has to postpone marriage or live in a rented apartment for a few years. This does not create big problems.

"In ultra-Orthodox society, such an approach cannot work. Marriage is critical from the point of view of the status of the individual. A father who wants an attractive son-in-law has a very short window of opportunity at his disposal. The prospects of marrying for a girl at age 20 have been reduced to almost zero, as everybody weds before this age."

Friedman compares this to what old farmers used to call "the apricot season." Apricots are tasty only during a short time. Something similar is happening in the ultra-Orthodox community, he says. Marriages are arranged by marriage brokers; young people do not choose their own partners, and those who remain unmarried for too long become increasingly less attractive. All of this adds up to a situation in which people simply cannot afford to wait to marry.

"There is tremendous tension among girls who reach marriage

age," he explains. "They all need husbands, and they have to compete for them. Men also compete for wives, but they have more time, because they marry at an older age.

"There is a domino effect. Soon after the first one of a generation marries, it becomes a general phenomenon. As the situation of those who remain becomes difficult, their parents have to mobilize resources very fast.

"In the brokered marriage, economic values become critical," Friedman says. "Haredi society is quite aware of the standard of living of the outside environment. It educates its sons to know their value on the marriage market if they are good students.

"The good yeshiva student is intelligent enough to understand the economic catch. If he has to go to kollel and put so many children through life, it is obvious that he cannot purchase a flat from his future earnings. His in-laws cannot help him financially, other than on the occasion of his wedding, as they have more daughters to marry off within a few years.

"Thus, the prospective groom has to see to it that on the occasion of his wedding he gets as much financial help as possible. A good yeshiva student who is an attractive marriage candidate will tell his prospective father-in-law that he has to supply him with an apartment, and sometimes also a car."

Although these demands may sound outlandish to outside observers, the parents of the prospective bride accept them. Everybody knows that even if they promise solemnly to help their son-in-law later, they will be unable to keep their commitments.

"The situation is strange, even tragic," Friedman says. "Those youngsters who realize the Haredi ideal continue to study as long as they can. When they have to marry off their daughters, they cannot compete with those who have left the kollel after two or three years, are making a living and have accumulated savings.

"The latter has a much better chance of getting a talented yeshiva student as a son-in-law than the fathers who are studying in the kollel and come with empty hands."

In essence, the ideal of long-term kollel study, coupled with the social pressures to have many children, work against those who pursue these objectives, Friedman says. Generally, the first child is born within one year of marriage, and the second and third children usually come in the second and third years, respectively. In most cases, the third child is followed by a break of a couple of years, and then another series of up to three children born in rapid succession. In most cases, that is the end of childbearing.

"Years later, this leads to a situation in which during a very short time families must marry off up to three or four children," Friedman says. "This is economically impossible for virtually everybody. It is one of the proofs that the system is close to collapse.

"In light of this, over the past 15 years ultra-Orthodox politics have had to change totally," he says. "In the past, the main concerns were the role of religion in the public arena of Israeli society, and education. Now the main problem of the ultra-Orthodox parties has become maintaining the institutional system their society has created."

This means obtaining massive funding from the Israeli government. Friedman stresses that the need goes beyond support for yeshivot and other Haredi institutions. It includes direct support to individuals. The catch is that as kollel life becomes more and more the norm, young people begin to generate productive income at a later stage in life, thereby reducing their potential opportunity to accumulate savings.

"Even those who are fortunate enough to get a well-paying job do not have the time to build up savings to support their children. Most face even bigger problems. They have studied at the kollel and have not received a general education. Thus, they must compete for a limited range of jobs with their peers. When their children reach marriage age, they face impossible economic challenges."

To date, Friedman says that problems have generally been resolved, with great difficulty, through government aid in the acquisition of apartments. Since the 1950s, he notes, the Israeli government has built large numbers of apartments. While they were hardly an economic success, the empty housing ultimately provided an answer to the needs of many Haredi families.

"When many flats remained empty, the government had to fill them," Friedman says. "The Haredim realized they could buy very cheap apartments in towns such as Ashdod or Ofakim, because no demand existed for the units. This resulted in the movement of many ultra-Orthodox to the country's periphery.

"There, they created additional institutions. Starting a yeshiva does not require any great preparations," Friedman says. "Some tables, chairs or benches and copies of the Talmud are all you need. That makes such institutions highly ambulant.

"In the past few years, the building process has repeated itself," he says, noting that the government overbuilt for the demands of aliya from the former Soviet Union. In the process of building for 400,000 immigrants, he notes, building another 10,000 units for the Haredi community is not so difficult.

"Initially, the Haredim went to non-Orthodox towns, where they found a place in society," Friedman says. "They fulfilled the roles of teachers, rabbis, kashrut supervisors, etc. and earned a living by providing some of these services to the local non-Orthodox society."

In recent years, this process took what Friedman characterizes as "a wrong turn." The previous government, which wanted to establish settlements in the territories, promoted the idea of building an entirely Haredi town, which would not be part of a larger community.

"The first such town was Emanuel," he says, adding that the media originally did not understand the basic problems of Haredi society, so they presented the town as a great opportunity for a high quality of life. "They did not understand that it would essentially be a society of kollelim, with all of the resulting economic problems.

"A municipality needs taxes in order to provide and maintain its infrastructure," he explains. "Most of those who study in kollelim pay little or no taxes. They often receive financial support from the government. On the other hand, due to the many children in Haredi society, they are a major burden on a municipality's infrastructure. The municipality must provide much more social and educational services than for other sectors.

"A visit to Emanuel today reveals a collapsing community," Friedman says. "Its municipality has a very limited budget, which leads many residents to leave. That, in turn, enhances the very problematic situation of a society which cannot manage its social costs. Emanuel is proof that Haredi society as such is not economically viable."

This has been proven in other Haredi towns, too. Friedman says that Betar, near Jerusalem, was built according to the same principle. Today, its several thousand inhabitants know that the town cannot support itself. If it were part of Jerusalem, he notes, it would benefit from the city's infrastructure.

But all of these bad experiences are not enough to teach the planners and the Haredim themselves a lesson. In the Modi'in area, Friedman says, another Haredi town is being built. "Kiryat Sefer is going to be another economically unviable Haredi town. In all likelihood, the government will have to appoint a local council and support it with government money," he says. "The question is how long such a process can go on."

Even the long-established Haredi city of Bnei Brak cannot escape this fate. Friedman says it maintained a healthy economic infrastructure for years that was based on its good location near the main roads of Israel's most populated region. This location helped the town attract a lot of industry, which paid significant taxes to the city.

But today Bnei Brak is near bankruptcy. This can be attributed in part to poor municipal management, but the main reason is pure self-destruction. Many kollelim have taken over much of the city's industrial areas, replacing income-producing industrial concerns with institutions which cost—rather than generate—city funds.

But Bnei Brak's problems are not limited to its huge education outlays for its many children and adults who spend their days studying. Friedman points to great internal divisions, which manifest themselves in demands by every sect for its own schools and institutions.

All of these demands force the municipality to allocate more land and money for buildings and services than would be necessary without all of this divisiveness, he says. "This leads to major economic waste. No modern community, even a relatively wealthy one, can afford it."

One more factor contributes to the predicament of strengthening Haredi numbers and weakening economic stance. In line with global trends, quite a few non-Orthodox people become Orthodox.

"In the Israeli reality, one can hardly become Orthodox in a simple way," Friedman says. "One does not start one day to go to synagogue and put on phylacteries. The way to enter the Haredi community is complex. One has to familiarize oneself with many behavioral changes and one has to know so much that it is impossible to acquire this knowledge on a do-it yourself basis.

"When one becomes Orthodox, one goes to a specific institution and steps outside the economic system," he continues. "During a year or two, one need not provide a living for oneself, as if it were an economic moratorium from society. There are up to 10,000 people in such institutions at present, who also have to be supported.

"The opening of a yeshiva for those who return to religion provides additional jobs for kollel students. It offers them an opportunity for a profession, a way to make a living and the chance to raise their social status. But every new institution is an additional economic burden.

"Sephardi Jews have to some extent gone in the footsteps of Ashkenazi Jews. The result is increased ultra-Orthodox political power, a greater flow of money and more economic problems. We already have seen that what strengthens the position in the short run creates problems in the long run. Somewhere, there must be a limit.

"It is clear today that the combined effect of large numbers of children and the long economic moratorium of the Haredim cannot continue," Friedman sums up. "The more pragmatic political leaders of the Haredi community understand this. Students also understand that there is no simple solution. The rabbinical leaders, however, either do not understand or try to give the impression that they do not understand.

"What can be done about it? Students cannot leave the kollel early to follow the principles of the market. Their community takes a negative view of somebody who does not want to learn and prefers to seek a job to make a living.

"If you leave the kollel at an early stage, you face a difficult situation, because you have broken the norms of your society. You also have to serve in the army if you leave the kollel early, and then you have to find work. Those who have been accustomed to living in a system which finds solutions for them have problems finding solutions by themselves.

"They have lived their entire lives in institutions where they were told, 'be quiet, and we will take care of you.' Now they have to find their way in an alien outside world, which they fear very much."

To Friedman, the prognosis is fairly clear. "There may not be enough money to maintain existing institutions," he says. "Their debts are often crippling. What should they do? Close or go into bankruptcy? What will happen to their students?

"The only reasonable solution is institutional. Haredi leaders will have to reconsider their policies. They will have to change their approach and say, 'Not everybody can continue to study.' The earlier they do it, the better.

"They will have to become more selective, like universities. The best students will be accepted for kollel study, while the less talented ones will not. They should be encouraged to learn a trade while they are young."

But Friedman knows the community well enough to understand that this solution is problematic for at least two reasons. First, all of the young men who will not study in kollel will need an alternative occupation, and second, even if one is found, the shift will conflict sharply with Haredi values.

Friedman believes the first problem can be addressed by establishing technical schools for Haredim. This, in turn, poses a major financial problem, because it requires a substantial investment in infrastructure. The investment per person is much greater than that incurred in setting up a yeshiva. It is also more expensive to maintain a technical school than a yeshiva.

As to the second problem, Friedman says, "Selection assumes that the good pupils will go to the kollel and the others will go elsewhere. By saying this, the leadership would radically contradict what they have been telling students to date. They would have to change their society's value system totally by saying that there is a way to remain Haredi other than in the kollel.

"They would have to deny the most elementary value of their society by saying that one does not necessarily have to learn torah and that there is an option to be Haredi while studying for a profession and partaking in the economy of the modern world."

As he discusses it, the situation seems to grow increasingly complex. Even if the psychological barrier can be overcome, Friedman says, there are other critical challenges.

"How can one be sure that the most talented will go on to the kollel, and that the less talented will go to technical schools?" Friedman asks. "The reverse might happen. Those who are not very bright may prefer to learn in the kollel, while the very talented may say, 'I want to make a living. Why should I sit in the kollel and then have to seek charity for my daughters when they have to marry? If studying in the kollel is no longer a precondition for being a Haredi, then I can do better outside.'

"Academic society has developed a mechanism to prevent such a process. Those who study the most attractive professions get a higher reward later in life," Friedman notes. "Those who study law expect to make a lot of money in the future. Thus one can attract talented people. The kollel, however, does not prepare people for well-paid jobs."

There is no simple solution that bodes well for Haredi society. By introducing economics in the kollel society, all religious values would be turned upside down. The current situation cannot continue, he says, leading him to the pessimistic expectation that Haredi society will be changed by a socio-economic explosion, rather than an institutional approach.

YAAKOV GADISH

A Recipe for Kibbutz Survival

Y AAKOV GADISH has a very odd resume. He is a kibbutznik farmer who became a high-ranking government official. Today, he is a well-paid business consultant—and still a kibbutz member. It isn't unusual to find a kibbutz member who visits neighboring kibbutzim to share his ideas about increasing crop production, but how many of them consult in corporate boardrooms? Frankly, it's a profession usually associated with capitalistic city-dwellers, not with socialists who cast their lot in with a collective settlement. But Gadish is no traitor to kibbutz ideology; he is, in fact, just another of Kibbutz Yavne's income-generating branches, much like the hatchery or the watch factory.

Gadish was born in 1934 in what was then Poland and is now Ukraine. He fled the Nazi-occupied country in 1942, taking care of himself since the age of eight. He passed through many countries before reaching Palestine five months before World War Two ended in 1945 and became a Youth Aliya pupil.

When he was 16, Gadish joined Kibbutz Yavne. He worked in

the fields, but never forgot his education. Although he has no high school diploma, he went on to higher education. His first diploma, an M.A. in economics, came from Bar-Ilan University in 1974.

Over the years, he filled many economic posts in his kibbutz, and later on the national level. After serving as kibbutz treasurer, he went on to be coordinator of economic activities. In the mid-1970s, he was appointed head of economic activities of the religious kibbutz movement. In 1981, he became director of the budget division of the Finance Ministry, a position he held until 1984.

After being involved in major national decisionmaking, Yavne put Gadish and another kibbutznik in charge of setting up a new watch factory. After getting the factory off the ground, he was reelected to the post of coordinator of the economic committee.

As if his work experience hadn't been unconventional enough for a kibbutz member up to that point, Gadish set up an economic consultancy office in the kibbutz in 1988. It was—and remains—a one-man office, and it provides services on the open market.

Since he left the Ministry of Finance, Gadish has held many nonpaid public positions. He was a member of the Bank of Israel's advisory committee and a board member of M.I. Holdings, the company charged with selling the government's banking holdings. He is married and has five children and seven grandchildren. While not all his children are in the kibbutz, all his grandchildren are.

Within the small part of the country's population which lives in kibbutzim, Gadish is part of an even smaller grouping. Yavne is a religious kibbutz, one of just 17 in the country.

Although the kibbutz idea never really caught on among Orthodox Israelis, Gadish is convinced that his path is the best of all worlds. "I see in the kibbutz the realization of the perfect Jewish religious society," he says with confidence. "Rambam says that the greatest form of charity is to become a partner with somebody. The problems start when the partner abuses you."

He is anything but sanguine about the future. He calls himself a skeptic and a realist. That was underscored a few years back, when he was asked to speak to Yavne's members at an Independence Day celebration. He told the gathered crowd that the kibbutz's members in their 80s should be proud of what they had achieved.

"You will pass away with the knowledge that you have been successful," he told the older generation, but he had less certainty when it came to those who will still be alive in a quarter-century. He understands that the kibbutz movement is in a difficult period, which he attributes to the fact that today's consumer-oriented society stresses individualism before nearly everything else.

Kibbutz Yavne is in itself one of Israel's financial success stories. A collective settlement of people who have no money themselves, the kibbutz has several tens of millions of dollars in cash reserves in the bank. Despite this wealth, the general assembly turned down a proposal to allow kibbutz members to go abroad for a month once every four years; the members decided to stick to the previous rule of once every eight years.

In recent years, Gadish has published and spoken frequently on how the kibbutz movement should confront its present crises, which are of both economic and social natures. He has avoided the issue of his personal economic betterment. Despite the fact that his consultancy work brings a strong positive cash flow to the kibbutz, he says he has never even considered leaving the collective and working for his personal gain.

Instead, he downplays his economic contribution to the collective. "Only in a few situations can you identify how much a single member earns for the kibbutz," he says. "Usually, one is part of a much bigger activity where the individual contribution is less identifiable.

"Had I been head of the hatchery of Yavne and made good business deals, I might have made an even bigger contribution to kibbutz income than through running a consultancy," he continues, adding, "but it would not have been so transparent."

However, he insists that it's an irrelevant point. He made the choice many years ago to be a kibbutznik; that means he decided to work for the greater good, and to do all he can to help the collective.

Despite the ideological battering of the sector in recent years, Gadish continues to believe that the kibbutz creates a better society than man can reach on his own.

"Living as a kibbutz member doesn't come easily," he stresses, saying, "It requires a heavy price, sometimes it makes you very angry, but it is worthwhile. The kibbutz has tried to make people less egoistic and to educate them to find another meaning in life than to be a slave of their property or an addict to a career and self-fulfillment. It has also tried to build people who are free, because they are content with what they have." He proposes to let the future unfold as it will. "Ultimately, it is an intellectual exercise whether the kibbutz idea is viable, and whether this idea can bring added value to humanity more than the conventional way of life," he says.

"We are lucky that the kibbutz idea is not an abstract one. It has existed for 80 years. We have seen what it has contributed. "About 50,000 people have died to date after living their lives as kibbutz members. Today, another 50,000 kibbutz members have reached what elsewhere is called retirement age.

"Younger kibbutz members have lived many years in the kibbutz," Gadish notes. "Even people who left the kibbutz after a number of years have been influenced by it. It is a system which has worked for a prolonged period for a significant number of people.

"It can be evaluated at three different levels," he says. "The personal one, as I did before, that of the closed community and at the national level. If we are a bit more presumptuous, we can even see in it a wider, universal message."

Gadish claims that the national challenges which justify the kibbutz ideology remain salient. In his view, it's all a question of state of mind.

"Before independence, the kibbutzim helped determine the map of Israel," he says. "The country would have been dramatically smaller without the kibbutzim. If, before Israel's independence, 11 kibbutzim had not been established in the Negev, it would not have become part of the country.

"The border in the Jordan Valley was fixed because there were kibbutzim there. The only Jewish settlements between Tiberias and Jerusalem were kibbutzim. Upper Galilee is part of Israel because of its kibbutzim. Rosh Hanikra, Manara, Chanita, Dan, Dafna, Maayan Baruch and many other kibbutzim have determined the exact borders of Israel.

"Today, we face a national challenge in the aliya waves," he says, turning to the present. "Finally, we can fulfill our destiny. We may be able to save several million Jews. The rabbinate will not determine who is a Jew. That will be done by the anti-Semites calling a Russian Jew a Zhid."

Gadish suggests that Israel has ceased to be a goal-oriented society. If Israel were a healthy community, he says, it would see in the aliya a great challenge. "Four million Jews have had to absorb less than half a million Jews in recent years," he says. "It is a sign of sickness that we view this opportunity as a burden."

This leads Gadish to the conclusion that one has to search for ideological satisfaction within the smaller framework of the individual kibbutz.

Some kibbutzim have made an important contribution at this difficult juncture, Gadish says. They have set an example for the nation by offering new olim to make their first home in the Jewish homeland in a kibbutz.

"In Yavne, at any given time, we have 16 families of olim," he says. "They never stay in the kibbutz for more than a year, but they all stay in the country after they leave us. We do not select them on a religious basis or require an Orthodox way of life from them. We only ask that they not desecrate the Shabbat in public or bring non-kosher food into the kibbutz kitchen. What they do in their own rooms is their business."

Gadish is an idealist, but he is too much of a realist to ignore the massive pressures on the kibbutz community. "The processes which the kibbutz is undergoing are no different from those the state faces, or, in a larger sense, those which confront the Western world.

"The mood of the time is very much against us," Gadish says matter-of-factly. "People look for self-fulfillment and hedonism, which starts from the individual who asks what else he can receive. The kibbutz, which cannot be a consumer society, is constantly on the defensive.

"Man in the outside world wants to reach an equilibrium between his needs and the neighborhood's needs. The aim for self-fulfillment is very high. Everybody wants to be somebody."

He admits that this mood influences kibbutz members as well. People in the kibbutz read newspapers and watch television, just like anybody else, and they see how those in the outside world reach self-fulfillment.

"One person wants to be president, another mayor, a third one wants to head a labor committee, while yet another pursues a business career," he says. "The kibbutznik confronts that with his own reality of working on the production line of a plant or in the cotton field.

"The problem is particularly acute for those who return from the army," he says. "They may be about 30 years old, and they know what they are capable of. As officers, they have had important responsibilities. They have travelled the world as well, and then they come home and are offered jobs selecting chicks in the kibbutz hatchery."

Today's global trends reach the kibbutzim at a moment when

they are being led by the third and fourth generation. These young leaders were born into an exceptionally good life, Gadish says. For them, like for all of Israel's younger generation, the existence of the state is a given.

"I know how it was when Israel had not been established yet," he says. "My children do not understand this. They think that Israel is a stable part of the universe and cannot imagine a world without it. Those who haven't lived in another reality cannot understand it. The kibbutz cannot escape this changed attitude.

"Indeed, the kibbutz concept is based on something totally different from society at large," he continues. "It is a system of great sacrifices. I am speaking about those individuals who have above-average capabilities and contribute to the community of the kibbutz. It is no great altruism that those who have few capabilities want to share with others.

"The general mood had led to many changes and a desire for more," he says. "There were two reasons why some kibbutzim introduced payment in the kibbutz dining room. First, the fact that food was free led to a lot of waste. Second, some kibbutz members felt like servants when asked to serve others in the dining room. If, however, they collect money for the food, then they have turned the kibbutz dining room into a restaurant and have raised their personal status. This approach permeates kibbutzim, but is largely fictitious.

"If the electrician's activities are turned into a profit center where people pay for service, then the public will not bother him for unimportant things," Gadish says, explaining the rationale. But he adds quickly that it isn't so easy. The approach has more disadvantages than advantages, he says, as everyone will see when the electrician begins to refuse certain jobs because they won't add to his bottom line.

"He will spend a lot of time on bookkeeping, because he thinks that he has to take decisions," Gadish continues. "That may be good for a business community, but while he does all of those irrelevant calculations here, the kibbutz factory's production line suffers greatly. One should realize that kibbutz members have, as it were, a basic partnership contract with each other."

Gadish terms this petty sort of profit center approach "introducing paganism into the kibbutz ideology. With these pseudobusiness concepts we have introduced false deities in the collective, for which we prostrate ourselves. But this approach does not contribute anything to the wellbeing of the collective. It only leads to confusion."

He claims that these ideas did not emerge in individual kibbutzim. They came from the central kibbutz organizations, where people developed disastrous concepts. For some of the senior figures, large central organizations such as Hamashbir and Tnuva were not large enough. They wanted to be international traders, to run worldwide businesses.

"These people have caused the kibbutz idea major damage," Gadish says. "In the 1970s, the kibbutz movements were rich. They had major savings, built up by the labor of three generations. They always worried about big financial surpluses. In less than ten years, they wiped out the pile of money and turned it into a deficit.

"These technocrats did not have the mentality to be movement leaders," Gadish charges angrily. "They were out for fulfillment. They transferred this unhealthy approach to the kibbutz system. When a kibbutz came to the central organization with an investment program of $2 million, the technocrats belittled it and said, 'Come with a program of $6 million, or else we have nothing to talk about.'

"The same people came up with other alien ideas, such as that of the profit centers," Gadish says. "They wanted to introduce absolute decentralization in the kibbutz, as if the whole institution was mainly a business entreprise and not an ideologically-based community."

Gadish stresses that he is not an opponent of change per se, but he says, "In Yavne, we have not changed our basic approach over the last 50 years. It is a kibbutz which works well. People have been in the army and watch television like others. Our youth has been outside, and some of them returned. What is already problematic, and will become increasingly so, is to maintain the idea of vertical rotation."

Gadish uses himself as an example to explain his approach. He has always felt it right to return to the cotton fields as a laborer after holding management positions, in order to renew what he terms his "work permit." After completing a stint as a senior Finance Ministry official and a period as the head of the new watch factory, he worked in the fields for a year.

He understands that this ideology may not be suited to anyone beyond the first or second generation. They made and continued the kibbutz revolution, Gadish says, and they were motivated by a burning ideological fire propelled by the knowledge that they were creating something new. He admits that the young generation today has no such fervor.

One of the imperatives for kibbutz society's survival lies in grasping a basic change in approach: Gadish stresses that kibbutzim do not have to produce products that are loaded onto trucks and delivered to market. "Products" often can be put in envelopes or copied onto diskettes. More than 60 kibbutzim have adapted this approach to their own production, and he is convinced that the number will grow.

Another top priority is understanding the need for diversity in occupation paths. Gadish notes that this has limits: a kibbutz cannot survive if most of its members hold jobs outside the kibbutz. "If that happens, we cannot maintain services inside the kibbutz in an orderly form," he says. "Once you bring people from the outside to provide services, you create distortions in the kibbutz social fabric, even if all income is pooled.

"A kibbutz can live with reasonable inequality," he says, "but it cannot live equitably in a nonequitable kibbutz society. It is not viable to go outside to work with your private car and earn what you can, then to come home and trade your city clothes for shorts and sandals. To go to the dining room and be served by Russians or other new immigrants is too much of a distortion of the kibbutz ideal."

Gadish says that nothing can change people's desire for self ful-fillment in their work, in or out of the kibbutz. In an odd way, the country's high unemployment rate actually helps stem the flow of kibbutzniks to outside jobs: if they cannot find work, they will settle for a job in the kibbutz itself. The unemployment statistics will change over time, but Gadish says kibbutzim must strive for diversification and new models of work within the kibbutz.

These new models can include forming cooperatives of engineers or other professionals from one or more kibbutzim. They could work outside the kibbutz but be subject to the obligations of the kibbutz. One example: when the kibbutz needs such a person for a job at home, he would be required to arrange his schedule accordingly. If the same engineer is elected kibbutz secretary, he can take leave for a year or more from his job.

This model is not as revolutionary as it may sound. Gadish points out that lawyers and other professionals often take a leave in order to work in government service.

Gadish learned many of these lessons during his stint at the Finance Ministry. During a long doctors' strike, he was called upon to negotiate.

"One of their representatives said to me, 'You are a kibbutznik. We do not want to hear a single word of ideology, morality and human-ism. All we want is more money,'" Gadish recalls. He still shakes his head when he retells that story.

While he understands that these are difficult times for the collec-tive perspective, he remains certain that the time will come when what he calls "our type of idealism" will rebound. "We see it with our children," he says. "Even in good kibbutzim, many children do not remain. But when somebody comes back, he returns as a total kibbutznik, not as a reformer."

He cites conversations he has had with children of Yavne members who now live outside the kibbutz. "They said they did not know whether they would return to the kibbutz," Gadish recounts. "They also said that we should not try to buy them by making the kibbutz less collective. If they do return, they said, they wanted to return to a real kibbutz, not a watered-down version."

That kind of talk makes Gadish happy. The movement's moral and social strength comes from its ideology, and he dismisses any efforts to dillute the ideology in an effort to draw more supporters.

This hard-line approach is not without risks, though. Gadish raises the question of whether or not kibbutz society can survive long enough to greet the next wave of idealism with open arms. "Will we be ideologically dead before that time?" he asks.

There is a very real risk that the movement will not survive, or that its ranks will shrink significantly before it enjoys a resurgence. But neither of these scenarios convinces Gadish that reform is the path of choice. "The kibbutz's unique idea is to break the direct link between the contribution an individual makes to society and what he receives from it," he stresses. "Every member should contribute according to his ability, and in turn the kibbutz should give everybody according to his need."

That has been the golden rule of kibbutz life since its inception, and Gadish sees it as crucial to the movement's survival. "The problems and the beauty of the kibbutz idea are all contained in this basic idea," he says.

The whole movement is based on this principle, and Gadish warns that any deviation from it will kill the kibbutz idea. He is unmoved and unconvinced by reform-minded kibbutz members who advocate greater individualism as the key to survival.

"There have always been many variations on the collective idea," he says. "One is the collective moshavim. Originally, they wanted to produce together and consume separately. In other words, produce like a kibbutz and consume like private people. In this type of settlement, the collective idea is breaking down rapidly and they strive toward more and more privatization."

The mere fact that other types of communities are moving toward greater individualism convinces Gadish of nothing. He states flatly that he believes a kibbutz should be expelled from the kibbutz movement if it changes the rules of compensation to reflect a personal profit motive.

Don't get him wrong; Gadish has nothing against the personal profit motive. It just has no place on the kibbutz scene.

"A community which wants to create a link between the contribution of the individual and his income can be anything but a kibbutz," he says. "Such a community should go its own way and be a collective moshav, or anything else."

This is not a game of spite in which Gadish seeks to cut off those whose ideas are different than his own. He sees it as a very real battle for survival. He claims that a silent majority of kibbutz members today believe in the basic idea that there should not be a connection between an individual's contribution and reward, and he believes that if these new-fangled ideas make inroads, many disillusioned idealists will leave.

For this and other reasons, Gadish steadfastly opposes moves to make kibbutz members pay for their meals or for services rendered. Any attempt to cut back on collective services poses a threat to the community, he says.

"These changes are the beginning of a lengthy struggle which may last a decade or two, until the property of the kibbutz is divided," he warns gravely. "You have to understand that the kibbutz is a voluntary agreement. We are not a missionary movement. I am not trying to convince anyone to leave their private lives behind and join us."

While some advocates of reform in the kibbutz movement say

these changes are the only way to preserve membership at current levels, Gadish insists he is not concerned about numbers.

"The kibbutzim are an invention of Jews in Israel," he says. "Less than three percent of the Jewish population lives in kibbutzim today. We have always been a small movement. In the future it may go down, to two percent or even less. So what? But if you do not define where you stand now, the movement may find itself with one-third of its present numbers ten years from today."

Gadish's commitment to kibbutz ideology does not imply a commitment to defend all mistakes that have been made in the past. He denounces the trend toward living beyond the community's financial ability, saying, "There are many people in the world who earn less than they want and have to live from what they can earn.

"I often say to the heads of the kibbutz movement, 'You have 286 kibbutzim and you think you have to keep them all alive. That is a mistake. If you were to decide not to support the worst ten of them, you would give a signal to the others that they have to play by the rules. I refer mainly to those who do not want to mend their ways, and become the parasites of the movement.'"

Each kibbutz should do all it can to help weaker kibbutzim, Gadish allows, but there must be limits. "I am against giving guarantees to other kibbutzim," he says. "I am against a situation where I am responsible for somebody else regardless of what he does. He may jump in the water with a block on his foot and call for help. If I try to save him, he will pull me down. That is immoral and hopeless. You have no choice but to let him drown."

He has spoken publicly against the movement's willingness to seek handouts and subsidies. In one of his stronger speeches, at a movement gathering, he said bluntly that the way to kill the kibbutz movement is to give it a two billion shekel subsidy. "The message that entails is that you can be irresponsible," he says. "It is dangerous to tell lazy people that they do not have to work."

But Yavne has a different kind of problem: what to do with its surplus income. Gadish is convinced the kibbutz has to become more charitable. "Each year, we host in the kibbutz a two-week camp for deaf-mute children," he says. "This may be one way for us to continue to function as an economically oriented community and at the same time find useful outlets for the surplus money we earn."

Perhaps Gadish sums up his warnings about the economic well-being of kibbutzim best when he says, "I think we should concentrate much more on solidarity within each kibbutz than in the movement. The movement's strength has to remain in those activities which all kibbutzim have in common."

But from his viewpoint, the biggest test facing the kibbutz movement is the social-ideological one, not the economic one. He sees nothing strange about his conservative view on the future. After all, he says, "Once a revolutionary carries out a revolution, he becomes the most conservative adherent of that specific revolution."

He is quick to add, however, "Society has no choice but to adapt itself to its environment. But an institution that attempts to change its basic character is doomed to fail."

Glossary

Following is a selection of words and terms that the interviewees use in their discussions about Israel's future:

Aguda/Agudat Israel *The oldest ultra-Orthodox political party*

Aliya Hebrew: *immigration to Israel; literally "to go up"*

Am Segula Hebrew: *the Chosen People*

Ashkenazi/m *Jews who trace their roots to Eastern European communities; includes large communities of Jews from Poland and Russia*

Bnei Hebrew: *sons of; often used in names of synagogues*

Canaanism *Secular anti-Zionist movement that emerged in pre-State Palestine, which considered diaspora Jews entirely distinct from those in Palestine*

Curia Italian: *public administration of the Papal Court*

General Zionists *Precursor of the Liberal Party, which subsequently merged with Herut into the Likud*

Halacha Hebrew: *Jewish religious law*

Hamashbir *Centralized buying organization for kibbutzim and moshavim; its importance has waned in recent years*

Haredi Hebrew: *ultra-Orthodox Jew*

Histadrut *Large Israeli trade union*

Inquisition *Tribunal of Catholic Church established to identify and punish heresy*

Kibbutzim *An Israeli invention; communal settlements based on socialist principles. They began as agricultural communities, but today engage also in industry*

Kiddush Hebrew: *religious blessing over wine*

Kollel Hebrew: *Talmud school for married men*

Kosher *Jewish dietary laws*

Labor *Center-left political party*

Likud *Center-right political party*

Luftmensch *Yiddish: literally someone up in the air; i.e., without a solid economic base*

Mapai *Precursor of Labor Party*

Meretz *Alliance of three left-wing parties*

Minyan/im *Hebrew: quorum of ten people required for a communal religious service*

Moshav/im *These settlements, in which a large part of property is private, began as largely agriculture-based communities, but today many moshavniks hold every type of job imaginable*

National Religious Party (NRP) *Modern Orthodox Zionist party*

Olim *Hebrew: those who immigrate to Israel*

Payot *Hebrew: sidelocks worn by ultra-Orthodox males*

Progressive Party *A small center party, which traditionally allied itself with Labor*

Project Renewal *Initiated by the Israeli government in the late 1970s, the program entailed diaspora communities adopting and assisting Israeli communities*

Rambam (Maimonides) *12th-century Jewish philosopher and physician*

Reconquista *The Christian's Medieval reconquest of Spain*

Sabra Hebrew: *a native-born Israeli; also cactus fruit, known for being prickly on the outside and sweet on the inside*

Seder Hebrew: *literally "order," this is the name given the traditional service and meal that mark the beginning of Passover*

Sephardi/m *Jews who trace their roots to pre-Inquisition Spain, Africa and Asia*

Shabbat Hebrew: *the Sabbath*

Shas *Ultra-Orthodox haredi political party that emerged in the 1980s and has played the kingpin role in governments led by both Labor and Likud*

Shoah Hebrew: *the Holocaust*

Talmud *Compilation of Jewish oral law, consisting of Mishna and Gemara*

Teshuva Hebrew: *repentence*

Tnuva *Large Israeli dairy cooperative*

Vaᶜad Leumi *General council of the Jews in pre-State Palestine*

Yeshiva Hebrew: *Talmud school*

Yishuv Hebrew: *literally "settlement," the term used when referring to the Jewish community of pre-State Israel*

Yordim Hebrew: *Israeli emigres, literally "those who have gone down"*

Youth Aliya *Framework for young people who came to Israel alone, or whose families were unable to care for them. Many participants were adopted by kibbutzim. Today, some disadvantaged sabras enroll in the program*

Zhid *Derogatory term for Jews*

Notes

Twenty Years After Oslo

1   *Israel's New Future: Interviews* (Jerusalem: Rubin Mass, Jerusalem Center for Public Affairs, 1994).

2   Manfred Gerstenfeld, interview with Abba Eban, "Challenges in the Aftermath of Peace," in *Israel's New Future*, 25.

3   See for instance Manfred Gerstenfeld, "Israel's Future Revisited Ten Years Later: The Poverty of Predictions," in Michel Korinman, John Laughland, (Eds.) *Israel on Israel* (London: Valentine Mitchell, 2008).

4   Rainer Münz, "Europe: Population Change and its Consequences: an Overview," *The Berlin Institute for Population and Development*, December 2007.

5   Reza Moghadam, "New Growth Drivers for Low-Income Countries: The Role of BRICs," *Strategy, Policy, and Review Department*, International Monetary Fund, January 12, 2011.

6   Peter Dominiczak and Steven Swinford, "David Cameron: Relationship with EU is unacceptable," *The Telegraph*, May 13, 2013.

7   "Hungary Must Abide by EU Values, says MEPs," Press Release, *European Parliament*, July 3, 2013.

8 Kate Connolly, "Angela Merkel: youth unemployment is most pressing problem facing Europe," *The Guardian*, July 2, 2013.

9 Jonathan Masters and Greg Bruno, "U.S. Domestic Surveillance," *Council on Foreign Relations*, June 13, 2013.

10 Jeffrey Price and Jeffrey Forrest, *Practical Aviation Security: Predicting and Preventing Future Threats* (Oxford: Butterworth-Heinemann, 2008), 78–79.

11 Manfred Gerstenfeld, interview with Irwin Cotler, "Existing Tools to deal with Iran's Crimes," in *Demonizing Israel and the Jews* (New York: RVP Press, 2013), 45.

12 AFP, "Iran's Hassan Rowhani rules out halt to uranium enrichment programme," *The Telegraph*, June 17, 2013.

13 Hanif Zarrabi-Kashani, "Iran Election Update," Middle East Program, *Woodrow Wilson International Center for Scholars*, May–June 2013.

14 Joseph Logan, "Last US Troops Leave Iraq, Ending War," Reuters, December 18, 2011.

15 Toby Helm, "David Miliband's farewell blast at west's failings in Iraq and Afghanistan," *The Observer*, July 13, 2013.

16 "Testimony by Cynthia J. Arnson: Director Latin American Program, Woodrow Wilson International Center for Scholars," *Senate Foreign Relations Committee, Subcommittee on the Western Hemisphere*, December 1, 2010.

17 Alain Juppé and James R. Rubin, "The Arab Spring: A Conversation with Alain Juppé," *Council on Foreign Relations*, September 19, 2011.

18 Thomas L. Friedman, "What does Morsi mean for Israel?," *The New York Times*, July 3, 2012.

19 Duncan Pickard, "Approaching Consensus on the Tunisian Constitution," *Atlantic Council*, July 3, 2013.

20 Shlomo Cesana, "Tunisia's New Constitution to oppose Zionism, ties with Israel," *Israel Hayom*, November 28, 2011.

21 "UN says Syria refugee crisis worst since Rwanda," *BBC News*, July 16, 2013.

22 Helene Cooper, "Washington Begins to Plan for Collapse of Syrian Government," *The New York Times*, July 18, 2012.

23 "Syria death toll now above 100,000, says UN chief Ban Ki Moon," *BBC News*, July 25, 2013.

24 Associated Press, "In Syria, infighting between al-Qaida groups and mainstream rebels undermining revolt," *The Washington Post*, July 15, 2013.

25 Ben Rhodes, "White House Statement on Syrian Chemical Weapons Use, June 2013," *Council on Foreign Relations*, June 13, 2013.

26 AFP, "Russia Claims Syrian rebels have used sarin gas," *The Telegraph*, July 9, 2013.

27 "Syria chemical weapons 'most worrying terror threat to UK,'" *BBC News*, July 10, 2013.

28 "Report: Israeli Submarine strike hit Syrian arms depot," *The Jerusalem Post*, July 14, 2013.

29 Dimi Reider, "Syria: The View from Israel," *European Council on Foreign Relations*, June 20, 2013.

30 Reuters, "IDF reinforces Golan border with eyes on Hezbollah," *The Jerusalem Post*, July 10, 2013.

31 Jodi Rudoren, "Israel Finding itself Drawn into Syria's Turmoil," *The New York Times*, May 22, 2013.

32 "Blast rocks Egypt's gas pipeline to Israel, Jordan," Reuters, July 21, 2013.

33 David Wurmser, "The Geopolitics of Israel's Offshore Gas Reserves," *Jerusalem Center for Public Affairs*, April 4, 2013.

34 Dore Gold, "Morsi and the future of the peace treaty," *Israel Hayom*, July 29, 2012.

35 Chris McGreal, "Turkish PM accuses Israel of practising state terrorism," *The Guardian*, June 4, 2004.

36 Eli Yossi, "Prime Minister Recep Tayyip Erdogan's Visit to Israel: The View from Turkey," *Tel Aviv Notes No. 132*, May 5, 2005.

37 Steven G. Merley, *Turkey, The Global Muslim Brotherhood, and the Gaza Flotilla* (Jerusalem: Jerusalem Center for Public Affairs, 2011), 7.

38 "Turkey," *The World Factbook, Central Intelligence Agency*, July 10, 2013.

39 "Israel," *The World Factbook, Central Intelligence Agency*, July 10, 2013.

40 Mitchell G. Bard, "Modern History of Israel: The Partition Plan," *Jewish Virtual Library*, 2013.

41 "The Khartoum Resolutions," *Israel Ministry of Foreign Affairs*, 2013. http://mfa.gov.il/MFA/ForeignPolicy/Peace/Guide/Pages/The%20Khartoum%20Resolutions.aspx.

42 Suzanne Goldenberg, "Barak's Peace Plan Rejected," *The Guardian*, December 1, 2000.

43 Manfred Gerstenfeld, interview with Dore Gold, "Europe's Consistent Anti-Israeli Bias at the United Nations," in *Israel and Europe: An Expanding Abyss* (Jerusalem: Jerusalem Center for Public Affairs, Adenauer Foundation, 2005), 60.

44 Michael Omer-Man, "This Week in History: Gaza Disengagement Begins," *The Jerusalem Post*, August 19, 2011.

45 Ian Black and Mark Tran, "Hamas Takes Control of Gaza," *The Guardian*, June 15, 2007.

46 Steven J. Rosen, "Olmert Details his Offer to Abbas," *Middle East Forum*, December 1, 2009.

47 Natan Sharansky, "3D Test of Anti-Semitism: Demonization, Double Standards, Delegitimization," *Jewish Political Studies Review*, 16:3–4 (Fall 2004).

48 Manfred Gerstenfeld, interview with Hans Jansen, "Protestants and Israel: The Kairos Document Debate," *Demonizing Israel and the Jews*, 76.

49 Manfred Gerstenfeld, interview with Justus Reid Weiner, "Muslims Drive Out Christians from Palestinian Territories," *Demonizing Israel and the Jews*, 73.

50 www.palwatch.org.

51 www.palwatch.org/main.aspx?fi=157&doc_id=9308.

52 www.memri.org.

53 www.camera.org.

54 http://honestreporting.com.

55 www.ngo-monitor.org.

56 http://spme.org.

57 Herb Keinon, "In J'lem, Obama asserts Israel's right to defend itself," *The Jerusalem Post*, March 21, 2013.

58 Mitchell Bard, "American Public Opinion Toward Israel," *Jewish Virtual Library*, May 2013.

59 Ethan Bronner, "Beyond Cairo, Israel Sensing a Wider Siege," *The New York Times*, September 10, 2011.

60 "Text: Obama's Speech in Cairo," *The New York Times*, June 4, 2009.

61 Douglas Bloomfield, "Why Obama's Popularity is Rising in Israel," *The Jewish Week*, May 10, 2013.

62 "Full text of Obama's speech in Jerusalem: 'So long as there is a United States of America, ah-tem lo lah-vahd,'" *Haaretz*, March 21, 2013.

63 Khaled Abu Toameh, "PA's Abbas accepts PM Hamdallah's resignation," *The Jerusalem Post*, June 23, 2013.

64 Manfred Gerstenfeld, interview with Dore Gold, 54.

65 library.fes.de/pdf-files/do/07908-20110311.pdf.

66 Ibid., 49.

67 European Union Demographics Profile 2013, www.indexmundi.com/european_union/demographics_profile.html.

68 fra.europa.eu/fraWebsite/material/.../AS-WorkingDefinition-draft.pdf.

69 Wilhelm Heitmeyer (red), *Deutsche Zustände. Folge 3* (Frankfurt am Main: Suhrkamp, 2005), 151. [German]

70 "Kritik an Israel nicht deckungsgleich mit antisemitischen Haltungen," gfs.bern, March 28, 2007. [German]

71 "Antisemittisme i Norge? Den norske befolkningens holdninger til jøder og andre minoriteter," *The Center for Studies of the Holocaust and Religious Minorities*, May 30, 2012, [Norwegian] www.hlsenteret.no/publikasjoner/antisemittisme-i-norge.

72 Gunnar Heinsohn and Daniel Pipes, "Arab-Israeli Fatalities Rank 49th," *Daniel Pipes Middle East Forum*, October 8, 2007.

73 For instance: European Commission, "Iraq and Peace in the World," *Eurobarometer Survey*, No. 151, November 2003, 78 and "BBC poll: Germany most popular country in the world," *BBC News Europe*, May 23, 2013.

74 Professor Joshua Teitelbaum and Lt. Col. (Ret.) Michael Segall, *The Iranian Leadership's Continuing Declarations of Intent to Destroy Israel 2009-2012* (Jerusalem: The Jerusalem Center for Public Affairs, 2012).

75 Manfred Gerstenfeld, *Israel's New Future*, 16.

76 Michael Horowitz, "The History and Future of Suicide Terrorism," *Foreign Policy Research Institute*, August 2008.

77 Manfred Gerstenfeld, "Double Standards for Israel," *Journal for the Study of Anti-Semitism*, 4/2 of Volume 4/2, 2012, 616–618.

78 Jibran Ahmad, "U.S. drone, Pakistan air force strikes kill 19 militants," Reuters, July 14, 2013.

79 Michael J. Boyle, "The Costs and Consequences of Drone Warfare," *International Affairs* 89: 1, 2013, 1–29.

80 Steven R. David, "Fatal Choices, Israel's Policy of Targeted killing," *Mideast Security and Policy Studies No.51*, The Begin-Sadat Center for Strategic Studies, Bar Ilan University, September 2002.

81 Justus Reid, Weiner, "Targeted Killings and Double Standards," *Strategic Perspectives Number 9*, The Jerusalem Center for Public Affairs, 2012.

82 Irwin J. Mansdorf and Mordechai Kedar, "The Psychological Asymmetry of Islamist Warfare," *Middle East Quarterly*, Spring 2008, 37–44.

83 Richard Kemp, "A salute to the IDF," *The Jerusalem Post*, June 15, 2011.

84 Amos N. Guiora, "Teaching Morality in Armed Conflict: The Israel Defense Forces Model," *Jewish Political Studies Review*, 18:1–2, Spring 2006.

85 "2000: Suicide Bombers Attack USS Cole," http://news.bbc.co.uk.

86 "Congressional Research Service Memorandum: Terror Attacks by Al Qaeda," March 31, 2004.

87 Stephen Charles Nemeth, "A Rationalist Explanation of Terrorist Targeting," *University of Iowa*, 2010.

88 Nathan Guttman, "Israel's Airport Security, Object Of Envy, Is Hard To Emulate Here," *The Jewish Daily Forward*, January 6, 2010.

89 Badi Hasisi, "Ethnic Profiling In Airport Screening: Lessons From Israel, 1968–2010," *American Law and Economics Review*, Advance Access, September 17, 2012.

90 "Attempted Terror Attack on Northwest Airlines Flight 253," *United States Senate*, 11th Congress, 2d Session, Report 111-199, May 24, 2010.

91 Badi Hasisi, "Ethnic Profiling In Airport Screening: Lessons From Israel, 1968–2010," *American Law and Economics Review*, Advance Access, September 17, 2012.

92 "Begin Hints that Mitterrand Remark Paved way for Terrorists' Attack," *The New York Times*, August 11, 1982.

93 "Israelis Assail Greek Leader for Likening them to Nazis," *The New York Times*, June 26, 1982.

94 Per Ahlmark, *Det öppna såret* (Stockholm: Timbro, 1997), 200. [Swedish]

95   Ina Huynh Matihsen, "Exhibition by the Norwegian artist Gullvåg," *Norway, the Official Site in Jordan,* The Norwegian Embassy in Amman, January 30, 2011.

96   Per Gudmundson, "Mona Sahlin, hakkorsen och Hamasflaggorna," *Gudmundson,* January 15, 2009, http://gudmundson.blogspot.com. [Swedish]

97   "Israelska flaggan brändes," *Dagens Nyheter,* January 10, 2009. [Swedish]

98   Per Gudmundson, "Rödflaggat," *Gudmundson,* January 13, 2009, http://gudmundson.blogspot.com. [Swedish]

99   Per Gudmundson, "Swedish Leading Social Democrats in Rally with Hezbollah Flags," *Gudmundson,* January 10, 2009, http://gudmundson.blogspot.com. [Swedish]

100   Erik Svansbo, "Folkbladet uppmärksammar 'bloggkupp,'" *Svansbo,* January 14, 2009, http://blogg.svansbo.se. [Swedish]

101   Per Gudmundson, "Rödflaggat," *Gudmundson,* January 13, 2009, http://gudmundson.blogspot.com. [Swedish]

102   "U.N. chief Ban hails bin Laden death as 'watershed,'" Reuters, May 2, 2011.

103   "World leaders condemn Yassin assassination," *The Sunday Times,* March 22, 2004.

104   "UN Commission on Human Rights Adopts Resolution Which Condemns Continuing Grave Violations of Human Rights in the Territory, Including the Tragic Assassination of Sheikh Yassin," United Nations Press Release, *If Americans Knew,* March 24, 2004.

105   www.unwatch.org.

106   www.eyeontheunblog.com.

107   Anne Bayefsky, "Another scandalous session of the UN Human Rights Council," *The Jerusalem Post,* May 29, 2013.

108   Judy Maltz, "November 4, 1995: Yitzhak Rabin assassinated," *Haaretz,* June 16, 2013.

109   Interview with Moshe Landau, *Haaretz,* October 6, 2000.

110   "Shinui," The Israel Democracy Institute, http://en.idi.org.il/tools-and-data/israeli-elections-and-parties/political-parties/shinui/.

111   "Population of Israel: General Trends and Indicators," *Israel Ministry of Foreign Affairs,* December 24, 1998.

112 Danielle Ziri, "CBS Report: Israel population hits 8 million," *The Jerusalem Post*, April 14, 2013.

113 "Israel: High Income OECD," Data, *The World Bank*, 2013.

114 Leon Lazaroff, "China to Capitalize on Nasdaq Jump With Tech IPOs, BNY Says," www.bloomberg.com, May 7, 2012.

115 Hezi Sternlicht and Israeli Hayom Staff, "Israeli high-tech start-ups sold for combined $5.5 billion in 2012," *Israel Hayom*, January 8, 2013.

116 Clyde Haberman, "Dozens are Killed as Israelis Attack Camp in Lebanon, *The New York Times*, June 3, 1994.

117 "Summary of Operation Grapes of Wrath Press Conference- 15-April-96," *Israel Ministry of Foreign Affairs*, April 15, 1996.

118 "Cabinet Communique," *Israel Ministry of Foreign Affairs*, October 17, 2004.

119 Avi Issacharoff and Amos Harel, "Recollections of Israel's Operation Defensive Shield, ten years later," *Haaretz*, March 30, 2012.

120 "The Second Lebanese War," *the Knesset*, 2009.

121 Michael Herzog, "Operation Pillar of Defense (Gaza – November 2012): Objectives and Implications," *Jerusalem Center for Public Affairs*, January 21, 2013.

122 Asa Kasher, "A Moral Evaluation of the Gaza War: Operation Cast Lead," *Jerusalem Center for Public Affairs*, February 4, 2010.

Introduction

1 Ruth R. Wisse, *If I am Not for Myself* (New York: The Free Press, 1992), 94.

Other Books by Manfred Gerstenfeld

Revaluing Italy, with Lorenzo Necci (Italian), 1992.

Environment and Confusion: An Introduction to a Messy Subject, 1993.

Israel's New Future: Interviews, 1994.

The State as a Business: Do-It-Yourself Political Forecasting (Italian), 1994.

Judaism, Environmentalism, and the Environment, 1998.

The Environment in the Jewish Tradition: A Sustainable World (Hebrew), 2002.

Europe's Crumbling Myths: The Post-Holocaust Origins of Today's Anti-Semitism
(Foreword by Emil L. Fackenheim), 2003.

American Jewry's Challenge: Conversations Confronting the Twenty-First Century
(Foreword by Jonathan Sarna), 2004.

Israel and Europe: An Expanding Abyss?, 2005.

European-Israeli Relations: Between Confusion and Change?, 2006.

The Abuse of Holocaust Memory: Distortions and Responses (Foreword by
Abrham H. Foxman), 2009.

Anti-Semitism in Norway (Foreword by Finn Jarle Saele) (Norwegian), 2010.

American Jewry's Comfort Level: Present and Future, with Steven Bayme
(Foreword by David A. Harris), 2010.

The Decay: Jews in a Rudderless Netherlands (Dutch), 2010.

Judging the Netherlands: The Renewed Holocaust Restitution Process, 1997-2000 (Foreword by Stuart E. Eizenstat), 2011.

Demonizing Israel and the Jews (Foreword by Rabbi Marvin Hier), 2013.

Books Edited:

The New Clothes of European Anti-Semitism, with Shmuel Trigano (French), 2004.

Academics against Israel and the Jews (Foreword by Natan Sharansky), 2007.

Israel at the Polls 2006, with Shmuel Sandler and Jonathan Rynhold, 2008.

Behind the Humanitarian Mask: The Nordic Countries, Israel, and the Jews (Foreword by Gert Weisskirchen), 2008.

Israel at the Polls 2009, with Shmuel Sandler and Hillel Frisch, 2008.

Monograph:

The Autumn 2005 Riots in France: Their Possible Impact on Israel and the Jews, 2006.

www.ingramcontent.com/pod-product-compliance
Lightning Source LLC
Chambersburg PA
CBHW062201270326
41930CB00009B/1611